To Howard,
Frien

7

MW01283593

et !

A CIVIL WAR DIARY

WRITTEN BY DR. JAMES A. BLACK,
FIRST ASSISTANT SURGEON, 49TH
ILLINOIS INFANTRY

EDITED BY

BENITA K. MOORE

authorHOUSE®

AuthorHouse™
1663 Liberty Drive, Suite 200
Bloomington, IN 47403
www.authorhouse.com
Phone: 1-800-839-8640

First published by AuthorHouse 9/12/2008

ISBN: 978-1-4343-9368-5 (sc)
ISBN: 978-1-4343-9367-8 (hc)

Library of Congress Control Number: 2008905518

Printed in the United States of America
Bloomington, Indiana

This book is printed on acid-free paper.

DEDICATION

To My Husband David, who did as much of the work as I.

David G. Moore

CONTENTS

PHOTO OF DR. JAMES A. BLACK

This *photograph* of James A. Black was *probably taken in the latter months of* 1863, while he was in *Memphis, Tennessee. James was 28 years of age.*
James Black enlisted in the Union Army at age 26. His personal characteristics were identified as: Height 6 feet 3 inches, Red Hair, Blue Eyes, and Light Complexion. James makes reference to his weight in the 170's.
Soldiers paid for their own photographs. Photographs were often sent home to family and friends and many were exchanged with fellow soldiers.

BIOGRAPHY OF DR. JAMES A. BLACK 1835 - 1902

THE EARLY YEARS

James A. Black, the second child of ten and the eldest son of Willis and Emilla Hensley Black, was born July 2, 1835, eight miles east of Salem in Marion County, Illinois. Little is known about the early life of James Black other than he received a public school education at a rural district schoolhouse and later attended Salem College. At a point he taught school for three terms in Marion County, although the grade level and dates of his teaching career have been lost to history. Sometime thereafter, under the guidance of Dr. William Hill of Salem, James began an apprenticeship in the study of medicine. In 1860 James established a medical practice in Keensville, Wayne County, Illinois, where he lived and boarded with a local farmer, John Keen, Sr. The 1860 census shows James owning real estate valued at $300. and personal property valued at $150. His occupation was listed as "Physician."

This scant outline of James' early years presents more questions than answers about his personal life; and until additional primary sources or written personal accounts are discovered any biographer is relegated to conjecture about what was likely to have been, and general descriptions of life in this geographical area and time period. In 1961 Harry Black, a local historian and family genealogist, wrote, "All trace had been lost of Willis Black's descendants until the author began to compile his genealogy, yet at the time of the Civil War and a number of years after [they] were well known in the Salem, Illinois, area. Willis Black owned a large acreage east of Salem, Illinois, as well as property at Omega, Illinois, and in the town of Salem itself." Indeed, it seems strange that a near void in pre Civil War information about the Willis Black Family does exist. Perhaps, hopefully, the Civil War Diary of James Black will inspire a forthcoming of additional information concerning events about the prominent Willis Black family and James A. Black, in particular.

THE WAR YEARS

In the fall of 1861 James Black postponed his medical practice and returned to Salem to join the Union Army. On October 19, 1861, he enlisted as a private for a three year term with the 49th Illinois Infantry Regiment. At Camp Butler, a military training facility located near Springfield, Illinois, James, age twenty-six, was mustered into the Army on December 31, 1861, as a Private in Company D., and immediately began his training as a Union soldier. The first entry in his diary is dated January 1, 1862.

The military seemed to be a good fit for James Black as he quickly received promotion to Corporal, then Sergeant. After one month of training his regiment was transported to the field of battle and in the passing of two more months the regiment engaged in ferocious fighting in two decisive battles, Fort Donelson and Shiloh. Soon thereafter any thoughts of a quick war or personal military glory faded. James understood this would be an arduous and long struggle to the end. Likewise, with the eminent and growing medical concerns, and with the recognition of James' medical background he was soon assigned as an orderly to the regimental hospital. Shortly, James was dispensing medicine and tending to the sick of the regiment. After independent study and successful completion of an Army medical examination for surgeons, James A. Black received a commission in December, 1862, as Assistant Surgeon, 49th Illinois Infantry Regiment.

The task of Assistant Surgeon was most demanding. When necessary, assistant surgeons were to accompany men into battle, attend to the wounded and sick and, if necessary, make arrangements for transportation to the regimental hospital. The regimental surgeon normally remained at the regimental hospital and medically treated soldiers as they arrived. So it was with James Black, although there were many more duties to perform. The major block of James' time as assistant surgeon was consumed with treating illnesses, diseases, and other common medical concerns of the soldiers. James became acutely aware of the menace of inadequate sanitation practices, deplorable medical facilities, poor drinking water, improper diet, bad cooking habits and poor personal hygiene. Although surgeons were somewhat helpless in their effort to rectify the pressing medical concerns, most, including James, never waned in their effort to seek improvement.

Apart from his personal preoccupation with the war, James had family concerns. His younger brother, Frank, helped to organize a Southern Illinois regiment and was commissioned Lieutenant Colonel in the 111th Illinois Infantry Regiment. Frank's regiment served in the Eastern Theater of the war, but both brothers strove to keep close contact through personal correspondence. Frank was wounded in battle, but recuperated and rejoined his regiment before war's end. After the war James and Frank retained their close ties and remained lifelong friends. Frank outlived James by three years.

January 22, 1864, major tragedy struck the Black family. While accompanying a U.S. Deputy Provost Marshal and acting in the capacity of Deputy Sheriff, Willis Black, James' father, tried to arrest two Union deserters in Marion County. Willis Black was shot and killed. James was notified of the death of his father but was unable to get immediate leave for home. However, he used his military connections to acquire information about the murderers and informed other family members of his acquired information. After leave was granted James returned home to assist his mother with financial affairs and settlements. James made mention of the death in his diary without identifying his personal emotions or how he coped with his grief.

In March, 1865, James was granted another leave and returned home for some pleasant personal business. On the rainy Wednesday evening of March 15, 1865, James married Missouri Jane Moody of New Middleton, Illinois, in a simple church wedding with friends and family in attendance. As a side note of interest, James made no reference in the diary to his impending marriage until the day of the event, although in retrospect there were many hints to the astute reader. James referred to Missouri Jane as Zue.

Before James' tenure as a surgeon in the field came to a close he personally witnessed considerable suffering of military personnel and civilians alike. The causes of the suffering varied--some were man-made while many were simply natural to humans. Antiseptics were unknown, anesthetics were scarce, epidemics were rampant. Apart from battlefield and accidental injuries, diseases, respiratory ailments, dysentery, and lice, were all too common with little medical treatment or relief that really worked. James was aware of such and he worked hard to find solutions, generally with little success.

In the spring of 1865 James was detached from his regiment and served as a Post Surgeon in Smithland, Kentucky, where he encountered a different set of frustrations and problems. Here he dealt with military bureaucracy, large scale inoculations, routine physical exams, numerous contagious diseases, and strict Army regulations required considerable paper work. He did not cherish this duty.

The surrender of the Southern Army brought great joy to many, but not all soldiers would return home immediately. There was still much to be done and the 49th was involved in the military gearing down process. Because of his surgeon/officer status James was among the final group to be mustered out of the regiment on September 9, 1865. A final pay and a ceremonial discharge at Camp Butler, Illinois, September 15 made it final.

POST WAR YEARS

James was now a civilian, a married man, and thirty years of age when he began to execute his dreams of a new life in a different place. By horse and buggy Zue and James left Salem in mid October, 1865, for Fillmore, Montgomery County, Illinois, to establish Dr. Black's medical practice. In 1867 he relocated his practice to Mulberry Grove, Bond County, and remained there until 1871 when James and Zue made their final move a few miles south to Fairview, a recently established community, later renamed Pleasant Mound. Pleasant Mound, Bond County, became home for the young couple, where they reared their ten children, and lived the remainder of their lives.

One block south of the main street in Pleasant Mound, James purchased one square block of picturesque land overlooking a serene meadow. Here he and family lived and his medical practice shared the site. It was fitting that the Civil War Surgeon chose such a beautiful, peaceful location on the Illinois prairie to be his home, his permanent site for his lifelong medical practice.

James A. Black, M.D. was a successful and beloved physician. One can only wonder as to the number of babies he delivered, the number of house calls he must have made in this rural community, or the number of patients he guided to recuperation, or added to their quality of life. Although his work and his family consumed much of his life, he usually found time to express his Republican views if one wanted to hear them. He served as Assessor of Pleasant Mound Township and school treasurer and was active in the Baptist Church at Pleasant Mound. True to the man he gave back to his community. Needless to say he was a lifelong proud member of Post No. 301, G. A. R.

Dr. James A. Black died of stomach cancer in his home at Pleasant Mound on June 1, 1902, aged 66 years, 10 months and 29 days. He was buried in the Maxey Cemetery, a rural cemetery a few miles northwest of Pleasant Mound. Zue and James had ten children, three sons and seven daughters. One son and two daughters died in infancy. When James died he left his wife, two sons, five daughters, two grandchildren, two brothers and one sister. Missouri(Zue) Jane Black died February 26, 1917, aged 75 years, 4 months, 14 days. Zue was buried next to her husband.

THE MAN

Surgeon James A. Black's diary is a splendid daily record of the war as seen from his unique vantage point. However, the diary is far more than an accounting of his experiences and observations. It is so well written that it reveals to the interested reader his personal attitudes, his values, his fears, his pleasures, his frustrations, and his failures. Once the diary is read, the careful reader will acquire great insight into the man, almost to the point one might believe he has met him, knows him.

In many ways James A. Black was a product of his time. He so valued the basic comforts of life--good food, personal comfort, reliable shelter, agreeable weather--as he also cherished family, friends, home and all the privileges that went with each. His written expressions reveal a strict adherence to a rigid morality, not too dissimilar to the traditional Protestant code of conduct. He openly disapproved of gambling, card playing, drinking, excessive profanity, immoral conduct by either sex, or those who economically took advantage of the less fortunate. James was not a tolerant man if tolerance infringed on his belief of right and wrong. Church attendance was important to James and many of his close associates were churchgoers, as illustrated by his close friendship with the regimental chaplain. Church attendance was just expected from a good Christian. The Sunday sermons were important to James as they presented cause for personal reflection, or a reinforcement of his spiritual beliefs. He believed personal behavior, not what the individual proclaimed to believe, was the best measure of man. Even though James was a moralist and a man of convictions, he usually did not rush to judgment; but once he made an unfavorable decision about an individual's behavior he was slow to forgive.

James' attention to detail is worthy of note. He methodically kept track of personal correspondence, both written and received, in his diary as he also noted the cost of items purchased and the fairness of price. He kept records concerning his military pay, the money and goods he sent home, his financial transactions with fellow soldiers as well as his personal expenses. He was frugal but had few qualms about his rare extravagances especially concerning his occasional dining out, or the cost of a few valued personal possessions. Money was important to him but not at the expense of friends or personal comfort. Undoubtedly, James not only understood his personal financial situation, he also understood the value of knowing such, of keeping accurate records. The fact that James kept a daily entry, four-year diary during the war tells us volumes about his commitment to accurate record keeping.

One has only to read the diary of James Black to understand the heart and soul of a strong Union man. His strong dislike of northern copperheads, his appreciation of southern Union sympathizers reveal his deep convictions regarding secession. The preservation of the Union was foremost to James even if his belief required extreme personal sacrifices, untold hardships, or a willing participation in a war to its rightful conclusion. He never wavered in his beliefs that the war was necessary and just, although at times he showed major concerns about what he believed to be improper conduct of the war by particular military leaders. Usually accepting of military limitations or mistakes, he was never accepting of incompetence. He respected and admired good military leadership even when he disagreed with their tactics. He shows obvious admiration of the leaders who learned from battlefield experience, who adapted as the war required. He admired General Grant for his ability to grasp the situation at hand as he admired General Sherman for his ability to motivate his men, although he did express reservations when General Sherman used a scorched earth policy in the Meridian Campaign. Likewise, his detestation of incompetence was equally as obvious when General Banks was in charge of the Red River Campaign. As a surgeon in the field and almost from the beginning of the campaign, James Black questioned decisions that placed undue hardships on the soldiers or decisions that unnecessarily placed the men in harms way. His daily entries are almost a list of indictments against General Banks. Interestingly, almost one hundred fifty years later most historians agree.

Conversely, James was not always in sync with many of his fellow soldiers. Indeed he was a good soldier and adhered to the military way, while at the same time he was in a personal learning mode and pursued self improvement. He valued learning as illustrated by his constant desire to read and acquire new reading materials, to draw from it as he improved his writing skills, his vocabulary, his spelling and punctuation. His intense study to pass the surgeons' examination, his careful observations of battlefield tactics, and his endeavor to engage in meaningful conversation with friends are but a few examples of his desire to improve his intellect. His appreciation of theater when the opportunity presented itself, his desire to attend lectures or speeches, his love of music wherever he found it, reveal much about his love of cultural activities. There could be little doubt that the underside of the Civil War Surgeon was laced with a love of learning while his inner being craved culture.

Although James A. Black was a product of his times, his environment, and his opportunities, it was his ardent desire for a better life that made him the man he became. One can only imagine the numerous good qualities, his weaknesses and quirks that are now lost to history. Indeed, James would have been an interesting man to know.

TO THE READER

One can only imagine his thoughts and emotions when James A. Black sat at his desk to write the final transcription of his diary. With pen dipped in ink and writing in his ornate cursive handwriting he began the task of transcribing a four-year daily account of his experiences and observations during the Civil War into one durable oversized book. The final product was an impressive 395 page handwritten accounting.

James A. Black never stated in writing his purpose for keeping a diary. Whether he had a grand intent in mind or if he merely followed a whim to document a part of his life is not clear. James was a private, disciplined person with a considerable appreciation for learning, and the diary may well be an extension of his personality. It is also possible the diary simply reflects his penchant for details and record keeping. His written record of events, his use of exact names and locations, his persistent insertion of details concerning weather, financial transactions, military equipment and procedures, and many other daily observations push one to believe James was simply writing a personal record for himself. Publication goals or desire for personal recognition were unlikely, as such never came about even in the face of opportunity.

Additional speculation concerning the purpose of the diary will likely continue as many readers will surely develop their own thoughts and, in fact, the reader's conclusions may be as valid as those of the editor. What seems to be more significant is that a document so long lost to history has now reemerged 142 years hence. Regardless of the intent and more significant to history, the diary is now available for all who want to read and learn about a Southern Illinois man who served and fought in the Civil War for the Union cause.

The value of the diary as a primary source is indisputable--it documents the military and personal activities of a soldier/surgeon in the western theater of the Civil War. The diary is also of value to readers other than historians. Not unlike a novel, although not with a polished writing style, the reader must guard against reading too fast, must overcome his desire to know what happens next. Fellow soldiers and civilians alike become the characters in a plot of war. The reader knows the final outcome but the suspense of daily events, the inevitable struggles, the joys, and the fate of the many characters remains in doubt until the end.

The language in the diary is also worthy of attention--so much so that any change by an editor would diminish the overall value to the reader. Indeed, after reading the diary a linguist or critical reader alike may obtain a sense of the 150 year evolutionary changes in writing style. Two separate words in the 1840's may become hyphenated or compound words today. Word meanings may change. James states, "Soldiers and civilians were sitting in church promiscuously." Today such a description would conjure up an interesting mental image when in fact he used the old meaning of promiscuously which meant intermingling. Similarly, many of the words he uses may have archaic meanings today, but were quite vibrant words at the time.

Sentence structure, spelling, capitalization, and sometimes grammar may vary from modern usage. On occasion it is difficult to match object with verb, or to determine what the prepositional phrase modifies, but rarely is there doubt about what James intended to communicate. He wrote as he was taught to write in the 1840's, and he wrote his diary without benefit of dictionary or manual of style. In fact, when all is said and done the reader will most likely stand in awe of James A. Black's ability to write, to communicate his thoughts and feelings to a reader.

THE TRANSCRIPTION

There is little doubt that, if possible, any primary source should be presented without modification. The foremost problem to that end is what is a totally correct transcription. Written in cursive the handwriting is beautiful in form but difficult to read without some uncertainties. Writing with pen dipped in ink requires the proper touch of pen to paper as well as the proper handwriting. Even for the experienced and exacting writer, ink may blot with the slightest hesitation of movement. Words must end with a graceful lessening of pressure and letters must be spaced properly to prevent a darkened overwrite. Periods, commas or any brief contact with paper require graceful hand movement even when the pen is exact with ink. Certainly the technique of handwriting during the mid nineteenth century required more time, more forethought, more patience, and a different skill than writing today.

There were other concerns that made a transcription difficult: unintended dots, blots, and darken specks are found throughtout the diary. The vowels a, e, o, were often difficult to discern. The upper and lower case were not always detectable to the eye. The correct spelling of many words, especially names and local geographical areas, was unknown to James, and to his credit he used reasonably accurate phonetic spelling. Quotation marks were sometimes used in a different manner. Company "D" was written Co. "D,,. Contractions varied regarding the location of the apostrophe. Didn't might be written as did'nt, although this was less common in the latter parts of the diary. The colon and semicolon were seldom distinguishable. Abbreviations were not always consistent. It should be no surprise that time has taken a toll on a handwritten 142 year old diary. Many other minor concerns could be noted, although they serve little purpose to the reader.

As previously stated great care has been taken to preserve the spirit and accuracy of this original work and to parallel the original diary in every manner. Solely for the purpose of enhancing readability, a few minor modifications were made. The following is a list of those modifications:

1. Italics(*Italics*) indicate uncertainty in the transcription of a word.

2. Brackets[Brackets] are used by the editor to give explanation or to add clarification. Brackets were not used in the original diary.

3. The regimental roster was used for the spelling of soldiers' names. However, the rosters were not always correct. An example of roster error was the misspelling of Capt. Louis Krughoff of Co. C, 49th Regiment, Nashville, Ill. The roster read Kurghoff.

4. Periods and commas were sometimes indistinguishable in the original diary. The transcription reflects the punctuation mark most resembled with no regard to correct punctuation other than at the end of sentences.

5. Periods and commas are removed from the daily headings. Removal made no difference in meaning.

6. If a sentence had no period and the first word of the following sentence was not capitalized, an extra space is added between words to help the reader recognize separate sentences.

7. Toward the end of the diary an equal symbol (=) was used at the end of a few sentences. This symbol is included in the transcription, although its meaning could not be determined.

8. Frequently an elongated curvy line was inserted at the end of a sentence. Explanation for its probable meaning was not found. The curvy line in the transcription is represented by a tilde(~) symbol.

9. The spelling of "Cavalry" is consistent in the transcription, although the proper spelling of the handwritten word was in question at times.

TITLE PAGE WRITTEN BY DR. JAMES A. BLACK

DIARY
JANUARY 1, 1962 - DECEMBER 31, 1865

WEDNESDAY JANUARY 1ST 1862
Camp Butler Illinois

On duty for the first time in the U.S. Service. I was detailed for guard, and chosen from the ranks by Tricillion Act. Reg't. Adj't. as orderly at Reg't. Hd. Qrs. for himself and Wm. Cogan Serg't. Major. had to keep up fires and read the papers. light duty, I think.

The Com Officers of Co. "D,, gave us an Oyster Supper all went on swimingly [very well] and we conclud they are a clever set of fellows.

THURSDAY JANUARY 2ND 1862
Camp Butler Illinois

Drilled in squad drill, at the usual hours forenoon and afternoon. We carried bread from the Old camp, distant 3/4 mile. The commissary is still over there. Snow and ice plenty alternately. The 5th & 7th Ills. Cav. at the Old camp near the lake. not drilling much yet, too muddy.

FRIDAY JANUARY 3RD 1862
Camp Butler Illinois

The boys playing cards at every interval when off duty. from Revellie in the morning until Tattoo [a call sounded shortly before taps as notice to go to quarters] at night and sometimes even later. drilled in squads at the usual hours morning and evening most of the day in fact. Stalbrands battery and the 32nd and 46th Ills. Infty. are here yet.

SATURDAY JANUARY 4TH 1862
Camp Butler Illinois

Drilled in squads as we will necessarily have to do for some time yet owing to the inexperience of the men and the carelessness with which some of them seem to drill. We still carry bread from the Old Camp. Nothing in the way of news to day. We have many inconviniences here

SUNDAY JANUARY 5TH 1862
Camp Butler Illinois

Recruits still coming in, the company will soon be full if we remain here and the Officer continue to work as energetically in the future as they have in the past. good deal of Shenanegan in camp stealing recruits from one another, after they are brought in before they are mustered in.

I was in quarters all day trying to write, but owing to the romping of the boys it is hard to do. wrote A.K.A.

MONDAY JANUARY 6TH 1862
Camp Butler Illinois

Drilled fore and afternoon by 2nd Lieut. E.B. Harlan. he marched the entire company over to the Old Camp to get bread. Snow on the ground except in the roads where it has been worn out by the Cavalry and Muddy. great many horsemen stewing about on horseback.

TUESDAY JANUARY 7TH 1862
Camp Butler Illinois

Still drilling. I imagine an awkward lot of recruits, going through the evolutions of drill would be laughing stock for old Soldiers if there were any here to enjoy the sport. Camp dull in consequence of the cold weather, and the change of life from civil to Military. Wrote J.F.B.

WEDNESDAY JANUARY 8TH 1862
Camp Butler Illinois

Co. "D,, had a splendid dinner in honor of the Victorious battle fought at New Orleans Jan. 8th 181_. Capt. J.W. Brokaw Maj. W.W. Bishop, and 2nd Lieut. E.B. Harlan dined with us. (Serg't. F.A. Niles' Mess.) The dinner was made up by the boys of the Co. as a setoff to the Com Officers supper of New year's

THURSDAY JANUARY 9TH 1862
Camp Butler Illinois

Very wet and sloppy in consequence of the snow thawing out and running off. No drill to day too much water and mud. Only out on dressparade

The 46th Ills Infty. fussing about not getting their pay. talk of their mutinying. Not doing any more duty etc. until paid off. It will be strange if they don't go longer without pay before they are out of the service. I wrote to J. R. Higgason

FRIDAY JANUARY 10TH 1862
Camp Butler Illinois

On guard to day for the first time. 1st relief, No. 43, Countersign "Dupont," night very cold. The Sharpshooters (__ Ills Infty.) left here for Quincy Illinois to day. Co. "D,, moved into barracks with Co, "C,, a German Co. The regiment now in contiguous barracks the[y] have not been so heretofore. We'll all talk dutch now.

SATURDAY JANUARY 11TH 1862
Camp Butler Illinois

Rumor says our troops are leaving Cairo Illinois for Columbus, Ky. prospect considered good for a fight there soon. The Paymaster has come to pay us off for the first, together with other troops at this camp, and a welcome visitor he is if he does it, for money is scarce. camp very dull.

SUNDAY JANUARY 12TH 1862
Camp Butler Illinois

Out on inspection with knapsacks and blankets for the first time since I've been here in camp. tis rumored that fighting is now going on at Columbus, Ky. considerable anxiety manifested in regard to the results. Many rumors in camp in consequence of it.

MONDAY JANUARY 13TH 1862
Camp Butler Illinois

Too cold to drill to day except in quarters. we have a few old guns and were drilled by the Serg'ts some of them about as green as the ballance of us. No dressparade this evening in consequence of the extreme cold weather. The boys put in the time playing cards from early morn til late at night. though I think there is but little gambling going on among them.

TUESDAY JANUARY 14TH 1862
Camp Butler Illinois

The Paymaster is in camp to day paying off the 32nd Ills Infty. We had squad drill this afternoon and dressparade at 4.P.M. We have six roll calls per day now in order to keep the men about camp. some of them go to Springfield without leave. Snow falling briskly at 4.P.M.

WEDNESDAY JANUARY 15TH 1862
Camp Butler Illinois

On guard 1st relief No. 47. countersign "Buel" stock at the Q.M's. Snow two inches deep, cloudy during the day. Co."D,, drew the remainder of their uniforms to-day. I got a haversack and canteen. the barracks hanging full of overcoats knapsacks canteens extra shirts and drawers etc.

THURSDAY JANUARY 16TH 1862
Camp Butler Illinois

Our Reg't signed the payrolls and were paid off to day. I received $.31.63.cts. some mistake in making out the rolls. I got most three months pay for half a months duty, while some who came in months ahead of me got much less. I took dinner with Sal Brets in the __th Cavalry.

FRIDAY JANUARY 17TH 1862
Camp Butler Illinois

I went to Springfield to day with Hoss, Burrows, Brokaw, & O'Neill. I bought a vest and forgot the old one and left it in the hack we came to camp in.

We found Old Jas. Thompson in Springfield drunk we brought him to camp with us. Capt. J. W. Brokaw went home to day. I sent ten dollars to R.M.L. & J.F.B. money I borrowed before leaving home from them.

I wrote to J.F.B.

SATURDAY JANUARY 18TH 1862
Camp Butler Illinois

I sold my revolver to day for $.15.00 to a soldier Gen'l Van Renseller in camp to day to review the troops. all out on parade Infty, Cavalry, and Artillery. The first demonstration of the kind we have had since we have been here. Weather cloudy and drizzling rain.

SUNDAY JANUARY 19TH 1862
Camp Butler Illinois

I mist roll call this morning and was put on extra duty for it by Serg't F.J. Burrows I helped Ira C. Wiggins, John Peck, and Thos. Farro dig a grave for a brother of Corpl. M. Pate who came here on a visit I think and died. Two other graves being dug at the same time. weather wet and disagreeable.

MONDAY JANUARY 20TH 1862
Camp Butler Ilinois

1st Lieut. Jas. W. Cheney gone to Springfield to day. Serg't F.J. Burrows drilled us in Squad drill to day

The frost is still in the ground but the snow thaws out and makes it very sloppy getting about. and we have to carry most of the water we use from Sangamon river one quarter of a mile.

TUESDAY JANUARY 21ST 1862
Camp Butler Illinois

In compliance with yesterdays order we had Non-Com Officer's and company drill in the forenoon, and Com. Officers, and company drill, and dressparade in the afternoon Corpl. C.R. O'Neill and [I] boxed up our citizens clothes and got them ready to ship home. Soldiers not allowed to wear citizen's dress after they have been supplied with the blue.

WEDNESDAY JANUARY 22ND 1862
Camp Butler Illinois

C.R. O'Neill and I carried our box of clothing to Jam.town, distant one mile and left it to be shiped marked "W.H. Black Salem Ills.

The hack driver brought my vest around which I forgot and left in his hack last Friday, when we came from Springfield Ills.

THURSDAY JANUARY 23RD 1862
Camp Butler Illinois

On guard 1st relief, No. 16th countersign "Thomas." Weathe still and cold. I stood near where the cavalry keep their horses. Snow on the ground.

A man fell through the Railroad bridge over Sangamon river last night onto the ice and killed. supposed to be drunk don't know him.

FRIDAY JANUARY 24TH 1862
Camp Butler Illinois

I bought a Portfolio of the post Sutler [a civilian provisioner to an army post] to day for .50.cts. He is getting a large portion of the boys money for articles that are of little use to them, or at least, that migh be dispensed with without inconvinience to themselves. Rec'd a letter from & wrote to J.F.B.

SATURDAY JANUARY 25TH 1862
Camp Butler Illinois

We had Non-Com Officers drill A.M. and Com. Officers and company drill, and dressparade in the afternoon. A citizen drumed out of camp to day, by the boys for selling whiskey to soldiers. Some of whom are drunk whenever they can get the liquor. Served him right. The camp is cursed with hucksters and catchpennies [those who use sensationalism or cheapness for appeal] of every conceivable description.

SUNDAY JANUARY 26TH 1862
Camp Butler Illinois

Out on inspection at 8.A.M. with knapsacks blankets and clothing generally. We received our arms to day at 2.P.M. The Belgium Muskets, they heavy and clumsy. The boys drumed one of the frail fair ones out of camp to day from the hospital. Preaching in "Capt. Woods Co. "K,,"s barracks to night.

MONDAY JANUARY 27TH 1862
Camp Butler Illinois

On drill in the "Manual of Arms" for the first time to day, except what little drilling we have done with old guns from the guard house, occasionaly. C.R. O'Neill went home to day. I loaned him $.10.00 and sent $.5.00 by him to the I.O.O.F. to pay my weekly dues. I wrote to John Keen, Jr.

TUESDAY JANUARY 28TH 1862
Camp Butler Illinois

Drilling in the "Manual of Arms" in squads to day, in quarters. the weather being to cold to handle our pieces in the open air, especially while we are so awkward. beside[s] it is too Muddy to get out with any satisfaction now.

I wrote to R.M.L.

WEDNESDAY JANUARY 29TH 1862
Camp Butler Illinois

Drilled again in quarters. was out on dressparade this evening with knapsacks and arms for the first time. looks something more like Soldiering except our awkwardness in handling our pieces. Some of the boys mash their toes occasionally in "Order Arms." I bought a pinch back locket for .25cts. and a picture case for .40cts. to day. the camp is infested with peddlers of all kinds.

THURSDAY JANUARY 30TH 1862
Camp Butler Illinois

On guard. 2nd relief. No. 8. countersign "Scott." considerable passing as this is the gate next to the river and a bucket or a horse is sufficient to pass anybody. I had two pictures taken to day for .80cts bought a pr gloves (buck) $1.00. There are three picture galleries here. none of the artists good.

FRIDAY JANUARY 31ST 1862
Camp Butler Illinois

The 32nd Ills Infty Vols. left here to day for Cairo Illinois, with arms, Camp and Garrison Equipage the first Reg't I ever saw march with all of their traps on. hope we may follow in their wake, as Cairo is certainly a more comfortable place than this. It is too cold here for us to become efficient in drill during the entire winter. I took the Ear-Ache while on drill to day, and shook as with an Ague [a fever with shivering and chills] at night.

My first illness in camp, and I hope it may be my last as the noise & racket is about equal to my patience, when in the best of health. The nights are cold and with but two blankets each, and the little straw we have and the open barracks it is imposible to keep comfortable

SATURDAY FEBRUARY 1ST 1862
Camp Butler Illinois

Sick and lay in my bunk all day with cold and Ear-Ache. took no medicine hoping to get better without it, as their is but little to be expected from it under such untoward circumstances, but doomed it seems to disappointment. Many of the boys sick with Measles, quite a number dying with them. some sent to quarters before they are well, and relapse, and die.

SUNDAY FEBRUARY 2ND 1862
Camp Butler Illinois

I am convalecent this morning. I attended sick call for the first time, got a dose of Camp. Cath. Pills.

We received orders to prepare four days cooked rations for a move. We returned our arms, to day we are to be supplied with others when we get to Cairo Illinois. Every body's bussy to day.

MONDAY FEBRUARY 3RD 1862
Camp Butler Illinois

Up at 5.A.M. rolling up blankets and over-coats and packing knapsacks. Went to the Railroad at 2.P.M. I was detailed, and helped load Q.M. & commissary stsores. we started on a freight train at Sun down, reshiped at Decatur Ills. and passed Sandoval at midnight some of the boys stoped along the road. O'Neill & Col. Pease joined us at Centralia Ills.

TUESDAY FEBRUARY 4TH 1862
Cairo Illinois

We arrived here at 8.A.M. to day unloaded our baggage and stores and put it aboard a boat and crossed the Ohio to Fort Holt Ky. at 4.P.M. unloaded again, and went into log barracks left by some other Reg't. The Situation is low, and the river almost bank full at this place. Many men of the regiment very drunk to day. Cairo muddy.

WEDNESDAY FEBRUARY 5TH 1862
Fort Holt Kentucky
Divided the company into messes and built chimneys to the barracks, repaired the bunks, found but little straw in them. George Jennings over here to day.

We drew arms again to day. this time we got the Springfield Musket. Except the flanking companies ("A,, and "B,,) were armed with Enfield Rifles everything in order now. The men like these guns better than the ones they had before. not so clumsy.

THURSDAY FEBRUARY 6TH 1862
Fort Holt Kentucky
Finished our chimneys, cleaned our quarters and drilled in the "Manual of Arms." very green having had arms so little of the time, and the weather has been unfavorable most of that time. The river is on the rampage, and threatens soon to drive some of us out of our cabbins on the left of the Co.

FRIDAY FEBRUARY 7TH 1862
Fort Holt Kentucky
The river so high this morning as to drive us out of our barracks. We put up tents and moved into them. Prospect of an attack. We drew ammunition. Maned the fort, ordered to sleep "on arms"

Rec'd orders to cook rations and be ready to march to-morrow. I wrote to J.F.B.~

SATURDAY FEBRUARY 8TH 1862
Fort Holt Kentucky
Pulled up stakes and started up the Ohio River at 10.P.M. on the Str.s Alps, and Lake-Erie-No. 2. the Erie sprung a leak and reported sinking in the night, we removed men and baggage to the Apls and a barge in-tow, with considerable excitement. lost only a few guns and accoutrements. no lives lost.

SUNDAY FEBRUARY 9TH 1862
Paducah Kentucky

I was ordered by Col. Wm. R. Morrison to go on board the Lake Erie she having overtaken us this morning. found Lieut. Col P. Pease and about twenty men of the Reg't aboard.

We helped coal the boat for our breakfast, then started up the Tennessee River had a very pleasant trip arrived at Fort Henry at 5.P.M. it is a low earthwork on the left bank. the river is up to the works on one side. We stayed on board the Apls during the night in charge

MONDAY FEBRUARY 10TH 1862
Fort Henry Tennessee

I was fortunate enough to be on detail to help unload the plunder again. we had to wade water two feet deep with the things. Pitched tents. then went around to see the Fortifications good works on the north bank of the river, with some very heavy guns. but the situation to low to be formidable. Rebel barracks badly riddled by the gun-boats.

TUESDAY FEBRUARY 11TH 1862
Fort Henry Tennessee

We cleared off our camp ground. Rec'd orders at 2.P.M. to prepare two days rations and be ready to march at 4.P.M. I carried a box of ammunition from the river to camp half-a-mile. We started at 5.P.M. with 40 round of Buck & Ball, and two days rations in havesacks. Knapsacks on, we went five miles toward Ft. Donelson and camped.

WEDNESDAY FEBRUARY 12TH 1862

Moved at Sun-up. reached the vicinity of Fort Donelson at 1.P.M. and formed in line of battle to receive a cavalry attack, but it didn't come. We move around towards the right. left our knapsacks, changed positions several times. some shelling but no casulties in our Reg't. Eat Raw bacon & Hard tack to day. the head of our Brig fired into after dark. we lay on our arms. in sight. Rebs.

THURSDAY FEBRUARY 13TH 1862
Fort Donelson Tennessee

Up at daylight, and formed at Sunup in 1/4 mile of the rebel works. in the front line at 8.A.M. maneuvered until noon. at 1.P.M. we were moved up under cover of brush, very close to the rebel works. then charged to within 30. yards of the Rebel works, and held the position one hour and ten minutes. Capt. J. W. Brokaw was killed, Jake Moore, O'Neill, Bishop, Smith Taylor Weldon Barton and Sawyer were severly wounded, of Co. "D,, Col. Morrison was wounded & taken off the field. The Reg't lost 14 men killed, 37 wounded, and _ missing.

FRIDAY FEBRUARY 14TH 1862
Fort Donelson Tennessee

The fight continues. Gun-boats and forts [guns] seem to be engaged. artillery heavy. frequent charges made during the day on the rebels lines. Weather cold. Men trying to build an earthwork for some artillery in front of our Reg't shelled heavily by the enemy. I was on guard at night every alternate hour. the hardest night in the service.

SATURDAY FEBRUARY 15TH 1862
Fort Donelson Tennessee

Heavy artillery firing all day. hard fighting on the right of us in the morning. we were moved back, and a battery was lost on the right. the enemy seem to be massed on the right, to break our lines. We were put farther to the left. I saw some of our company sleep in the snow when missles from artillery didn't go three feet above them.

SUNDAY FEBRUARY 16TH 1862
Fort Donelson Tennessee

The Fort was Surrendered at an early hour this morning with 15,000 prisoners. The troops that were engaged in the fight marched into the works and viewed the fortification and their contents. The Rebels standing by way side our band playing "Dixie" We stacked arms & I eat dinner with some Rebels in their camp today

MONDAY FEBRUARY 17TH 1862
Fort Donelson Tennessee

Prisoners being sent off for the north to day. We pulled up stakes and moved to an open field in the extreme East part of the camp near the river. the ground is very muddy. We supplied ourselves with rebel tents and many other things from their camps such as cooking vesels, dishes, cups, pans, etc. We also procured some eatables meat, corn meal, and potatoes. they were not so near starved out as we supposed them to be.

TUESDAY FEBRUARY 18TH 1862
Fort Donelson Tennessee

Went to the west side of camp to day for the ballance of our plunder. Prisoners still being sent north to spend the winter and see the country. On guard at the commissary and forrage pile. The ground at the western portion of the fortification is rough and very broken. some brush on it, and many deep ravines.

WEDNESDAY FEBRUARY 19TH 1862
Fort Donelson Tennessee

Rained all day. I lay in camp and cooked dinner for our mess. We(me) cut and carried Oak Bushes to make beds of, to keep our blankets out of the mud.

Jacob Moore died from wounds received last thursday and was burried to day by the boys of the company. I rec'd a letter from T.C.B.

THURSDAY FEBRUARY 20TH 1862
Fort Donelson Tennessee

In quarters most of the day. I received my sachel with part of my things by N. Washburn from Ft. Henry. I lost one blanket, a pr. boots, pr. pants, a hat & shirt. Stolen by some cowardly wretch who played sick and stayed behind. we were out on battallion drill and dressparade this afternoon.

FRIDAY FEBRUARY 21ST 1862
Fort Donelson Tennessee

J.K. Rainey & _ Cunningham came into camp before breakfast this morning from home, to see the sights of a battlefield. Lieut. E.B. Harlan

and twenty men detailed from our Co. to bury dead rebbels I was among
the detail. it was a mistake of the Adjts. it should have been 20 men from
the Reg't. I helped bury one Jonnie, the bushes litteraly cut to pieces. J.F.
Black came to camp this evening from home.

brother

SATURDAY FEBRUARY 22ND 1862
Fort Donelson Tennessee

Thirty four guns fired at the fort in commemoration of the birth day
of Gen'l. Washington.

Frank and [I] visited the 48th Ills. Infty. saw Capts. Stephenson and
Lydick, and others, acquaintences of Cos. "B,, & "I,, Then went over a
portion of the field to see the marks left upon the different objects

SUNDAY FEBRUARY 23RD 1862
Fort Donelson Tennessee

Lay in camp all day. Visited by Wm. Milner. cooked and washed
dishes, and waited upon the men generally. A praiseworthy perhaps, but
disagreeable position. going to try and do better than cook tomorrow.
Goshorn and I are conspiring against a couple of Corporals for the
position of Sergeants.

MONDAY FEBRUARY 24TH 1862
Fort Donelson Tennessee

Promotions being the order of the day. Jas. W. Cheney was made
Captain of Co. "D,,. E.B. Harlan 1st Lieut. A.S. Rowley 2nd Lieut. T.O
Hoss Elected 1st Serg't. F.J. Burrows 2nd serg't. S.C. Goshorn 3rd Serg't.
& Jas. A. Black 4th Serg't from the ranks over O.W. Brokaw. 5th Serg't
I ran against Corpls F.A. Niles & Geo Howard got a majority over both
of them.

TUESDAY FEBRUARY 25TH 1862
Fort Donelson Tennessee

Heavy frost this morning, a bright clear day. I was put on camp
guard as Serg't for the first time this evening. The wind blew hard from
the west and commenced raining at midnight. disagreeable then till day.
had to go around to the men's quarters and wake them up when the
reliefs were put on. One man of Co. "I,, left his post without leave and I
reported him to the Adjt.~

WEDNESDAY FEBRUARY 26TH 1862
Fort Donelson Tennessee

I lay in camp and slept most of the day. The Officers making out the muster and pay rolls for friday. Weather clear to-day. We had battallion drill and dressparade. I tried to learn my place as Serg't. and learned that I did'nt like the place of left guide on drill.

THURSDAY FEBRUARY 27TH 1862
Fort Donelson Tennessee

I was out on Non Com Officers drill for the first time. we also had company & battallion drill and dressparade, to day. not much time spent in idleness when the weather is so we can drill. Though our ranks have been sadly depleted during this month, the casualties of the fight together with the consequent hardships, privations & exposures.

FRIDAY FEBRUARY 28TH 1862
Fort Donelson Tennessee

Inspection to day, also muster for pay. O.W. Brokaw returned from home. he took the corpse of his father home. The cold wet weather, with scant and unwholesome diet have increased the sick to near two hundred, besides those sent off sick & wounded. Many a man who was stout and rugged a month ago is now a debilitated wreck.

SATURDAY MARCH 1ST 1862
Fort Donelson Tennessee

Out on Non Com Officers drill and dressparade to day. Weather clear and bright. hope we may be moved from here soon to a place better adapted for camping purposes. When it rains every thing is mud, and water suitable for drinking and culinary purposes is very scarce. Wood is scarce and has to be carried a long ways to cook with and for warming. I wrote to C.R.O'N

SUNDAY MARCH 2ND 1862
Fort Donelson Tennessee

Raining. I went [to] the Hospital, (an old building poorly adapted to the wants of a hospital and badly supplied) to get some medicine for Wm. Holmes and to see old Mr. Cunningham.(sick there) Several of the boys sick from sleeping on the wet ground & using bad water. Mostly <u>diarrhoius</u> [diarrheas].

MONDAY MARCH 3RD 1862
Fort Donelson, Tennessee
Weather cloudy and windy as usual. We received Orders to prepare three days cooked rations and be ready to march to-morrow morning. every body busy to-day. All anxious for the move. the prospects are in our favor as we <u>cant worst ourselves much,</u> and <u>may improve in a location</u> and water.

TUESDAY MARCH 4TH 1862
Fort Donelson Tennessee
"Struck tents" and moved out of the works at 8.A.M. and waited near by until noon for the ballance of the command to get ready. We marched over bad roads and fields in the direction of the Tenn. river above fort Henry. rained & snowed in P.M. Was very disagreeable. we camped after night on the ridge between the two rivers.

WEDNESDAY MARCH 5TH 1862
Stewart County Tennessee
Marched at 9.A.M. Past the Iron works. at 1.P.M. have marched far enough to be at the river now. I suspect that we have been misled. The Artillery left Ft. Donelson this morning overtook us at noon to day. we reached the Tenn. river at dark after a hard days march, and camped. we put up three tents for the Co.

We found the river high, water running three feet deep, for a space of five hundred yards between us and the river.

THURSDAY MARCH 6TH 1862
Metal Landing Tennessee
Lieut. E.B. Harlan and I went back [down] the road half a mile to a citizens, (Mr. McCuthen) and got a warm breakfast for .25cts. We crossed the slough to the landing most of the men went over in wagons. I crossed on the top of a rail fence. the rails covered with ice making it a very slow process. we went abord the Str. Ft. Wayne and crossed the river.

FRIDAY MARCH 7TH 1862
On board Str. Fort Wayne

We recrossed the river and went three miles up. we landed at Paris Landing awhile to day. the boys broke into a warehouse and got some whisky, and other articles tobaco, calicos, Lawns [fine sheer linen or cotton fabric], shoes, augers, Peas etc. after we crosst the river we went ashore and I cooked some of the Peas for dinner. The river is full of boats Maj. W.W. Bishop says there are 82.

SATURDAY MARCH 8TH 1862
On board Str. Fort Wayne

The Q.M. issued clothing to day. I drew pr Shoes & pr Socks. We lay by the shore all day waiting for other troops to arrive and get on transports. boats still coming up the river.

Most of the troops seem to be coming from Fort Donelson. more work to be done somewhe[re] soon rumored that we are going to Florence Alabama.

SUNDAY MARCH 9TH 1862
On board Str. Fort Wayne

Lay by the shore in the A.M. was detailed with four men to help clean off the decks of the boat. I cooked and washed in the forenoon, and in the afternoon. We went down to Fort Henry for coal. remained there until after night then went back to where started from in the morning.

Not many troops at Ft Henry. I think the fort has been dismantled of its guns.

MONDAY MARCH 10TH 1862
On board Str. Fort Wayne

We started up the river in company with nine other boats, destination unknown. I lost my pocketbook last night, containing one dollar and forty cts. and as much of a loss as ten fold the amount would be at any other time, as I am quite unwell, and not partial to "hard tack", even in health.

TUESDAY MARCH 11TH 1862
On board Str. Fort Wayne

Going up the Tenn. river to day Corpl. M. R. Kell joined us just from home. I borrowed some money ($.) of him. we have hard fare, many of the men sick with diarrhoeas, almost universally from change of water I suppose. Lat[e] night opposite Savanah. Hardin Co. Tenn. I recieved a letter from J.F.B.

WEDNESDAY MARCH 12TH 1862
On board Str. Fort Wayne

Lay opposite Savanah all day. fifty six Steamers lying here loaded with troops and munitions of war. J. Mason, Wm Clemens, Wm Peters, Eph Williams, and Wm Musgrave joined us to-day. We crossed the river to the north side to get some ammunition and recrossed again afterwards.

THURSDAY MARCH 13TH 1862
On board Str. Fort Wayne

We lay opposite Savanah until evening then crossed over and landed, and disembarked the 49" Ills with the 3rd Brig. 1st Division. I was detailed to help unload the boat, taking off wagons, mules, Q.M. & Commissary stores etc. it has been my fortune since we started from Camp Butler Ills to help handle this plunder almost everytime it has been moved. I have done considerable hard work at it.

FRIDAY MARCH 14TH 1862
Savanah Tennessee

I was detailed again with Eight men to clear off a camp ground pitched tents. rained in P.M. ballance of the Division gone up to Pitsburg Landing. A.K. Dement shot at a rabbit to day. Col. P. Pease said "he" would make an example of a man, by ordering him out and having him Shot, one of these days" We cut oak bushes to make beds. I am not well.

SATURDAY MARCH 15TH 1862
Savanah Tennessee

Weather cloudy. we are camped in a hollow. Short of provisions. the boys buying some from the citizens corn meal, chickens, potatoes, eggs, etc. we received a mail once more to day. I was fortunate enough to get half doz. letters. viz. [that is to say: namely] F.M.A., A.K.A., S.J.B. Wm B., S.B.A & J Keen, Jr. "When it rains it pours."

SUNDAY MARCH 16TH 1862
Savanah Tennessee

We drew some flour to day and had some "slap-jacks" Detailed for guard, with thirty men from the Reg't, but I being a supernumerrary, I returned to camp after posting the men. A Lt. of the 29" Ills Infty. officer of the guard. We got some more mail to day. I received a letter from J.F.B. and wrote J.F.B. & J. Keen, Jr.

MONDAY MARCH 17TH 1862
Savanah Tennessee

I was fortunate enough to be detailed again to day to clear off another camp. The Col. has found that our present camp dont meet the requirements of the service. We pulled up and moved repitched our tents, and traded some coffee for two chickens, and I cooked them. The best meal we have had in the Co. for two months. The citizens seem disposed to be friendly, and come into camp with marketing.

TUESDAY MARCH 18TH 1862
Savanah Tennessee

I went to the country with Corpl Howard to day and got dinner. bought some chickens, eggs, and corn meal. not much to be had in the country. We returned to camp and commenced doing well and living respectable, dont think there are any rebel troops in this neighborhood.

WEDNESDAY MARCH 19TH 1862
Savanah Tennessee

Lay in camp and cooked chickens and eggs for breakfast. I washed my clothes the hardest portion of a soldiers duty for me to perform. I had rather cook three days, than wash one. Engaged a bushel of meal to be brought in by a country-man for us.

THURSDAY MARCH 20TH 1862
Savanah Tennessee

I went out to a John Blacks with Serg't O.W. Brokaw on horseback. left our horses with an old man and had to ferry horse creek, half mile wide in a canoe. we eat dinner then went visiting. we bought bushel corn meal and returned to camp. Orders to be ready to move at 8.A.M. to-morrow.

FRIDAY MARCH 21ST 1862
Savanah Tennessee

Up at 3.A.M. cooked rations. packed knapsacks. struck tents at 11.A.M. and went aboard the Str. H Chouteau I was detailed with six men to load our wagons, Mules, horses, & Stores on the boat. I can always count on getting such a job. 2nd Serg't F.J. Burrows is detailed at Reg't Hd. Qrs. 3rd Serg't S.C. Goshorn is always either to drunk or to Sick. 5th Serg't O.W. Brokaw pretends to be doing duty with the Q.M. And Corporals are Sinecures [positions that require little or no work].

SATURDAY MARCH 22ND 1862
Pitsburg Landing Tennessee

Disembarked at 10.A.M. and marched out two and a half miles from the river. near the Shiloh church. Lt Harlan cleared off this camp. And we pitched tents and went to cooking for the mess. Water is excellent here, but to far off. have to carry drinking water about one quarter of a mile from a nice spring.

SUNDAY MARCH 23RD 1862
Shiloh Tennessee

In camp all day resting from our recent harrassing movements. had dressparade in the evening. The sutler is in camp now. I drew $.1.00 worth of Sutler tickets. Some of the boys spending all their wages with the sutler buying nuts, candies etc. that are of little use to them.   I wrote to S.B.A. & R.M.L.~

MONDAY MARCH 24TH 1862
Shiloh Tennessee

In camp all day. Capt. Cheney received half a dozen cartrage Revolvers to-day. he kept one. and let Lt. Harlan, Lt. Rowley, Serg't Hoss, Serg't Brokaw, and myself each have one at $.14.00, with each a box of 100 cartridges. He sent to Worchester Mass. for them. We are camped on level ground, in open timber land.

TUESDAY MARCH 25TH 1862
Shiloh Tennessee

Out on battalion drill in an open meadow the colonel has a drillmaster who rides along with him and tells him what commands to give, and how to give them. I saw Col. S.G. Hicks out on the field drilling the 40" Ills Infty. I visited several regiments. there seem to be a great many troops here. we are briggaded with the 17" Ills Inft, 29" Ills. Inft. and 43rd Ills Infty Commanded by Col. L.F. Ross of 17" Ills.

WEDNESDAY MARCH 26TH 1862
Shiloh Tennessee

We are drilling every day now. I saw a fine display of Infty & Artillery on the meadow drilling to day I think Brig. Gen'l John A. McClernand's entire Div. drills on that meadow. it is very level and contains about acres. I drew $.2.00 in Sutler tickets to day making $.4.00 in all I owe him.

THURSDAY MARCH 27TH 1862
Shiloh Tennessee

Capt Cheney, Hoss, Dickson, Brokaw, and I went out and practiced pistol shooting to-day. Rowley & Harlan not out. John Chapman came over to our camp to day visiting he belongs to the 40" Ills Inft. the 40" are about half mile farther to the right than we are in another Brig.

FRIDAY MARCH 28TH 1862
Shiloh Tennessee

Weather fine and pleasant. I visited the 48." Ills. Infty. We went out on drill I acted as left guide for Co "A,, had a dispute with the O. Serg't. A.K. Dement in regard to making a "left turn".~

Bob. Martin came from home he is clerking for P.P. Hamilton Sutler. he brought papers & letter from J.F.B.

SATURDAY MARCH 29TH 1862
Shiloh Tennessee

Weather very fine & pleasant. As Saturday is Soldiers wash day I went to the Spring and washed my clothes.

It is hard work washing in one kettle without a wash board. I had rather do any other work we have to do in camp. I would hire it done but havent the money to pay for it. The health of the men is improving since we have been here not many of our company sick now~

SUNDAY MARCH 30TH 1862
Shiloh Tennessee

Had inspection to day of arms & knapsacks, with blankets and clothing in them. I went over to the 40" Ills. and saw Slow Barnhill (Adj't.) Chapman John Higgason, and Beard's boys and some other acquaintances. their Reg't seems to be in good health, and fine spirits.

MONDAY MARCH 31ST 1862
Shiloh Tennessee

Cloudy and raining in the forenoon. We drew five days rations. Played ball with a lot of the boys. they are beginning to have some life about them again. the health and spirits of the men has improved materially since we left Fort Donelson and got off of those steam-boats. Lieut Thos. Kelly of the 40" Ills. visited us to day he is looking very well.

I find Salem boys in quite a number of regiments. Marion County need never be ashamed of her numbers, nor, of the character of the men who represent her in the Army. her representatives will compare favorably with those from any other county in number and character. And Illinoians seem to have established a good reputation in the estimation of the troops from the other states who were at Donelson.

TUESDAY APRIL 1ST 1862
Shiloh Tennessee

The sky clear. weather warm and pleasant. company drill A.M. and battallion drill and dressparad P.M. Lieut. McGaine Act' Reg't Adjt. was embarrassed and made a mistake on parade. Three gun-boats went up the river to day on a reconaisance

WEDNESDAY APRIL 2ND 1862
Shiloh Tennessee

Company drill in the A.M. in the skirmish and bayonette exercise. No drill in the P.M. the meadow occupied by the 2nd Division. Col. S.G. Hicks visited our camp this evening

THURSDAY APRIL 3RD 1862
Shiloh Tennessee

Drilled at the usual hours to day. The boy[s] returned from the Savanah Hospitals to day. some of them looking much better. I was visited by Serg't James McClure of the 3rd Iowa Infty. Clark came to-day with a stack of sutler goods for P.P. Hamilton there has not been many goods in camp since here

FRIDAY APRIL 4TH 1862
Shiloh Tennessee

Weather showery, we were caught in the rain while on drill to day. it did'nt only rain but it poured. We enjoyed seeing the Col.(Pease) get his good clothes wet. Long Roll beat at Sun-down. we fell into line and moved out a piece with the Brig. remained two or three hours and returned. Rebels said to be coming in force.

SATURDAY APRIL 5TH 1862
Shiloh Tennessee

No drill saturday being wash day since we have been here. We drew five days rations to day and baked a lot of buscuit[s] on Capt. Cheney's stove. Weather very pleasant. I was over to Shiloh church this morning and saw and heard a splendid brass or silver Band play, all mounted on white horses, blong to Ohio Cavalry. I saw some Rebels in the church. the Cavalry skirmished with the rebels to day. They are coming.~

SUNDAY APRIL 6TH 1862
Shiloh Tennessee

Long Roll beat at 7.A.M. our Reg't formed a line and were attacked. the briggade not formed. T.O. Hoss, John Wilson, Wm. J. Gray, J. Smith, John Ward, Geo. Howard, S. Bacon, R.A. Grunendike, John Hook, C.W, Rodecker, Wesley Simmons, J.D. Echols, were wounded almost at the first fire. Timothy Baldwin afterwards and died. we were forced back until 4.P.M. we held our ground.~ Capt. Cheney and I on Picket guard at night.

MONDAY APRIL 7TH 1862
Shiloh Tennessee

Ordered to "move steadily forward and retake the ground we lost yesterday," by Gen'l John A. McClernand. Joined on the left of Gen'l.

Smith's command. supported artillery awhile, then crossed an open field under the enemies fire of grape & canister. almost to their guns. then ordered to recross the field. Then we moved to the left obliquely and attack[ed] and drove the enemy beyond our camp. fresh troops pressed them farther. we halted at our camp.

The Reg't lost 17. killed and 99. wounded

TUESDAY APRIL 8TH 1862
Shiloh Tennessee

A false alarm, and stampede, with some of the men. we formed in line and waited an hour or two there was firing in the front but no attack. some of the stampeded men did'nt return until noon Details were made for briggade guard a thing though[t] of rather too late.~ details were made to bury the dead; from our Reg't Lieuts. Doll, Co. "C,, and Rogers, Co. "A,, were burried at dark by their companies.~

WEDNESDAY APRIL 9TH 1862
Shiloh Tennessee

We shot off and cleaned up our guns, and burried the dead about camp. during the two days fight our Reg't lost 17. men killed, 99. Wounded, and missing. John W. Bullard, Mathew Pate, & Jas. Thompson of Co. "D,, were among the missing. I went over to the 48th Ills. to day. I saw 134. rebels burried in one trench, and 23. in another. I went to the 15th Ills. and got my musket which I left in exchange for a rifle.

THURSDAY APRIL 10TH 1862
Shiloh Tennessee

The weather cool. we went over to the rear of our drill ground and cleared off another camp. The Reg'ts moved to it at Sun-down. There is a very disagreeable Stench pervades the entire neighborhood from the carcasses of the horses slain in the battle. Rebels said to be coming. we drew ammunition.

FRIDAY APRIL 11TH 1862
Shiloh Tennessee

A battery moved into our old camp, and we moved to the camp prepared yesterday. raining. pitched our tents. and [I] went in and took the Roll-Book and commenced acting in the capacity of Orderly Serg't.

as Goshorn is drunk and sick alternately and hence incapacitated for duty.

SATURDAY APRIL 12TH 1862
Shiloh Tennessee

I went to the commissary and drew rations. divided the company into four equal messes then divided the rations among them. not half supplied with cooking utensils. and but one or two good cooks in the Co. I wrote letters for Burt & Flake and wrote to J.F.B.

SUNDAY APRIL 13TII 1862
Shiloh Tennessee

Our Brig. went out on parade and heard Orders read by Adjt Ryan of the 17th Ills Infty. A prayer offered by the Chaplain of the 29th Ills. Infty. And a Speech by Brig. Gen'l. John A. McClernand and a Capt of the 17th Ills. Was visited by Drs. Elliot, J.K. Rainey, & Castle and J.P. Scott. went out on the battle field and picked up some bullets etc. to send home as trophies. Many citizens here getting bullets, *casses*, guns etc.

MONDAY APRIL 14TH 1862
Shiloh Tennessee

Weather fine. spent most of the day in camp. was called to see a sick man in Co. "F,, took J.K. Rainey with me. Our Surgeons stampeded the first morning of the fight and have not ventured to return to camp yet.

The din of battle seems rather to harsh for their sensative feelings. they are rather ornamental.

TUESDAY APRIL 15TH 1862
Shiloh Tennessee

I took out the company and drilled them for the first time. and was on dressparade as orderly the first time this evening. J.K. Rainey & Castle left for home, carrying trophies of different kinds.

We have poor water again and not very much of it. are using at present out of a little branch.

WEDNESDAY APRIL 16TH 1862
Shiloh Tennessee

We drew five days rations this A.M. and beef P.M. Edd L. Merritt in camp to-day. Lieut. A.S. Rowley rejoined the company. Capt Cheney and I went to the 15th Ohio Infty to get our tents. which Capt. loaned them just after the fight. they beiging [being] without. and we having a Surplus at present.

THURSDAY APRIL 17TH 1862
Shiloh Tennessee

Fine spring weather. the leaves on the trees as large as the palm of my hand. I drilled the company in A.M. Col. L.F. Ross 17th Ills. drilled the battallion this P.M. he is a much better drillmaster than Col. Pease. There [are] ten regiments on the drill ground at one time. a gread deal of energy Manifested in drilling. though some make but little progress Capt. Dearing our drill master is gone.

FRIDAY APRIL 18TH 1862
Shiloh Tennessee

The rebels said to be advancing. two or three Brigs sent out. canonading heard in the direction of Corinth, probability of an other fight soon.

I took a team and went after our tents again to the 15th Ohio Infty. got it this time except the poles. so much for our favor.~

SATURDAY APRIL 19TH 1862
Shiloh Tennessee

Raining and camp dull. nothing of importance going on in camp. a perfect monotony it seems. we cooked eat and lay in camp all day.~

Saw Samuel Bradford he is ta[l]king of going into the service. we have but little inducement to offer here. our sick are without medical attendance.

SUNDAY APRIL 20TH 1862
Shiloh Tennessee

Weather very disagreeable. raining most all day Lieut. E.B. Harlan went to the hospital boat sick to-day Capt Cheney & Lieut. Rowley left our mess and started one of their own. John Jenkins came into ours again. I took our sick up to a Doctor of some other regiment.

MONDAY APRIL 21ST 1862
Shiloh Tennessee

Col. Wm R. Morrison rejoined the regiment to-day. he is still lame, though he will stir things up a little here, and look after the interests of the men. Lt. Col. Pease will drill them. and thats as far as he goes. We have been without a Surgeon since the fight.

H. Austin rejoined the company to day. James P. Lindermann detailed for clerk at Brig. Gen. John A. McClernands Head Quarters, yesterday.

TUESDAY APRIL 22ND 1862
Shiloh Tennessee

Weather very fine, again. we drew five days rations ninty pounds fresh beef fore quarter. I washed my clothes to day. Wm Clemens sick with Erysipelas in the face. Had battalion drill this evening. Col. Pease got fuddled, this evening, and got the left in front, and had dressparade without correcting the mistake.

WEDNESDAY APRIL 23RD 1862
Shiloh Tennessee

I went to Col. Morrison and got a pass, and went to the river to see Lieut E.B. Harlan he is sick on the Str. Emerald. he is short of money and dispirited.

I saw the gun boat Tyler bring a rebel Steamboat down the river to day with the stars-and-bars flying under the Stars-And-Stripes. its a capture.

THURSDAY APRIL 24TH 1862
Shiloh Tennessee

Pulled up stakes and moved four miles in a South westerly direction.(toward Corinth). We left our tent for the sick of the company.(the best we had.) We divided our mess among the ballance of the messes. for want of a tent, our camp is out in a open field. there are very many troops about here.

FRIDAY APRIL 25TH 1862
Camp Stanton Tennessee

Raining most all day and night. Troop[s] are still coming out. One Briggade went forward on a reconnaisance to-day. trying to learn somthing of the enemies where-abouts, circumstances and the locality of the country. There are some earthwork in front of us. with some 24. Pdr's and the 11th and 48th Ills Inft supporting them. there is an open field of perhaps one hundred acres here, used as a camp ground.

SATURDAY APRIL 26TH 1862
Camp Stanton Tennessee

The weather very pleasant. I went to the 48th Ills and [saw] the boys and the fortifications the first that this army has thrown up Col. Phillip B. Frank's Reg't. 30 Ills Infty. arrived here to-day. We drew five days rations. prospect of a move as we generally move when we have most to carry.

SUNDAY APRIL 27TH 1862
Camp Stanton Tennessee

The boys raised a fuss this morning, threating to go to the river and clean out the Quartermaster, Jim Davis. Col. Morrison arrested Serg't. Joe Lucas Co. "G,, Lawrence Allerding Co. "A,, and Ira C. Wiggins Co. "D,, and sent me with them to the Brig. Officer of the Day. I left them with Lt. Bliss officer of the guard. Rec'd letters from Lyde & J.F.B.

MONDAY APRIL 28TH 1862
Camp Stanton Tennessee

Lieut Rowley drilled the company to day. after which we held an Election in the company to fill the vacancy made by Serg't F.J. Burrows promotion to Serg't Major. Serg'ts Goshorn, Myself & Brokaw were each raised one grade. Corpl. McKinney Elected fifth Serg't. & Nathan E. Lever Elected Corporal. troops moving towards Corinth.

TUESDAY APRIL 29TH 1862
Camp Stanton Tennessee

It rained again to day. I had a chill last night and sick to-day from the wetting I got during the night. Rec'd orders to be ready to move at 10.A.M. to day. We struck tents and moved out on the Corinth road three miles, and camped on a hill just at the beginning of some low marshy looking ground. we are in a thick woods this time with considerable underbrush. Cant see far to the front.

WEDNESDAY APRIL 30TH 1862
Camp_____Tennessee

We are now moving a short distance every few days and there is no special name given to each camp, but all designated or denominated alike the"Camp in the Field." Hence I will designate them by the distance from the Tennessee River at Pitsburg Landing, styling this "Camp 8. miles out." We mustered for pay to day. then moved a half mile to the right, across the road, and put up tents. After clearing off the under brush, we are now in good shades.

THURSDAY MAY 1ST 1862
Camp 8 Miles Out Tenn

I went to the Surgeon this morning and got some Quinine & Opium for Diarrhoea & Intermittent and took it lay in quarters most all day sick. Col. Pease had another attack of the Clearing-Mania to day and ordered a detail to clear off the camp as though we were going to spend the summer here.~ the weather is warm and pleasant here at this time. there is no citizens living about here.

FRIDAY MAY 2ND 1862
Camp 8 Miles Out Tenn.

The teams went to the river for more rations in compliance with an order requiring five days rations to be kept constantly on hand ahead. Capt. Cheney went in charge of the teams to day. Lieut Harlan has left Pitsburg Landing. gone down the river and perhaps home.

SATURDAY MAY 3RD 1862
Camp 8 Miles Out Tenn.

We were up in line of battle at 2.A.M. and remained until daylight, in readiness for an attack. Rec'd Orders to turn over our tents to the Quartermaster except two to the Co. (which was done during the day.) and to prepare four days cooked rations and be ready to march at 8.A.M. to morrow.~

SUNDAY MAY 4TH 1862
Camp 8 Miles Out Tenn.
Marched at 10.A.M. towards Corinth, the country is hilly and broken. we went four miles and camped it rained on us most all day and during the night. John Jenkins and I slept under an old fly on the ground and got thoroughly drenched. we are in a little open field on a hillside. I am still quite unwell.

MONDAY MAY 5TH 1862
Camp 12 Miles Out Tennessee
Ordered to report the company for Picket-Guard at 8.A.M. we went and marched from place to place until 1.P.M. we reached the Picket-post I remained up most all night along the line which was near a bayou, or Slough, at the edge of an old field. the weather was clear and chilly. no disturbance on the line has been no fighting for several days except it was a cavalry skirmish~

TUESDAY MAY 6TH 1862
Camp 12 Miles Out Tenn
Relieved off Picket at 1.P.M. no excitement on the line. we came in and slept the ballance of the day. camp is either extremely dull or I am very stupid; perhaps both.~ We have good water here a very good Spring under a very big hill not far off. somebody killed a sheep~

WEDNESDAY MAY 7TH 1862
Camp 12 Miles Out Tenn
The first Division out on review to day   Gov. Yates and Genl. McClernand present. the Governor made a little speech and promised to remain until after the battle of Corinth and take the Illinois men home that were wounded with him. I got very sick had to leave the ranks for a shade, and wate until dark.

THURSDAY MAY 8TH 1862
Camp 12 Miles Out Tenn
I was sick and in quarters most of the day Priv. I.Y. Barton returned to-day he was wounded and sent of[f] from Donelson. Boys drawing clothing to-day. Nothing of interest in camp. no news of importance. no

mail. no late papers. the mail is very irregular and uncertain and seldom arrives.~

FRIDAY MAY 9TH 1862
Camp 12 Miles Out Tenn

I lay in camp all day sick. it seems I cant get well. the Surgeons have no facilities for taking care of the sick, or are not disposed to interest themselves for the welfare of the sick. I get medicine about one day in nine. there are two or three Hospital tents hauled along with the regiment and the sick are scattered about through the companies taking care of themselves as best they can.

SATURDAY MAY 10TH 1862
Camp 12 Miles Out Tenn

I went to the hospital by directive of Doctor Marlow to be sent to the river to-morrow. I found the Hosp't tent with a lot of brush big enough for filling up a mudhole in the road. and a [lot of] other sick men in there. Col. Morrison (had on uniform and) was on dressparade for the first time to-day.

SUNDAY MAY 11TH 1862
Camp 12 Miles Out Tenn

I was sent back with nine other men in two ambulance by Surg. Wm. H. Medcalf to the hospital boat. We were first put on the Str Fanny Bullet, then on another boat, and taken four miles up the river to Hamburg, and there put ashore, without any one to tell us where to go or what to do. We found the Hospital.

MONDAY MAY 12TH 1862
Hamburg Tennessee

We are in Hospital, such as it is--in Ward No. 25., and Mess No. 10. we are lying in a Sibley tent, on the ground, without Straw even. the tents are in an old corn field and the furrows and ridges run through our tent just as the plow left them in laying the corn by, with the rains since on them.

TUESDAY MAY 13TH 1862
Hamburg Tennessee

The Surgeons here belonging to the army seem to be careless, cross and indifferent as to the welfare of the soldiers. there are some citizen Physicians here who are very kind and attentive. there is one here from Springfield Illinois. I think a small man and a german in charge of our ward. We have tolerable fair rations, soft-bread, coffee, soup, potatoes, meat, rice etc.~

WEDNESDAY MAY 14TH 1862
Hamburg Tennessee

In Hospital. Two Surgeons sent here by the Sanitary commission are alone worthy of the positions they hold, so far as I have been able to observe. The Surgeons here belonging to the army seem capable of eating sanitaries [items related to health] sent here by benevolent people at home for the sick, and of neglecting patients.~

THURSDAY MAY 15TH 1862
Hamburg Tennessee

I am getting better, though to nature be the praise ascribed, for the Surgeons have no claims upon my convalecence, as I have had no medicine. Some of the boys are getting discouraged Peyton Smith Co. "I,, is in tent with me with Rant Fever and makes a great deal of complaint cries like a boy.

FRIDAY MAY 16TH 1862
Hamburg Tennessee

Peyton Smith and others Sent off down the river to Hospitals in their respective States. I dont want to go prior to the taking of Corinth. I think I will be able to join the Reg't soon. the Hospital and everything pertaining to it, is full of vermin. even the adjacent woods are infested with them.

SATURDAY MAY 17TH 1862
Hamburg Tennessee

The 25th Ward was broken up to day and I was sent to Ward No. 2. much better place the ground is smooth and dry. the tents have been ditched and I got a matress to lay on there is a ward master here to wait upon patients that were not able to wait upon themselves. I met with a cavalry man here sick on the bed next to mine with the fever by the name James Black.

SUNDAY MAY 18TH 1862
Hamburg Tennessee

Able to walk about a little and wait upon myself a little, a very essencial qualifications in this Hospital. I walked down to the river this evening and saw the gun Boat Tyler here. there are a great many sick here quite a large field of hospital tents and generally full~

MONDAY MAY 19TH 1862
Hamburg Tennessee

Convalesing. am able to eat a slice of bread, two small potatoes, a spoonfull of gravy and a cup of tea, a Sick soldiers ration in hospital The Surgeons made a flying visit through our tent to day and sent off some boys down the river to other hospitals, and then to their homs.

TUESDAY MAY 20TH 1862
Hamburg Tennessee

I am gaining strength but very slow can walk but a short distance at a time. I am very tired of the place and will leave it as soon as posible the vermin are to plenty here for this place to hold me long after I get well enough that I can walk from Pitsburg Landing to the Reg't.

WEDNESDAY MAY 21ST 1862
Hamburg Tennessee

Heavy firing heard to day in the directions of Pope's Division many rumors in camp in regard to matters at the front. I think I will be able to leave this place soon for the Reg't. There are perhaps 1000 men sick here now. I saw John Cleverstine and John W.D.F. Cansey here they will not return to the Reg't if they can avoid it as they are undoubtedly working for a discharge.~

THURSDAY MAY 22ND 1862
Hamburg Tennessee

I asked the Surgeon to let me go to the Regiment to-day. says I may go to-morrow I got my pass some of the 61st Ills Infty. here going with me. all seem determined on leaving here at the earliest posible moment. I had rather endure the hardships and privations of camp life, than the vermin here

FRIDAY MAY 23RD 1862
Hamburg Tennessee

We left the Hospital, went to the river, and got on board the Str. White Cloud, and went to Pitsburg landing. I found John C. Wilson & M. Washburn there with the teams for rations. I went out with them to the Regiment there was a great many teams on the road going & coming. It was about fifteen miles out took us until night.

SATURDAY MAY 24TH 1862
Camp 15 Miles Out Tenn.

The Reg't came in off Picket. I washed my clothes and cleaned my guns, which was very rusty & dirty. I divided rations between the messes which has been drawn by Goshorn the boys are very much down on him. the Regiment is behind a line of good earthworks. I recd letters from C.R.O'N, A.K.A., & J. Keen, Jr.~

SUNDAY MAY 25TH 1862
Camp 15 Miles Out Tenn.

Lay in camp most of the day not very stout yet and sick in the P.M. Gen'l. John A. Logan's Picket drove in by the rebels to day. prospect of a fight soon. C.R. O'Neill returned to day going to try to get a discharged. Wm Musgrave returned also to day. We had inspection of arms and dressparade.~ Col. Pease is trying to prevent gambling among the men and officers, a hard undertaking.~

MONDAY MAY 26TH 1862
Camp 15 Miles Out Tenn.

I wrote a letter to Aunt Harriett for C.R. O'Neill to day Q.M. issuing clothing. I drew a Shirt. Went with F.J. Burrows over to the 48th Ills Infty. they are at the next line of works in our rear 1 mile. Eat supper with Capt. Lydick saw them on dressparad Capt Galbreath officer of Picket. yesterday I wrote to J.F.B. & J. Keen, Jr.

TUESDAY MAY 27TH 1862
Camp 15 Miles Out Tenn.
I went with C.R. O'Neill to Gen'l McClernands Hd Qrs to get the Div. Surg's approval to his discharge. he was absent and we did'nt get to see him to day.~ We are very scarce of water here, and what we have is warm and muddy. beside[s] it is full of tadpoles and wiggletales.

WEDNESDAY MAY 28TH 1862
Camp 15 Miles Out Tenn.
We received orders this morning early to be ready to march at 7.A.M. with four days rations in haversacks, and one hundred rounds of ammunition. We moved through Logan's Works in the direction of the M&O R.R. Gen'l. W.T. Sherman gained and held his position. Gen'l Logan on his right and we on the extreme right of our lines. firing heard in the P.M.~

THURSDAY MAY 29TH 1862
Camp Near Corinth Mississippi
Went to the R.R. for water with Jim Gray Col L.F. Ross fired artillery over us at a rebel Picket post. there was heavy firing in the direction of Corinth, and Picket firing on the lines during the day. Our C. & G Equipage was brought up to Sherman's old camp to day and left there as we have no works yet on our part of the lines. the Pickets got to friendly along the line, and would meet, and trade knives and play poker. Ross broke it up~

FRIDAY MAY 30TH 1862
Camp Near Corinth Mississippi
We moved at Sunup to the M.&O. R.R. and I went on Picket with most of the company. Heavy Explosions heard and dark smoke seen in the direction of Corinth to day. rumors say the fort has surrendered. Our Reg't are building earthworks on the west side of the R.R. to day, to be ready for an attack.~

SATURDAY MAY 31ST 1862
Camp Near Corinth Mississippi
Corinth is evacuated this morning. the rebels gone in different directions. Many of them will doubtless be picked up by our Cavalry,

as they are in pursuit.~ We were releived off Picket this morning by the 17th Ills. Infty. Co. "G,, killed a deer on the lines this morning.~ We returned to Gen'l Sherman's old camp to day, and took possession of it. we found water extremely scarce and bad. we carry it from one mile, to one mile and a half. get it from the creek. We have no news from the fleeing enemy, nor from our cavalry in pursuit. We have been one month and one week on this campaign its casualties have been large though few in proportion have been slain by the enemy. hardships, privation and disease have thined our ranks, and prostrated our army.

SUNDAY JUNE 1ST 1862
Camp Near Corinth Mississippi

A detail made to clean off camp ground to day. Alfred Beard came over to our lines and stayed an hour. he belongs to the 40th Ills Infty they are in advance of us now. C.R. O'Neill went to Corinth to day to see the place. he says the works are not very strong. not as good as he expected to find. are inferior to ours here.~

I lay in camp and wrote to J. Keen, Jr. & J.F.B.

MONDAY JUNE 2ND 1862
Camp Near Corinth Miss.

Capt. Cheney went to Corinth to day, and I drilled the company. Serg't. McKinney undertook it and could do nothing with the men they would not obey him. All the companies out at the same time. we are now behind strong fortifications built by Gen'l. W.T. Shermans. Division. I wrote to A.K.A.

TUESDAY JUNE 3RD 1862
Camp Near Corinth Miss

Fred Niles, Wm Flake, & Silas Dickson went to Corinth to day, and were arrested for picking up an old carpet, and kept under guard for it awhile~

Capt. Cheney drilled the company to day.~ The rebels are said to be scattering in every direction. many of them will go to their homes, and stay there.

WEDNESDAY JUNE 4TH 1862
Camp Near Corinth Mississippi
We received Orders at 6.A.M. to be ready to move at 7 1/2.A.M. with two days cooked rations. we moved at 10.A.M. in a nort[h]erly direction on the Purdy road. we went three miles and camped in consequence of a swamp, having to be corduroyed Col. Morrison is sick and in an Ambulance

THURSDAY JUNE 5TH 1862
Camp in the Woods Tennessee
We moved at an early hour toward Perdy. Col. Morrison was sent to Pitsburg Landing yesterday or to day sick Col. Pease is Sick also. Maj Bishop in command of the Reg't. Capt. Cheney called Ira C. Wiggins to account to day for stealing Sugar from the mess while we were on picket, to make lemon ade.~ We reached Purdy late in the day a very pretty little place of 1000 inhabitance. we camped close by.~

FRIDAY JUNE 6TH 1862
Purdy Tennessee
The 48th Ills Infty were put in our briggade. the 61st Ills rejoined it to day they were sent some time since to repair the road between Corrinth and Shiloh~
We moved at 8.A.M. and reached Bethel at noon pitched tents. found numerous Springs of excellent water. Bethel is a very small place on the M.&O. R.R.

SATURDAY JUNE 7TH 1862
Bethel Tennessee
I got a pass C.R. O'Neill and I went to the country on a foraging expedition. he fainted by the way side and turned for camp. I went two miles from camp to Thos. Gills, and got some Huckleberry pies and returned to camp
Companies "D,, & "F,, detailed for Picket with a battery of Artillery. We were posted on Tatum's hill.~

SUNDAY JUNE 8TH 1862
Bethel Tennessee

On guard. I went to camp and shaved. then went with Capt Cheney to Mr Tatum's and engage[d] dinner. returned at noon and eat dinner. an avowed secesh girl waiting on the table. The old man is turning his coat he will be a good Union-man in a very short time. he think this is a bad locality for a rebel.

MONDAY JUNE 9TH 1862
Bethel Tennessee

Capt. and I went back to Tatums and got breakfast. we were releived off Picket by Co.s "C,, & "I,, returned to camp, and I went to the spring in the afternoon and washed my clothes There are a great many troops here, reorganizing. one of those springs here will furnish water for a large army. this railroad will doubtless be put in order soon from here to Columbus Ky

TUESDAY JUNE 10TH 1862
Bethel Tennessee

Capt. Jones Co. "F,, left for home to day. Lt Col. P. Pease Lt. A.S. Rowley Co. "D,, received leaves of absence to day, and Corporal C.R. O'Neill his discharge. Corpl Howard rejoined the Co. yesterday. I bought a hat to day of Wash Morrow, Co. "I,, for $.2.50cts some of the boys who are teaming, from here to the river buy articles of clothing there from Sutlers and bring here for sale to the boys~ I wrote to J.F.B.

WEDNESDAY JUNE 11TH 1862
Bethel Tennessee

Col. Pease, Lt. Rowley and C.R. O'Neill left for home to day. F.J. Burrows and I got a pass and went to the country to day. Eat dinner at Thos. Gills then bought some honey and buttermilk and brought to camp. The former I divided with Col. Haynie,_the latter I shared with Maj. Bishop~

THURSDAY JUNE 12TH 1862
Bethel Tennessee

I lay in camp all day and read "Midshipman Easy." took a list of the clothing wanted by the boys of the company. The days are very warm and the nights quite cool. the health of the men is beginning to improve since we came here. the duty is light and no drilling now~

FRIDAY JUNE 13TH 1862 SATURDAY JUNE 14TH 1862

Bethel Tennessee

Editor's note--James Black transcribed the same information he wrote for June 10 and June 11 to June 13 and June 14. Subsequently, no entry recorded for these dates.

SUNDAY JUNE 15TH 1862

Bethel Tennessee

The 43rd & 61st Ills Inft left for Jackson Tennessee the "Articles of War" read to the companies to day by order. There was church in Bethel to-day many citizens in I was to preaching some of the citizens came to camp with the officers for dinner. two took dinner with us. they seem to be about one century behind~

MONDAY JUNE 16TH 1862

Bethel Tennessee

Capt Cheney and nine men went on Picket to day. We moved camp to day up on the hill west I put up Capt's tent for him. we are now probably located for the summer. it is the best and most convinient camp we have had since in the service. water in abundance. wrote F.M.A.

TUESDAY JUNE 17TH 1862

Bethel Tennessee

Windy and cloudy to day. camp dull & monotonous Many citizens in trading chickens butter Eggs etc. for Coffee. I bought some for our mess~

The natives have been using Rye, and other substitutes for coffee. none in the country for sale at any price. no goods of any descripthion in the country for sale. the citizens live on the[ir] own products here now~

WEDNESDAY JUNE 18TH 1862
Bethel Tennessee

It rained this morning. there were many citizens in camp to day I met with a Miss. Black. selling Chickens Butter Corn bread & Eggs plumbs etc. No relation of mine by the way. I bought some buttermilk at .05cts. pr. qt. Our teams returned from Jackson Tenn. No news~

THURSDAY JUNE 19TH 1862
Bethel Tennessee

I detailed the whole company to day for guard and fatigue. the duty is very heavy just now. rations have to be hauled from Pitsburg landing twenty odd miles for the command here comprising the 48" & 49" Ills. Inft. Co."I,, 11" Ills. Cavalry and Kidd's Battery 14" Ind. Artillery.~

FRIDAY JUNE 20TH 1862
Bethel Tennessee

I drew five days rations F.J. Burrows and I got a pass and went out to old Mr. Gills and gathered blackberries. Capt Cheney gone out to the country. Serg't Goshorn gone down about Iuka to the 21st Ills Infty to *Iuka*
see some of his friends

I was left in charge of the Co.

SATURDAY JUNE 21ST 1862
Bethel Tennessee

Drew two days fresh beef. Lay in camp and read the "Rebel Scout." Nothing of interest in camp we have no news. no papers here to read or if one should happen to reach camp it is the mearest accident if we get to see it. there are so many anxious. beside it having to come by way of Pitsburg Landing it is several days old~ Old Mr. Gill and ladies in to see dressparade.~

SUNDAY JUNE 22ND 1862
Bethel Tennessee

Preaching in camp to-day. I was detailed with thirty men to unload the Cars. the road is open now. Dr. A. Marlow married yesterday and gone to Ills~

I was detailed to-day for duty in the Hospital by request of Dr. Wm H. Medcalf Surgeon of the Reg't to act in the capacity of Hospt Steward. I wrote to <u>B.N.B.</u>

MONDAY JUNE 23RD 1862
Bethel Tennessee

On duty in the Hospital. I gave medicine to twenty or more men belonging to different Reg'ts in Hospt. here~ One man of the 12" Mich Infty died to-day here.

I made requisition and drew five days rations for thirty seven men. the doctor orders more rations drawn than we have men about the Hospital.~

TUESDAY JUNE 24TH 1862
Bethel Tennessee

E.W. Charles is playing sick. I went with Dr. Medcalf to the Reg't. this morning to attend sick call.

A dance in town this evening at Milt Simon's, it was broken up, and they went out side the lines and reorganized, and went "on with the dance." and in their actions said, "Let Joy be unconfined."

WEDNESDAY JUNE 25TH 1862
Bethel Tennessee

M. Washburn in the guard house to day for going outside the lines without leave or pass. Thos. Smith and Saddler rejoined Co. "D,, yesterday. Smith was wounded at Fort Donelson and has not been with us since until now.~ I attended the sick in the hospital to day and E.W. Charles went with Dr. Medcalf to attend sick call at the Reg't.~

THURSDAY JUNE 26TH 1862
Bethel Tennessee

I went to the Railroad with Seventeen convalecents to send them to Jackson Tenn but no room on the train. The 14" Ind. Battery were out practicing to day and threw two shells into camp, though neither of them exploded. hence there was no serious results in consequence~

FRIDAY JUNE 27TH 1862
Bethel Tennessee

Drew five days rations for Hospital to day. and Dr. Marlow Act Ass't Surg. 49" Ills Infty and I took an inventory of the Medical & Hospital property to-day preparatory to making out Quarterly Returns to the Surg. Genl. I sold $.19.00 worth of rations to day to citizens to get money to buy butter Eggs Chickens etc.

SATURDAY JUNE 28TH 1862
Bethel Tennessee

It rained hard at Sunup. There was a Mass Meeting out in the country to day. Many went from camp to it Capt Stephenson made a speech. There is talk of raising a regiment here in this neighborhood. Officers had a meeting in Camp~

SUNDAY JUNE 29TH 1862
Bethel Tennessee

Lieut. E.B. Harlan rejoined the company to day. has been absent since the 20th day of April. Sick.~ C.R. O'Neill came to day from home brough me three shirts, two pr drawers one pr. Socks and one Hdkf~

Preaching in camp A.M. & P.M. by a citizen a large congregation principally Citizens. Their curiosity brings a large portion of them. They have been told that the "Yankees have horns."~

MONDAY JUNE 30TH 1862
Bethel Tennessee

The Regiment Mustered for pay to day. an article I am much in need of as I have not been paid since January at Camp Butler Ills. Capt. L. Kurghoff Co. "C,, 49" Ills. Infty. is drilling one hundred picked men from the Reg't for a drilling match to take place on the 4th of July between the 48 & 49" Ills Infty Vols at the Cellebration at this Post.~

TUESDAY JULY 1ST 1862
Bethel Tennessee

The 48" & 49" Ills. Infty. have marching orders. they are to go by way of Columbus Ky. they went to the Railroad but there was no train came to take them, and the Order was countermanded, and they returned to

Camp. The chances were thought good for Richmond Va. I was to be left at the Hospital for the time. until some other troops arrived and arrangements made

WEDNESDAY JULY 2ND 1862
Bethel Tennessee

Dr. Medcalf and E.W. Charles went to Jackson with the expectation of getting home on a sick leave I prescribed for the sick in the hospital this morning while Dr Marlow attended sick call at the Regt all goes on smothly. health reasonably good.

THURSDAY JULY 3RD 1862
Bethel Tennessee

A. Ward and I went to Pitsburg landing to day, for Medical & Hospital supplies and sanitaries in an Ambulance. There are but few men or boats there now. we returned to within four miles of Bethel having attended to our business and traveled thirty six miles to day~

FRIDAY JULY 4TH 1862
Bethel Tennessee

A National Salute fired. Cellebration on hand. Speeches made by Stephenson, Mayfield, and others

Match drill between the 48" & 49" Ills. Then came a little "heel & toeology." by Soldiers and Citizens on the ground under an arbor prepared for the occasion. I rec'd letters from J. Keen Jr A.K.A. & B.N.B. wrote B.N.B. & A.K.A.

SATURDAY JULY 5TH 1862
Bethel Tennessee

I directed John Keen, Jr. to collect some money for me, by moral Suasion if he could, but by law if he must during the wheat Sales. As I will have to settle up my business down there very close to realize any thing.~ told him to settle with hard cases at his own discretion~

The days are warm. and the nights cool the health of the command is improving. I wrote John Keen, Jr.

SUNDAY JULY 6TH 1862
Bethel Tennessee

The cavalry sent out in the direction of Pochahauntas on a scout the rebels are threating to burn the place. It is south of the Memphis and Charleston Railroad and is consequently on contested ground between the two armies, and its at long range from here~

MONDAY JULY 7TH 1862
Bethel Tennessee

Serg't Wm. G. McKinney was Shot accidently this morning at 3.O'clock, and his thigh broken, by James Davis Co. "K,, 49" Ills Inft. while on Picket. He was sent to the Jackson Hospital. Lt. E.B. Harlan accompanying him. The 7" Kansas Cav.(Kansas Jayhawkers.) past here to day for Corinth Miss.

TUESDAY JULY 8TH 1862
Bethel Tennessee

Orderly Serg't Thos. O. Hoss rejoined the company to day. was wounded Apl 6" at Shiloh and absent since then. Dr. Medcalf & E.W. Charles returned from Jackson to day. did'nt get home on sick leave as they expected the doctor came back with his lip down.

Lt. Harlan returned from Jackson Tenn.

WEDNESDAY JULY 9TH 1862
Bethel Tennessee

I saw L.D. Skilling on the train to day going home. he had been down about Corinth or Iuka.

I went to the Reg't to see C.R. O'Neill. Sick he is in the Sutler's Dep't selling goods for P.P. Hamilton since his return to camp this time. The weather very warm and every thing dull in camp. some sickness in consequence of warm days and cool nights.

THURSDAY JULY 10TH 1862
Bethel Tennessee

The weather extreemly warm, and the camp exceedingly dull. I bought some buttermilk of Mr. Kanoodle to day.(Dr. Marlow's intended father-in-law.) I made a Register of patients in Hospital to day the first ever made in this hospital or in the 49" Ills Infty.~

FRIDAY JULY 11TH 1862
Bethel Tennessee

I went out to the country, with F.J. Burrows and others, to gather Blackberries. we found them plenty and very fine three miles from camp in a westerly direction. roads dry & dusty and very rough and considerably broken.

We returned to camp. I wrote to Wm. Holmes & J.F.B.

SATURDAY JULY 12TH 1862
Bethel Tennessee

The Signal corps practicing to day with their white flags. Sold 61.lbs of ham at 12 1/2cts pr lb. $.7.62 1/2cts. and bought Chickens Eggs & butter. drew Rations again to day. we have to purchase our Sanitaries here for hospital purposes. hence we sell the ration we cant use~

SUNDAY JULY 13TH 1862
Bethel Tennessee

C.R. O'Neill Sick and went to the cars to go home but the train did'nt come from Corinth Miss.

Preaching in camp to day by Com. Sergeant Bundy of the 48" Ills Infty. there is no Chaplain in either of the Regts here. the Chaplain of the 48" Ills, Robt. H. Manier, has gone into the Sutler's business, it is more profitable and better adapted to his peculiar inclination~

MONDAY JULY 14TH 1862
Bethel Tennessee

I requested Dr. Wm. H. Medcalf to relieve me to day from duty in the Medical Dep't and let me return to the company. Surgeons are spunging their board off the inmates of the Hospital, and have been doing so during my stay here. C.R. O'Neill left for home. P.P. Hamilton returned to the regiment

TUESDAY JULY 15TH 1862
Bethel Tennessee

Had a shower this A.M. the weather continues very Warm. camp very dull, a great want of events.

I bought a Doz chickens to day we continue to eat just the same as though events were of a livelier nature. Jacob Scott of 14" Ind. Batt. died this A.M. Dr. Medcalf has a kind of Post Hospital of this.~

WEDNESDAY JULY 16TH 1862
Bethel Tennessee

I got a Pass and went to Jackson Tenn. to see Serg't McKinney he is apparently doing well some hopes entertained of his recovery. I saw Maj. W.W. Bishop there he is on a Court Martial. Jackson is a fine looking place, ornamented with trees and Shrubbry, and now with soldiers.

THURSDAY JULY 17TH 1862
Jackson Tennessee

I saw Capt. Berry & P.P. Hamilton on the train going north. I bought some clothing a pr Pants, a pr Shoes & a knife. I returned to Bethel. Lt. Rowley rejoined the Co. absent on sick leave since June 11".62. also Corpl Robt Fletcher from home quite a number of men and officers are rejoining the Regiment that have been absent for some time. some since Donelson~

FRIDAY JULY 18TH 1862
Bethel Tennessee

I was relieved from duty in the Medical Dep't to day at my own request, and returned to the company for duty. Thos. Smith returned from Jackson Tenn. sick. he has been waiting upon Serg't McKinney. left him doing well. improving. I went out on dressparade~

SATURDAY JULY 19TH 1862
Bethel Tennessee

I took Corpl. M.R. Kell and Thos. Smith to Hospital sick to day. The weather is pleasant again. I heard that Frank was going to Camp Butler with his men Soon to organize with some regiment. recruiting is a dull and slow business now in Ills. I rec'd a letter from R.M.L.

SUNDAY JULY 20TH 1862
Bethel Tennessee

I went on guard at the Provost-Marshals. Lieut. Ferd Stephenson of the 48" Ills Infty is Provost Marshal Orderly Serg't. A.K. Dement Co.

"A,, returned to day from home. was wounded at Shiloh and a[b]sent since that time a rebel Soldier and three Jews and numerous citizens in to day. I rec'd letter from C.R.O'N and R.M.L.

MONDAY JULY 21ST 1862
Bethel Tennessee

A row between some of the boys and Milt Simons in consequence of some of his disloyal sentiments, boastfully expressed. he was put in the Military Prison to prevent the Soldiers hanging him, and was sent off some where by the Comndg Officer or the Officer of the guard on the sly to keep him out of the clutches of the soldiers. this is not a good place to preach treason.

TUESDAY JULY 22ND 1862
Bethel Tennessee

Milt Simons was Sent to Jackson Tenn. by Corpl Howard for trial.~ Discharges came to-day for T.M. Smith, Orville Niles & Mr Cunningham all of Co. "D,, is quite a relief to them as well as the Co. as they have been a long time unfit for service, and suffering in camp from disease. Rec'd two letters from J.F.B.

WEDNESDAY JULY 23RD 1862
Bethel Tennessee

It rained last night and cloudy this morning~ The Rebels are said to be coming in force and only 13. miles off. the boys are busy cleaning up their guns and revolvers, as they propose to give them a warm reception when they arrive here. they are coming from a Southwesterly direction~

THURSDAY JULY 24TH 1862
Bethel Tennessee

Rebels said to be 2200 strong 12. miles from here and coming. every thing is ready and in waiting for them. Mr. Cunningham left for home~ S.T. Gray's father came to see the boys, to day. W.J. Gray was sent out with some men to get some gov. property, wagons etc.

FRIDAY JULY 25TH 1862
Bethel Tennessee
Wm. J. Gray and detail returned bringing in three Gov't Wagons, tents, and other property belonging to the U.S. which had been taken by citizens from about Shiloh, and along the road between there and Corinth where they had been broken and left during the Corinth Campaign, and converted to their own use.

I Rec'd letter from John Keen, Jr.

SATURDAY JULY 26TH 1862
Bethel Tennessee
On picket. Capt. Cheney officer of the guard Citizens came in and held a meeting to-day to organize a home guard. We were treated to day. citizens coming in gave us cider to drink and apples. The Countersign was "Maine," parole [a watchword given only to officers of the guard and of the day] "Curtis." The night cool and pleasant.

SUNDAY JULY 27TH 1862
Bethel Tennessee
On Picket yet. we are kept on two days at a time now. countersign "Cairo." parole "Mitchel." ~ I caught a Cavalryman trying to slip through the lines. We received orders to be ready to march at a moments warning. The Rebels threatning the line of the M.&O. R.R.

MONDAY JULY 28TH 1862
Bethel Tennessee
Relieved off guard by the 48" Ills. Returned to camp loaned my Revolver to Dr. A. Marlow to go up the road to see some of Co. "G,, sick they detached doing guard duty at a crossing of the R.R. between here and Jackson Tenn. weather cloudy with occasional showers, though pleasant.

TUESDAY JULY 29TH 1862
Bethel Tennessee
Court Martial convened here to day Lt. E.B. Harlan Judge Advocate, T.O. Hoss Clerk. The Q.M. is issuing clothing. I Sold a pair pretty worn

to A. Bishop $.2.00 and drew another pair. it rained in the evening and during the night.~

We have no fortifications here though there is frequent threatnings of an attack by the rebels the cavalry here are Vigilant and industrious.~

WEDNESDAY JULY 30TH 1862
Bethel Tennessee

The 48" Ills. Infty. left for Jackson to day. something to be done up there I think. little of the realities of War, to be experienced perhaps.

Serg't O.W. Brokaw returned from home. The rebels seem undetermined as to what desperate act to attempt. I wrote to R.M.L.

THURSDAY JULY 31ST 1862
Bethel Tennessee

Tevis Greathouse of Vandalia Ills. in camp pretending to take the Vote of Soldiers for, or against, the addoption of the New Constitution of the State of Illinois. It is conducted illegitimately. boys of fifteen years of age are permitted to Vote. I think the polls would be accidently lost however if they were even legal, as soldiers vote in opposition to the wishes of the men making the effort. Copperheads and rebel Sympathizers at home will learn by it that their friends in the army are not very numerous, if our Regiment can be taken for a criterion. The weather is pleasant and has been generaly during the month. not warmer than we have in Illinois usually at this season. the nights are cool~ I Rec'd a letter from B.N.B.~

FRIDAY AUGUST 1ST 1862
Bethel Tennessee

On Picket at Mrs Murrey's. Countersign "Springfield." Parole "Sanford." I got my Revolver from Dr. Marlow. Corpl. Howard's Wife went out riding to day with cavalry man whom she never saw before. they went to Purday for dinner then came in by our post. I think she is a fast woman. if should be permitted to desecrate the name of "Woman."

SATURDAY AUGUST 2ND 1862
Bethel Tennessee

On Picket. Countersign "Boonville." parole "Grant." The 49" Ills Infty Commenced building fortifications that we may be able to defend the place against any force that will probably attack Bethel is not well adapted to the purposes, of repelling an assault, it is too low.~~

SUNDAY AUGUST 3RD 1862
Bethel Tennessee

The 7" Mo. Infty. Stoped here to night on their way from Shiloh to Jackson Tenn. they commenced tearing down old houses immediately upon stacking arms, and a dozen of them were brought in under guard, before they had been half an hour for trying to run the lines.

MONDAY AUGUST 4TH 1862
Bethel Tennessee

The 7" Mo. Infty. left for Jackson this morning. Capt. Cheney, Lt. Harlan, Lt. Rowley, Lt. Houston, and I went to the creek and went through the motions of a swim in the mud. there is no stream of any considerable size in this vicinity. Turned over a Bbl [abbreviation for barrel] Crackers to the A.C.S.~

TUESDAY AUGUST 5TH 1862
Bethel Tennessee

I was in camp all day Read a novel, Entitled "The Golden Feather." yellow backed literature is the soldier's amusement. I drew five days rations for the Co. Corpl. F. A. Niles returned from Jackson Tenn. left McKinney doing Well.

Orville Niles went home.~ We had roasting ears and peaches for dinner. "Cheney's Crampers" have been in somebody's corn field & orchard~

WEDNESDAY AUGUST 6TH 1862
Bethel Tennessee

I went to the Post Quartermaster and got a coffin for John Bagget. Co. "D,,~ The Adjt. had an Orderly's call to day for the first time in the

Reg't. I washed my clothes to day~ Col. P. Pease rejoined the Regiment to day. he has been absent on sick leave since the 11th of June 62.~

THURSDAY AUGUST 7TH 1862
Bethel Tennessee

On Picket. countersign "Chipewa." parole "Scott." on post at the R.R. was ordered by Lt Harlan to the post at Mrs. Murrey's, Hd Qrs. of the line. I followed two suspicious characters into camp and reported them to the Provost Marshall and he made them give bond.~ Col. Morrison returned, absent since the 5" June.

FRIDAY AUGUST 8TH 1862
Bethel Tennessee

On Picket. countersign, "Ft Henry" parole, "Porten." Lt Harlan sick and went to camp. I took the countersign around the lines. Capt Cheney came out and stayed on the lines with us all night.

The weather pleasant, but the mosquitoes very bad. there is low swampy land out this way~

SATURDAY AUGUST 9TH 1862
Bethel Tennessee

Went with Capt Cheney, Lieut. Harlan, Lieut. J.B. Houston, Lieut. H.W. Kerr, and Serg't Goshorn, out to Cotton Ridge. ten miles in a Northeasterly direction, in a six mule Gov Wagon to hear Lt. Kerr make a Speech, but his courage failed him and he would'nt even make an apology. Lt. Harlan made a short speech, and about twenty men volunteered, for Tenn. Cavalry.

SUNDAY AUGUST 10TH 1862
Bethel Tennessee

Drew five days rations for the company to day Co. "F,, relieved at Henderson Station seventeen miles up the R.R. by Co. "B,, and Co. "G,, at Hooker six miles up the R.R. by a Co. of the 48" Ills Infty Vols. I lay in camp all day and eat peaches. Prospect of getting pay soon~

MONDAY AUGUST 11TH 1862
Bethel Tennessee

Serg't Wm. G. McKinney died at Jackson Tenn. to-day. I went to the Hospital and stayed while Dr. Marlow went to the country awhile. Dr. Medcalf asked me to accept of the appointment of Hosp't Steward, A lot of recruits came in to join the Reg't. organizing here.~

TUESDAY AUGUST 12TH 1862
Bethel Tennessee

Capt Cheney returned from Jackson sick. he brought us $.14.00 for company savings. I have a very disagreeable sty on my eye, and was not out on dressparade this P.M. There is a cavalry regiment recruiting here by Frseling Hurst, a Tennessean.

WEDNESDAY AUGUST 13TH 1862
Bethel Tennessee

Charlie Burrows came to day visiting from the 21st Ills. Infty. The 48" Ills. Infty. requested Col. I.N. Haynie to resign his commission as Colonel. rumor says he agreed to, if the Reg't desired him to do so. he is an active and vigilant commander but dont seem to have the good will of officers or men~

I brought some of the boys to task this evening for bad conduct while on dressparade~

THURSDAY AUGUST 14TH 1862
Bethel Tennessee

Charlie Burrows returned to his Regiment to day.~

The 2nd Mo. Infty. passed here to day on the cars, going north, they had a Black Bear, with them. there are many troops going north on the Rail road from Corinth now. I bought 43 lbs of flour from the Hospital. Wrote W.W.H. and Ella & Zue M to day~

FRIDAY AUGUST 15TH 1862
Bethel Tennessee

Drilled in the company to day. Then lay in camp and read. "The Scout of the Silver Pond,"~ we had another alarm at night. the regiment fell in line and filled up our Cartrage Boxes. four hundred Rebel cavalry said to be comming. they keep threatning but dont come.~

SATURDAY AUGUST 16TH 1862
Bethel Tennessee

We signed the payrolls to day. prospect of some pay. The 48" Ills. Infty. ordered out. also Cos. E. & H. of our Reg't. probability of a fight somewhere soon The nights are clear and very light. as fine a time for a night attack as I ever saw.

I rec'd letter from J.F.B.

SUNDAY AUGUST 17TH 1862
Bethel Tennessee

Sam'l McDonald left for home. The Pay-master came and paid off the Reg't. he paid me $.102.00 the first pay I have had since Camp Butler Ills. I paid my debts. was detailed and sent down to Corinth in charge of two prisoners. I stoped at the Tisharninyo House after delivering my prisoners to the provost marshall. I saw Thomas Huggins on his way to his Reg't the 22st Ills. Infty.

MONDAY AUGUST 18TH 1862
Corinth Mississippi

I bought a, (hunters Case, Silver) watch to day $.19.00 a gold Pen $.2.00 returned to Bethel a special muster to day by orders from the War Dep't, Washington

The guard house here is full of rebels now. Dr. A. Marlow married to day to a Miss Kanoodle living in the country three miles west of Bethel

TUESDAY AUGUST 19TH 1862
Bethel Tennessee

Maj. Bishop took us out and drilled us to day in battalion drill. some fine movements made. Col. Pease offered the position of Hosp't Steward to me to-day. I told him I would accept it if it was to be permanent. that I disliked running back and forth from the Co. to the Hosp't.

WEDNESDAY AUGUST 20TH 1862
Bethel Tennessee

Dr. Marlow left for Illinois to day to appear before the Medical Board of Examiners preporatory to being commissioned. I was detailed for duty at the Hospital to act in the capacity of steward or Ass't Surg. as circumstances may require, during Marlow's absence.~

THURSDAY AUGUST 21ST 1862
Bethel Tennessee

In Hospital. since I left it before it has been moved to the Reg't. is in tents now and is entirely regimental. John Schroll of Co. "D,, is very low with Dysentery~

Eph Williams returned from Jackson to-day. I paid him $.5.00 borrowed money, which I have had since we were at the front of Corinth. The Reg't was paid off then while I was at Hamburg~ I Rec'd letters from J.F.B and wrote to M.D.W.~

FRIDAY AUGUST 22ND 1862
Bethel Tennessee

Dr. Medcalf changed his place of boarding to-day from the Hospital, at the instance of Col. Morrison.

Ira C. Wiggins run away from camp to day and started home. Capt Cheney tried to catch him with the telegraph but failed so far as heard from. M. Washburn returned from home, this P.M. I wrote to J.F.B.

SATURDAY AUGUST 23RD 1862
Bethel Tennessee

I bought $.5.00 worth of postage stamps to day. Capt Cheney Started home I sent $.35.00 by him to Frank. but the train left him at Jackson and he returned. I think he was trying to run the "blockade." and take a "French." [an informal, hasty, or secret departure] There are not many leaves of absence granted now.~

SUNDAY AUGUST 24TH 1862
Bethel Tennessee

In camp all day giving medicine. John Schroll very sick not much prospect of his recovery.~ E.W. Charles out in the country as usual. O he will soon want to go north to appear before a medical board. he's got woman on the brain.~

The Camp is extremely dull.~

MONDAY AUGUST 25TH 1862
Bethel Tennessee

I went and saw Col. Wm. R. Morrison to day in refrence to my Stewardship. he said he would make me Steward if Marlow passed the board and vacates the position. he is steward never been commissoned Asst. Surg. of the Reg't Lt. J.B. Houston returned from Jackson failed to get home. The weather is quite pleasant Rec'd letters from J.F.B., R.M.L. & Lyde.~

TUESDAY AUGUST 26TH 1862
Bethel Tennessee
I sent J.F. Black $.35.00 by Express. A company of Tennesseeans came in to day. men examined and sworn into the U.S. service for Col. F. Hurst's Reg't. to be mounted and armed as cavalry. generally appear to be good men. I Rec'd letters from F.M.A. & A.K.A.~

WEDNESDAY AUGUST 27TH 1862
Bethel Tennessee
Dr. Medcalf authorized me to act as Post Surgeon as he proposes to act as an invalid and see if he cant get a Sick leave. though he has'nt much encouragement as far as he has tried it. The Surgeon in chief at Jackson cant see it. I wrote to F.M.A.~

THURSDAY AUGUST 28TH 1862
Bethel Tennessee
I prescribed at Sick call and in Hosp't this morning. The 49" Ills. Infty. went to Corinth to guard the train. Dr. Medcalf went along. Serg't Mode Co. "C,, was accidentaly shot through the ankle at Corinth to day. Regt returned at night. Lt. Houston and F.J. Burrows gone home. Clark came~

FRIDAY AUGUST 29TH 1862
Bethel Tennessee
The 48" Ills. Infty. were surprised and fell into line this morning by 49" Ills. Infty. firing off their guns while on drill. they being loaded from yesterdays excursion. Col. Haynie jumped on his horse and rode over to the scene of action and threatened to place Maj. Bishop in arrest. but it seems he had given the Major permission to fire them off. Dr. Medcalf returned from Corinth to day~

SATURDAY AUGUST 30TH 1862
Bethel Tennessee

A Mass-Meeting in camp to-day many citizens in. Speeches were made by Col. Haynie & Captains Stephenson and Greathouse of the 48" Ills. urging the Tenneseeans to enlist, fill up the regiment and help to "drive the invaders from the State." Rec'd letters from C.R.O'N & J.F.B.~

SUNDAY AUGUST 31ST 1862
Bethel Tennessee

There was a general review to day by Col. Haynie the troop out generally. also muster for pay all went off well. the troops made a good appearence. Dr. Medcalf out on his old stiff horse. trying to keep up with Haynie and staff but fails.

John Schroll Co. "D,, died to day of Dysentery. Rumor says there is fighting going on at Boliver Tenn. the Rebels seem determined to cut that road and destroy communication between Memphis and Corinth. they would make Corinth untenable by cutting off supplies~ Fortifications are being built here. 25. Negroes have been pressed and put to work on them. The general health of the Reg't is improving some but not good yet. fatigue is rather heavy. weather pleasant.~ I wrote to J.F.B.~

MONDAY SEPTEMBER 1ST 1862
Bethel Tennessee

Col. Haynie had 40 Negroes in camp to day cutting logs for fortifications and throwing up earthworks. Our men said to be fighting at Boliver and between there and Jackson Tenn. The rebels will probably attemp to cut the M.&O. R.R. above here, and also the Memphis and Charleston R.R. west of Corinth. I think it is a cavalry force that is threatning now.

TUESDAY SEPTEMBER 2ND 1862
Bethel Tennessee

All the available men on or about camp are on detail and on the works. cutting and hauling logs and putting them up. Col. Morrison returned from Jackson. Dr. Medcalf left for home yesterday says he has a child sick. I think his child has got a father sick. too much activity here.

WEDNESDAY SEPTEMBER 3RD 1862
Bethel Tennessee

Every body bussy. the work is going on with a rush. building a fort for the artillery and throwing up a line of rifle pits for the Infty. If they give us a few days, we will amuse them when they come. I examined ten men for the new Reg't forming here. prospect of a fight.

THURSDAY SEPTEMBER 4TH 1862
Bethel Tennessee

The long, Roll beat. all the various commands into line and ready 10,000 rebel cavalry said to be approaching. The Reg'ts moved inside the works. I moved the Hospital to the East and side of the camp and put up the tents so as to have every thing ready, when the[y] come.

FRIDAY SEPTEMBER 5TH 1862
Bethel Tennessee

Dr. Thos. Williams detailed to take charge of our Hospital during Dr. Medcalf absence. E.W. Charles went to Corinth to hunt up our medicine ordered some time ago and lost in transportation some where or how. We get our medicines from Columbus Ky now. and seems to be some uncertainty in the railroads bringing thing through correct.

The weather is very pleasant.~

SATURDAY SEPTEMBER 6TH 1862
Bethel Tennessee

Dr. Medcalf returned! I went to Corinth after our Medicines. I saw Green Beasley and Mathew Cunningham hunting their Reg't. (22nd Ills. Infty.) I bought a blouse coat for $.7.00 I put up at the Corinth House. There are a good many troops here and there seems to be considerable stir among them.~

SUNDAY SEPTEMBER 7TH 1862
Corinth Mississippi

Troops are being sent off up the road. towards Columbus. probably going to some other Dep't, perhaps that of the Cumberland. got my medicines put up and to the depot after considerable trouble, and running about. I see there is a large quantity of commissary stores in the warehouses here~

MONDAY SEPTEMBER 8TH 1862
Corinth Mississippi

The 2nd Mo. Infty. at the R.R. to go north. I had considerable trouble to get my boxes aboard owing to the throng of business sending troops. I went to Brig. Gen'l. McPhearson Supt of R.R. and he interceeded for me, and I got my boxes into the Baggage car. I found Dr. Medcalf under arrest for absence without leave.~

TUESDAY SEPTEMBER 9TH 1862
Bethel Tennessee

I found several of the boys with murcurial sore mouths in the hospital from Dr. Williams too frequent and long continud use of Calomel.~

The Q.M. Dept issuing clothing to day to the Reg't. Dr. Marlow returned says he passed the board all right. he came back with a new suit of clothes on and brim full of whiskey, and disposed to be fussy.~

WEDNESDAY SEPTEMBER 10TH 1862
Bethel Tennessee

The train from Columbus was fired into to day this side of Jackson and three men wounded. Mrs. Marlow was on the train. Mr. Kanoodle stayed in camp over night. I slept out under the fly. the weather is pleasant now. I Rec'd a letter from E.M.~

THURSDAY SEPTEMBER 11TH 1862
Bethel Tennessee

Peter Taylor went to Columbus after his wife.

The Cavalry went out to day towards Pochahantas the rebels said to be out there but they returned without making any discovery. the Rebels are probably citizens that are doing the mischief and know when to be still. I wrote to E.M.

FRIDAY SEPTEMBER 12TH 1862
Bethel Tennessee

The fortification are now complete or at least they have stoped work on them. they are reasonably strong in them selves but there are some hills at short range that command them. Dr. Marlow went out to the country to night. Lt Harlan is act. Post Adj't. said to be fighting at Corinth. I wrote to S.B.A.~

SATURDAY SEPTEMBER 13TH 1862
Bethel Tennessee

A mistake about the fight at Corinth yesterday~
Peter Taylor returned from Columbus but did not bring his wife. Col. Haynie suffered another scare and doubled the Pickets and sent the cavalry out to reconnoiter, and discover the whereabouts of the enemy, his strenght and any other information that may be of value to this command. I think he will shell the woods presently~

SUNDAY SEPTEMBER 14TH 1862
Bethel Tennessee

Dr. Medcalf sent John Lane to Columbus to day after medicine. now it will be an accident if he hears of either, John or medicine, in a month more. Mr. Kanoodle came in and spent the day with us. Dr. Marlow went out to the country to see his wife.
The weather is very warm now.~

MONDAY SEPTEMBER 15TH 1862
Bethel Tennessee

Troops moving in the direction of Corinth now. that seems to be the objective point now. the rebels from below are threatning. Our Reg't. and the 48" Ills. Infty both out on dressparade at the same time ours in the longest, considerably
I received a letter from J.F.B.~

TUESDAY SEPTEMBER 16TH 1862
Bethel Tennessee

Lt. E.B. Harlan circulating a petition to present to Col. Morrison asking that Lt. Harlan be made Adjutant of the Reg't. most of the line officers signed it for him. Our old Brig. (Col. Ross') went past here to day going toward Corinth Miss. Weather still very warm. I wrote to J.F.B.

WEDNESDAY SEPTEMBER 17TH 1862
Bethel Tennessee

We had a fine rain to day. There is a petition circulating to make Serg't. Wm Martin Co. "E,, adj't. it seems to get most of its supporters among enlisted men. Harlan is the proper man as time will show. Add. Ward went out and found some peaches to day. He brought Nick Burns in sick. I have been quite unwell to day.

I Rec'd a letter from John. Keen, Jr.

THURSDAY SEPTEMBER 18TH 1862
Bethel Tennessee

Another company of Tennesseeans came in to day for Col. F. Hurst's Reg't. Co.s "D,, & "K,, detailed, and sent to wards Corinth on the train to day going to guard a bridge below here. We Rec'd news to day of the fight in Maryland and Virginia. weather cool. I wrote to J.K.

FRIDAY SEPTEMBER 19TH 1862
Bethel Tennessee

Mrs. Marlow & Mrs. Partriage in camp to day Lt Harlan fell violently in love with the latter the other day but unfortunately she is married. Co.s "D,, & "K,, returned from down the Rail road to day. Serg't. Maj. F.J. Burrows & Wm Clemens returned from home to day. good news from the East. I wrote L.H.B.

SATURDAY SEPTEMBER 20TH 1862
Bethel Tennessee

Cheering news from the Potomac, also from Gen'l. Grant, Lt. Harlan tore the nail off his little finger in a scuffle with Capt Cheney this evening. he went to the Hospital to have it dressed and fainted and fell down on the floor Our Scouts reconnoitering to day.

SUNDAY SEPTEMBER 21ST 1862
Bethel Tennessee

Camp rather dull to day. the news not quite so good. our men are falling back on Corinth, from the Posts below there. a prospect of an attack some where soon in this part of the country. 40. Recruits came for our Regiment to day from Illinois. most of them for Co. "K,, from Wayne

Co. I heard a Negro preach to night in Co. "I,, 48" Ills Infty. pretty good sermon.~

MONDAY SEPTEMBER 22ND 1862
Bethel Tennessee

Co. "D,, building a house, or rather moving one in from the country somewhere and putting it up. I saw Wm. Keen, Wm Branson, Jasper Branson, Clark Anderson, and Gillum Harris. they came yesterday. Lt Harlan Went to Cairo to day and Lt. A.S. Rowley to Jackson. weather very fine. I rec'd letter from J.F.B.

TUESDAY SEPTEMBER 23RD 1862
Bethel Tennessee

The Artillery was drilling to-day. (Batt. "K,, 1st Mo. Light art.) Lt Rowley returned from Jackson to-day. Our army is still pursuing the Rebels on the Potomac. Gen'l Ross' (Our old) Briggade passed here returning to Jackson no fight this time.

I wrote to J.F.B. to day.~

WEDNESDAY SEPTEMBER 24TH 1862
Bethel Tennessee

Co. "A,, 49" Ills. Infty detailed and sent to guard a bridge four miles down the road towards Corinth. they took their C.C. & G.E. along going to stay I suppose. Lt Harlan Returned from Cairo brought me a cap $2.00. Col. Morrison went to Jackson and returned to day

I rec'd a letter from F.M.A.~

THURSDAY SEPT 25TH 1862
Bethel Tennessee

Co. "B,, 48" Ills. Infty. sent to McNairy Station to guard a bridge and a crossing there. Capt Cheney Hoss, Wilson, Lever, & Wiggins went to Jackson to day to Courtmartial. I.C. Wiggins, Moore & Peters. Old Mr. Gill's house was burned by soldiers who sliped out through the lines with their arms he has always been a notorious old rebel destroyed everything in the house. Col. Morrison Comndg Post.

FRIDAY SEPTEMBER 26TH 1862
Bethel Tennessee

T.O. Hoss & Wiggins returned from Jackson Wm Holmes rejoined the Co. to day he has been absent since last April. he came from St. Louis. E.W. Charles went to Henderson Station 17. miles north to get some chickens & Butter but he returned without getting any.

SATURDAY SEPTEMBER 27TH 1862
Bethel Tennessee

Trouble in camp to day in regard to the burning of Gill's house. Col. Haynie is trying to make some of the boys tell who did it he has Col. Hurst under arrest and confined to his Quarters Capt Cheney and the rest of the boys returned from Jackson to day. rec'd letters from R.M.L. & Lyde

SUNDAY SEPTEMBER 28TH 1862
Bethel Tennessee

All quiet in camp to-day. Capt. Thos. W. Morgan up to day from the bridge. I have been reading "Prairie Flower" & "L eni L eotr." to day. John Q. Maybry rejoined the Co. to day. he has been absent sick, for some time. I received letter from J.F.B. and wrote Lyde & M.A.

MONDAY SEPTEMBER 29TH 1862
Bethel Tennessee

E.W. Charles went to Columbus and Cairo to day to look up some old tents and Hospital stores that Dr. Medcalf left there last Winter, when we came from Camp Butler Ills. I borrowed $10.00 from Stephen Frump Co. "D,, to day and bought a pair of boots $.7.00. Money is scarce with me now and not much prospect of getting pay soon either that anybody knows of.~

TUESDAY SEPTEMBER 30TH 1862
Bethel Tennessee

I made Quarterly and Monthly Returns to day a busy day, and not much time to idle. there are strict Orders to remain in camp to night Some talk of the rebels approaching in force again from a Southwesterly direction. There seems to [be] reason to think there is a rebel force somewhere in a Southerly, or rather Southwesterly direction threatening this place or our line of communication. They seem desirous of destroying the M.&C. R.R. and the M.&O. R.R. and thereby rendering Corinth and our posts below there untenable and forcing us to fall back farther North.

I wrote to J.F.B.~

WEDNESDAY OCTOBER 1ST 1862
Bethel Tennessee

Rebel Generals: Price, Van Dorn, and Lovell said to be coming with 40,000 men Col. Morrison receiving dispatches confirming the report. they are in the direction of Oxford. The best indications of a fight since we have been here.~

E.W. Charles returned from Columbus to-day without the medicines or hospital property he trusted to their being sent.

THURSDAY OCTOBER 2ND 1862
Bethel Tennessee

The 29" & 31st Ills. Infty. came on the 2.A.M. train from Corinth. Our Scouts brought in three prisoners and say the rebels are crossing the Hatchie in force. the train was fired into between here and Corinth and returned the Tellegraph wire is cut below here. a fight close at hand now.

FRIDAY OCTOBER 3RD 1862
Bethel Tennessee

Heavy firing heard in the direction of Corinth. the 29" & 31st Ills Infty ordered out in the drection of Corinth. Our couriers returned one loosing his horse.(shot.) they seem to be coming in between here and Corinth. fighting very heavy I rec'd letters from E & Z.M. and wrote to Lyde.

SATURDAY OCTOBER 4TH 1862
Bethel Tennessee

The news from Corinth is flattering. the rebels got into the town by the cowardice of Gen'l Davies, and were charged by Gen'l Hamilton and driven back with heavy loss, and are being pressed by Gen'l Rosecrans. Tricillion's "iron clad" car went down the Railroad to-day.

SUNDAY OCTOBER 5TH 1862
Bethel Tennessee

The news is still cheering from Gen'l Rosecrans the Rebels have fallen back 20. miles with heavy loss There are a great many dead rebels on the field, and the fleeing foe is being hotly pursued and severely punished for his temerity. The loss of the enemy is eaqualed only by the foolhardy rashness with which it was made, letter from S.B.A. & wrote S.B.A. & E. & Z.M.

MONDAY OCTOBER 6TH 1862
Bethel Tennessee

Dr's Goslin & Williams of the 48" Ills. Infty. Dr. Marlow of 49" Ills. went to Corinth to help take care of the wounded The rebels still retreating and Rosecrans pursuing. our cavalry scouring the country and picking up and bringing in a great many straglers. The Rebels are considerably demoralized~

TUESDAY OCTOBER 7TH 1862
Bethel Tennessee

Dr. Marlow returned their being plenty of Surgeons there to attend the wounded. I had tooth Ache to day and had it pulled out by Dr. Marlow when he was about half full of whisky. no news from the front to-day camp dull no mail scarcely and but little news in the papers.~

WEDNESDAY OCTOBER 8TH 1862
Bethel Tennessee

There is a great want of Events in camp to-day to make time pass reasonably. Q.M. Serg't Edd. Nixon left for home. no particulars from the scene of action to-day. I received pictures from Frank to day in a letter from Columbus Ky.~

Rec'd letters from J.F.B. & M.D.W. wrote to J.F.B.

THURSDAY OCTOBER 9TH 1862
Bethel Tennessee

Major Mayfield 48" Ills. returned from the front to day. the fight still going on successfully Price is intercepted by Maj. Gen'l W.T. Sherman from Memphis Tenn. a lot of rebel prisoners going north to day on the train captured at Corinth and during the rebels Skedaddle~ It has been dear bought glory for them they will hardly come again~

FRIDAY OCTOBER 10TH 1862
Bethel Tennessee

Weather cool and raining to-day. Col Haynie refuses to sign any more provision Returns for our hospital. He wants Dr. Medcalf to report to Dr. Goslin his junior officer. letters pass & repass. Medcalf & Goslin ordered to report in person to settle the question of rank. Haynie Succumbs~

SATURDAY OCTOBER 11TH 1862
Bethel Tennessee

Made morning reports Per Order of Col. Haynie for the first time Medcalf requires Dr. Goslin to report to him, by Seniority of rank Haynie left for Jackson Col. Morrison in command of Post. John Jenkins cut his leg to-day with an ax.

Rec'd letter from J.F.B. and wrote to M.D.W.

SUNDAY OCTOBER 12TH 1862
Bethel Tennessee

The Rev. Mr. Lockwood called upon me to day. he expects to be Chaplain of our Reg't. Col. Hurst returned from the fight to day. he is released from arrest and restored to his command the 6. Tenn. Cavalry. Col. Haynie has been out ranked again~

MONDAY OCTOBER 13TH 1862
Bethel Tennessee

Col. Morrison in command of the Post at present. Dr. Marlow went out to a Schoolhouse in the country and got a heating Stove for our Hospital tents. as the weather is getting cool enough to require fires especially for the Sick. the health is tolerably good at present. some few Intermittents. I went to the depot and bought some papers.

I rec'd letter from J.F.B.~

TUESDAY OCTOBER 14TH 1862
Bethel Tennessee

I put up our stove in Hospital tent, to day. Col Hurst's Cavalry went out on a reconnaisance Col. Morrison's <u>Wife</u> came from home to day. Capt Stephenson returned from home. Weather pleasant but camp quite dull

I wrote to A.K.A.~

WEDNESDAY OCTOBER 15TH 1862
Bethel Tennessee

Commissions came to day for Sergt Wm Martin Co. "E,, as Reg'tl. Adj't. and for flag bearers L.R.H. Dobbleman of Co. "H,, as 2nd Lieut Co "F,,~ Co. "D,, building another house to-day. they [are] building good size houses two or three will be enough for the Co. Rec'd letter from J.K.~

THURSDAY OCTOBER 16TH 1862
Bethel Tennessee

The 48" & 49" Ills Infty. are building Quarters as though they expected to spend the winter here and by the way it is not very improbable either.~ Maj. Mayfield bade the 48" Ills. farewell he leaves to morrow. Lt Harlan says he will resign and leave the regiment. I rec'd letter from J.F.B. and wrote J.F.B. & J.K~

FRIDAY OCTOBER 17TH 1862
Bethel Tennessee

Maj Mayfield of the 48" Ills. Infty. left for home E.W. Charles went to Columbus Ky. again to-day Lt Harlan, Livesay, and Burggraf rejoined the regiment. A <u>ball</u> out at Mr. Gamble's four miles in the country. Lt. Harlan and the Provost Marshall went out. the "invaders has been driven from the state" alls safe now. our men go ten miles with impunity.~

SATURDAY OCTOBER 18TH 1862
Bethel Tennessee

I went over to the Picture gallery to day to see specimens. Dr Marlow over there and he was "Tightaly Stight". Adjt Martin bought his suit to-day. The Q.M. Dept. were issuing <u>Clothing</u>. I drew an overcoat, ps. Socks. Lt. W.W. Bliss Co. "G,, is Act Regtl Q.M.~

SUNDAY OCTOBER 19TH 1862
Bethel Tennessee

A Man drumed out of the Service of the U.S. for stealing. he belonged to Co. "I,, 11" Ills. Cavalry. Election in the 48" Ills Infty for Major of the Regt vice [in the place of] Mayfield resigned. candidates Capts Lydick, Stephenson, & Greathouse. the latter was elected. Koettgen Co. "C,, buried. letter from E.M. wrote J.F.B.

MONDAY OCTOBER 20TH 1862
Bethel Tennessee

I had a chill and high Fever to day. James Morrison Ex. Adj't came to day from home, to get his horse and see the Col. and the boys of the Regt. A detail of men to day went to work getting timber to build a hospital for the Reg't. at the request of Dr. Medcalf~

TUESDAY OCTOBER 21ST 1862
Bethel Tennessee

I had another chill to day. The chill and Fever lasted from 10.A.M. until late at night they treat a man very coolly in camp especially while the chill lasts. I have but little time to take medicine between time. I will comme[n]ce as soon as the fever is cool to night and continue it until the fever comes to morrow, or if I miss it until after the time has past~

WEDNESDAY OCTOBER 22ND 1862
Bethel Tennessee

I commenced taking Quinine Pills (gr.iii.) one evry hour, from 1.A.M., until late in the P.M. There is no use of half doing a thing. Tapering off, chills is apt to taper off the patient. I lay in bed with an over coat on most all day, and missed the chill. Weather pleasant.~ I Rec'd a letter from A.F.A.~

THURSDAY OCTOBER 23RD 1862
Bethel Tennessee

The Carpenters went to work hewing the timbers for the hospital to-day. it is to be 20. feet wide, by 56. feet long, inclusive of Surgeon's Quarters in front and a small Kitchen and dining room at the rear. Lt. Bliss is to furnish the lumber~ I Rec'd a letter from J.F.B.

FRIDAY OCTOBER 24TH 1862
Bethel Tennessee

I got a pass to go to Columbus Ky. with Lt. Harlan and run the blockade home but gave it up, for the present at least. the carpenters laid off the foundation of the Hospital the work is progressing Col Pease returned to day from, I wrote to A.F.A. & R.M.L.

SATURDAY OCTOBER 25TH 1862
Bethel Tennessee

Col. Wm R. Morrison Commanding the Post. Lt. Col. P. Pease Commanding the Reg't. and Maj. W.W. Bishop nothing to do but smoke cigars, drink whiskey, and buttermilk when he can get it, and tell yarns. a routine of business for which he is admirably adapted. He is to careless, negligent, and good natured to command. he wont enforce discipline in the command. No news in camp to day.

SUNDAY OCTOBER 26TH 1862
Bethel Tennessee

Anton Heese Married to day to a citizen lady, in the country. Dr Marlow and his wife were out to the wedding~ Peter Taylor stole the Key to the Chest to day and got into the whiskey and got very drunk~ Stohr was burried to day. died yesterday in hospital~

MONDAY OCTOBER 27TH 1862
Bethel Tennessee

I got a pass for Columbus to day, and was ordered to Cairo, with Lt. Harlan by Col. Morrison with verbal permission from the Col. to run the blockade Mrs Morrison went along going home we went up on the Str City of Alton. Lt Harlan got a new suit of clothes. we had an oyster supper.

TUSDAY OCTOBER 28TH 1862
Cairo Illinois

We left for Centralia at 4.A.M. I found Eliza then heard Parson Brownlow speak. went to Salem with Mason & family surprized all at home. We went to Uncle Tom's to a party, saw some of the officers of the

89

111" Ills Inft. Vols there. Lt Harlan stoped over night with me. Frank came in and we surprized him at home.~

WEDNESDAY OCTOBER 29TH 1862
Salem Illinois

I went over to the fair ground, and saw the 111th Ills. Infty. Vols. Lt Harlan went out home, to day George & Margret came to town to day. Ell & Zue came up to see me, and I went home with them. Frank, Bob, & Lyde came down and we spent a very pleasant evening

THURSDAY OCTOBER 30TH 1862
Salem Illinois

The 111th Ills Infty. went out on review to day a great many citizens out to see them. the Reg't looks large enough for a Brig. They have orders to cook rations for a move went to a party a[t] Mr. Castles in the evening I took E.M. every thing went off pleasantly, and we had a good time generally.~

FRIDAY OCTOBER 31ST 1862
Salem Illinois

The 111th Reg't Ills Infty. left camp early this morning for Tonti on the I.C. R.R. accompanied by many citizens and friends. There was considerable dissatisfaction manifested in consequence of their having to go on a freight train.

There was many a tearfull eye to-day, at the final parting. To soldier at home is romantic; -- but to take up the line of march, for an enemy's country; -- for the tented field, with its hardships, exposeures, and privations, perhaps for the battlefield, is of very serious import, -- comparing this scene, with that of the departure of other Regiments; that went to the scene of action, one short year ago; with equal numbers, vigor, and strength, and can now muster but half those numbers, tell but too plainly, that this parting, may well be serious. They left about noon. I returned to town, and spent a lonly evening. as most evry person with whom, I met, was melancholly.

SATURDAY NOVEMBER 1ST 1862
Salem Illinois

I went with Father & Mother out to Georges and stayed until evening, and returned to Salem. Uncle Mark Lovell came in hunting his horses, and went back without them. Ell and Zue came up to spend the evening and stayed all night at our house with us, to help "drive dull cares away." There's quite a calm now, since the 111" Reg't took its departure.

SUNDAY NOVEMBER 2ND 1862
Salem Illinois

I went to church in the fornoon, and to Sunday school in the afternoon and was put in charge of a class, and heard them recite~ I went down to Moody's in the evening and found the girls at home and spent the time very pleasantly. I wrote to F.J.B.

MONDAY NOVEMBER 3RD 1862
Salem Illinois

We have concluded to return to camp next Friday. Lt. Harlan went out home to day. I saw Robt. D. Easley to day. C.R. O'Neill in town. I bought a knife and prs of gloves. the citizens miss the 111" Reg. they have been here for some time. I Rec'd letter from J.F.B.

TUESDAY NOVEMBER 4TH 1862
Salem Illinois

Election to-day. the copperheads, Judges W.W. Pace and Esq Wm Haynie tried to rule soldiers out insisting that in joining the army we lost our citizenship. Emett Merritt sided with them, but they yie[l]ded the point. Merritt and Sam'l Tilden had a fuss. I went to the I.O.O.F. Lodge. paid the Sec. $.5.00.~

WEDNESDAY NOVEMBER 5TH 1862
Salem Illinois

I saw Lt Harlan's father to-day, he is a Quaker. Uncle Tom Black went to St. Louis. I saw Mr. S.P. Nave. Uncle Mark Lovell in town again. I took Supper up at David P. Myres, this P.M. The copperhead ticket ahead so far as heard from Old Merritt ahead of Schaffre. Since so many Union men have gone into the service the Whangdoodles have things their own way. I Re'd a letter from J.F.B.

91

THURSDAY NOVEMBER 6TH 1862
Salem Illinois

I had my overcoat fixed to day. pockets put in it, and things prepared to start back to [camp] tomorrow. Ell & Zue came up and spent the evening. Lt. Harlan came into town but dont want to return to camp tomorrow. Mary C. insists upon his staying until after Sunday, and he cant say no.

FRIDAY NOVEMBER 7TH 1862
Salem Illinois

Lieut. Harlan assumed command and we went out to Sam'l B. Arnold's The Misses Torrence were there, also Miss. Benton, and Mr Pruden's family came down and we had a splendid time. Lt Harlan walked out there to assist Miss Torrence into the wagon and she had come on foot, and he could do no less than take her home.

SATURDAY NOVEMBER 8TH 1862
Stringtown Illinois) near clay County Line

We went with Matt Arnold up to Torence's and made a visit, then the girls went with us to Prudens and took dinner and had a heavy time. -- Then I walked to Salem Harlan went home. I got ready and took the train for Odin. then changed for Cairo. The past ten days has been an Oasis in the past twelve months.~

SUNDAY NOVEMBER 9TH 1862
Cairo Illinois

I left for Columbus on the Str City-of-Alton. Met with Lt. John L. Stanley Co. "B,, 49" Ills Infty he had been home without leave and was very uneasy about the guards at the R.R. Depot but he had his sword on and no baggage and he sliped them. I stoped at Columbus. I took a horse-back-ride with J.F.B. & R.M.L. to the little Obine one Co detached there. we returned to camp.

MONDAY NOVEMBER 10TH 1862
Columbus Kentucky

Frank went and got a pole and put up for a flag, and hoisted the stars and Stripes over camp. I went down and drilled Co. "E,, 111" Ills Infty.~

saw the Reg't on dressparade. Capt. Clark acting Adj't he for-got himself and made a perfict failure left out half the parade~

TUESDAY NOVEMBER 11TH 1862
Columbus Kentucky

I went with Frank to see the fortifications Capt Lydick and Lt. Harlan (and Chark the sutler) came down. I got a pass took the train for Bethel, arrived and went to see all of the boys & Doctors. found things very much after the same old style. Rec'd letters from J.F.B., F.M.A., A.K.A. & J.K.~

WEDNESDAY NOVEMBER 12TH 1862
Bethel Tennessee

I commenced acting Hosp't Steward proper to day. E.W. Charles Ward-Master. I called upon Col. Pease, Col. Haynie, and saw Maj. Bishop. The Hospital building has been about completed during my absence, and is a great improvement on tents. I wrote to W.H.B. & F.M.A.~

THURSDAY NOVEMBER 13TH 1862
Bethel Tennessee

We moved into the new Hospital to day. we put up stoves in our tent. Dr.s Medcalf and Marlow occupy the front rooms of the building. E.W. Charles and I occupy a hospital tent and use it for a dispenseary. Sam'l Craig died to day. Ira C. Wiggins Co. "D,, was marched before the Reg't while on parade this evening, with his hands tied behind him, for, sentence Court Martial. Had an Oyster Supper. I wrote to J.F.B.~

FRIDAY NOVEMBER 14TH 1862
Bethel Tennessee

I was reading all day. Mr. Kanoodle's girls were in camp to day. Col Pease, Dr. Medcalf, and Capt. L.W. Moore & ladies went to Esq. Wilson's to day visiting. Col. Morrison promised to write to Adjt Gen'l A.C. Fuller for an order for me to go before the Medical board for examination for an Ass't Surg.

SATURDAY NOVEMBER 15TH 1862
Bethel Tennessee

I drew five days rations for the Hospital Dept. Mrs. Marlow went out home to-day. I Saw Dr. Wm. Hill he is on duty at Corinth with some Artillery not much to do and well suited in that perticular. I.C. Wiggins dodged the guards this evening, and hence postponed his public demonstrations

SUNDAY NOVEMBER 16TH 1862
Bethel Tennessee

Chaplain J.H. Lockwood preached at 10.A.M. to day at the Q.M.'s, and held prayer meeting at night I read most all day preparing for that Medical Board of examiners. I.C. Wiggons appeared on dressparade in his thrilling adventure for the third and last time to day.

I wrote to Lyde.

MONDAY NOVEMBER 17TH 1862
Bethel Tennessee

Col. Morrison wrote a letter to Adj't Gen'l. Allen C. Fuller to day for an order for me to appear before the Medical board of examiners preparatory to being commissioned Ass't Surg. of the Reg't. John Mason went home to day in citizens dress. Two negro women came to cook and wash for the hospital to-day. It is hard to get a good cook permanently for the Hospital most of the good ones can do better.

TUESDAY NOVEMBER 18TH 1862
Bethel Tennessee

One company of the 12" Ills Cavalry came to day. rumor says to relieve the 11" Ills Cavalry here. Had some washing done to-day. our darkies left. they were a nuissance, as those we have tried have all been only work long enough to get an oppertunity to steal something.

WEDNESDAY NOVEMBER 19TH 1862
Bethel Tennessee

Mrs Medcalf ironed my shirts for me to day and hemed my handkerchief. I am reading Neill & Smith prepairing for that dreaded quising that the future has in Store for me. I am reading Physiology at the Same time, mixing in a little anatomy, and practice.

THURSDAY NOVEMBER 20TH 1862
Bethel Tennessee

E.W. Charles got a letter of recommendation from Col. Morrison, Col. Haynie, Lt. Col. Pease Dr. Medcalf and Maj. Bishop, and started to Cairo to get a transfer to the Navy. he is dissatisfied in the Reg't I was made steward over him. Col. Haynie is gone to Jackson. Col Morrison Comndg Post.

FRIDAY NOVEMBER 21ST 1862
Bethel Tennessee

Frank J. Burrows and Thomas O. Hoss went to Columbus to day on a visit to the 111th Ills Infty stationed there. Mrs Bishop came to day from home to stay awhile with the Major. We have had quite a number of lady visitors in camp since we have been here, and our men seem to be disposed to settle present difficulties between themselves and ladies of this country, by marryinn them. they becom Union.

SATURDAY NOVEMBER 22ND 1862
Bethel Tennessee

E.W. Charles returned to day. could not get into the Navy for want of a discharge from the army. I saw the Misses Wilson in town this evening. I got a detail of men and cut and hauled wood for the Hospital to day the weather is getting cool enough to make fires very essential.

SUNDAY NOVEMBER 23RD 1862
Bethel Tennessee

I went to preaching at ten A.M. to day and heard Chaplain Lockwood preach at the Q.M.'s. Read Tom. Moore's Poetical works the ballance of the day. I read that and Burns alternately when I am not reading medicine. no news in camp, trains run irregular and brought us no mail to night.

MONDAY NOVEMBER 24TH 1862
Bethel Tennessee

Mrs. Pease went home to day. The Non Commissioned Officers organized for a daily drill and elected Col Pease drill master Capt Kurghoff Co. "C,, wanted to drill them but they signified their prefrence in the Col's favor. F.J.Burrows & T.O. Hoss returned from Columbus. I rec'd letters from J.F.B. & A.K.A.~

TUESDAY NOVEMBER 25TH 1862
Bethel Tennessee

I drilled with the Non-coms to day, by Col. Pease. Henderson Stationed Surprised and the garrison comprising Capt. Wm. P. Moore Lieuts John L. Stanley & A. McGregor and the company,(Co. "B,,) captured and taken off, by Rebel Gen'l Forrest, this morning. one man Killed.(of Co."B,,.) The 48" went up but they found no rebels. The 22nd Ohio Infty came here from Corinth. Co."F,, sent to McNairy. prospect of a fight. all astir.~

WEDNESDAY NOVEMBER 26TH 1862
Bethel Tennessee

The 48" Ills. Infty. returned, and boast of retaking Henderson. and there was not a rebel in the neighborhood when they arrived. beside a Reg't from Jackson beat them there. The 22nd Ohio went back to Corinth. the train came through from Columbus. I wrote to J.F.B. & F.J.B.~

THURSDAY NOVEMBER 27TH 1862
Bethel Tennessee

All quiet during the forenoon. Non Com drill by Capt. Kurghoff. We received two boxes of wine to day from Columbus ma[r]ked "Castir Oil"~ Camp astir at 10.P.M. prospect of an attack. the cavalry sent out to reconnoiter and discover if posible the nature of the enemy.

FRIDAY NOVEMBER 28TH 1862
Bethel Tennessee

No enemy discovered last night. all quiet to day. Except the stir among the women Mrs. Medcalf & Mrs. Marlow, left for home. this is not considered a very safe place by them. Wm Holmes Co. "D,, left to day for home. no longer a soldier lost his health, and partially his eye sight.~

SATURDAY NOVEMBER 29TH 1862
Bethel Tennessee

I got a detail and hauld wood again to day. we burn considerable wood now. the hills around camp were heavily wooded when we came here, but are now bare from the timber cut to build fortifications,

Quarters, fires etc. T.O. Hoss went up to Jackson. Wiggins wife came down. I made out a Monthly Return for November, and forwarded to the Medical Director. I Rec'd letters from J.F.B. & Lyde.

SUNDAY NOVEMBER 30TH 1862

It rained during the day. there was preaching in camp but I did not go. I read most all day. The Tellegraph is said to be cut between here and Henderson Station. Some small Command perhaps of rebel Cavalry prowling around the Country occasionly doing some mischief, or picking up a small and isolated Command, cutting the Telegraph wir or burning a RR bridge as an opportunity offers, we have now been here near Six Months with no fighting, and comparitively little to do Except Maintain a guard around our Camp, and do the necessary duty that naturally has to be done, draw rations, cook them and Eat. it [is]true we have fortified the Camp, built a hospital and made many improvements. necessary for our Convinience and Comforts, yet we have done no Campaigning during that time.

MONDAY DECEMBER 1ST 1862

Bethel Tennessee

Co. "K,, was Sent with the train to Henderson Station. Hoskins (Sutler) has got a new stock of goods. the boys are buying pretty extensively boots at $.8.00 pr. pair. the weather is getting disagreeable and wet. winter coming fast, and the men are improving their quarters in order to be ready for it when it comes. I wrote to J.F.B.

TUESDAY DECEMBER 2ND 1862

Bethel Tennessee

Battery "K,, 1st Mo. light Arty. came into camp to day from Corinth. put their guns in fort. Nonsense. a petition going the rounds for an election of field officers. Maj. Bishop wants to be Colonel. but I dont thing [think] he will succeed. Rained all day. I wrote to Lyde.

WEDNESDAY DECEMBER 3RD 1862

Bethel Tennessee

I drew some Sugar and hams for the Hospital. had my hair cut by Wiggins. I talked to Dr. Marlow about his sliping into the chest and drinking up the Wine. I took charge of the Key and locked up the chest. I am not well to day took blue pill. Rec'd a letter from E.M.

THURSDAY DECEMBER 4TH 1862
Bethel Tennessee
We vaccinnated the recruits of the regiment to day, and the negroes in camp. Sent to the country and got some chickens. I took a Stroll in the woods and cut my name in the bark of a beech tree half mile South East of camp in the creek bottom. Raining at bedtime~

FRIDAY DECEMBER 5TH 1862
Bethel Tennessee
Snowing this morning and cold. so much for the Salubrious climes of the "Sunny South" we were out of wood. I got a detail and had some hauled. We got a Keg of butter (100lbs.) from Illinois. We had a can of Oysters. were up 'til midnight the Moon was Eclipsed and E.W. Charles stayed up to see it. the night was clear and beautiful The Eclipse was total.~

SATURDAY DECEMBER 6TH 1862
Bethel Tennessee
Weather clear and beautiful. An order issued forbidding Soldiers going to the R.R. Depot, except with a pass, as camp is almost entirely deserted some evenings, and is not considered safe. Rec'd a box of Medicines from Columbus Ky. and more comming. I wrote to E.M.

SUNDAY DECEMBER 7TH 1862
Bethel Tennessee
Lieut. H.W. Kerr Co. "E,, 49" Ills. Started home without leave to day and was baged at Jackson Tenn. and sent back to his regiment. Col. I.N. Haynie promoted to Brig. Gen'l. He is in a fine humor. Batt. "K,, 1st Mo. out on inspection and review to day. made a fine appearance. Weather very pleasant.

MONDAY DECEMBER 8TH 1862
Bethel Tennessee
I drew rations to day for the Hospital. got a detail and hauled wood. O.W. Brokaw returned from Columbus Ky. has been there on a visit.

brings no news. I am doubtfull he did'nt make a very favorable impression there, with the members of the 111" Ills. Inft.~

TUESDAY DECEMBER 9TH 1862
Bethel Tennessee

Lieut. E.B. Harlan was detailed Ordnance Officer of the Post. Gen'l I.N. Haynie is making up his staff. Harlan want to be a member of the staff.~

Our Negro cook stole the Sugar to-day, and got caught in it. he not only claimed to be innocent but that he was religiously inclined. we dispensed with his services, and sent him on his way rejoicing.~

WEDNESDAY DECEMBER 10TH 1862
Bethel Tennessee

General inspection to day, of both Reg'ts by a Capt. Wilson of the 18" Ills. Infty. the 49" Ills made the best appearance, every thing in good order. I weighed 174 lbs. to-day. I too in good order. My health has been good during the past twelve months. Recd a letter from Lyde.

THURSDAY DECEMBER 11TH 1862
Bethel Tennessee

I called upon Col. Morrison to day and he wrote another letter for me to Adj't. Gen'l A.C. Fuller for an order for me to go before the Medical board of Examiners. And it is high time I was getting it too.~ Hoss & Burrows went to the country to day. I wrote to Lyde.

FRIDAY DECEMBER 12TH 1862
Bethel Tennessee

Batt. "K,, out on review. Lieut Welman, Lieut Harlan, and Lieut Green put under arrest by Brig. General Haynie for not finding a verdict in favor of Mr. Tatum for some lumber which he says our troops here have appropriated but not proven. Mrs. Marlow in camp~

SATURDAY DECEMBER 13TH 1862
Bethel Tennessee

Two companies from each Reg't and the Cav. Sent out to obstruct the roads between here and the Tennessee River. The Rebels thought to be coming from toward Savanah. Haynie released those three Lieuts from arrest thinks there ia a <u>probability of having use</u> for them soon the rumor is that <u>Haynie</u> is cutting the <u>front logs on the branch</u>. we had an Oyster Supper this evening~

SUNDAY DECEMBER 14TH 1862
Bethel Tennessee

Artillery out on inspection, to day. Lieut Rowley & T.O. Hoss went to Jackson. I went with Capt Cheney around the Picket <u>lines</u>, and rode Major Bishops <u>horse</u>. thought to be some prospect of an attack. the guards are very vigilant.

I Rec'd a letter from, and wrote to <u>J.F.B.</u>

MONDAY DECEMBER 15TH 1862
Bethel Tennessee

The Weather is cold, and it rained most all day Gen'l Haynie preparing to leave here soon perhaps to morrow. I made 300 compound Cath.' <u>Pills</u> to day. the allowance furnished is to small. The cavalry sent out on a reconnaisance and to see what is going on in the country.~

TUESDAY DECEMBER 16TH 1862
Bethel Tennessee

Gen'l I.N. Haynie and Staff left to day. Col. Wm R. Morrison took command of the Post, to day~ The artillery, practicing, getting range of the Surrounding <u>hills</u>. <u>they</u> made excellent shots~ I bought a looking glass to day $1.00. <u>Expecting an attack at Jackson to night</u>. Rec'd letter from <u>E.M.</u>

WEDNESDAY DECEMBER 17TH 1862
Bethel Tennessee

Prospect of a fight here another fort being built, on Tatum's <u>hill</u>. The cavalry sent out on a scout. <u>Dr. Marlow drinking to-day</u>. fell out with me and made an attack. but he was repulsed at all points, and finally withdrew from the scene of action with impaired vision, and a bunged up countenance. I reported myself to Col. Pease and we were both placed in arrest~

THURSDAY DECEMBER 18TH 1862
Bethel Tennessee

Rebels advancing on Jackson, fighting at Mifflin. Rebels said to be in force.~ Troops going from Boliver to reinforce Jackson. Frank Black & John Burrows came this evening from Columbus. The road is still open and in order. they saw no enemy~

FRIDAY DECEMBER 19TH 1862
Bethel Tennessee

I was releived from arrest this A.M. by Col. Pease. Heavy firing heard in the direction of Jackson The 48" Ills. Infty. was sent out to join Gen'l Dodge at Purdy at 2.P.M. enrout for Jackson. Heavy details at work on the fortifications on Tatum's hill, both by day, and night.~

SATURDAY DECEMBER 20TH 1862
Bethel Tennessee

E.W. Charles got his discharge from the Army "to enable him to join the Navy" Sold me his Anatomy (Gray's) and Medical Lexicon (Dunglison's) for $.9.00. Fighting said to be farther off and to the right of Jackson nothing reliable. The train went with provisions to Henderson.~

SUNDAY DECEMBER 21ST 1862
Bethel Tennessee

Frank Black & John Burrows left at noon on a hand car for Jackson. Tellegraph in working order from here to Jackson. Humbolt was captured by the Rebels. the Railroad is being torn up by them. they will cut off our supplies and leave us to forage off the country. it is a bad stroke of policy in them to destroy the road as we will subsist off their friends. run our negro off for Stealing.

MONDAY DECEMBER 22ND 1862
Bethel Tennessee

The rebels have taken Holly Springs and Said to be coming. I Rec'd dispatch from Frank Black at Henderson Station. The train came from Corinth and went to Jackson E.W. Charles left us to day for Cairo Ills. he will soon be in his long desired "Gunboat Service." I wrote E.M.~

TUESDAY DECEMBER 23RD 1862
Bethel Tennessee

Tom. O. Hoss & S. Dickson went to Jackson with prisoners. No News from the Scene of action. I saw Gen'l Dodge's forces returning to Corinth by the Railroad. they were not in the fight. the fighting was northeast of Jackson. The rebels have gone in the direction of Columbus Ky.~

WEDNESDAY DECEMBER 24TH 1862
Bethel Tennessee

I Sent to the country and got some chickens and Eggs etc. Hoss & Dickson returned no news. I got a detail and cut and hauled wood again for the Hospital.~ Dr. D.K. Green came this evening from Jackson. I am a little doubtful of my success, in the Examination.~

THURSDAY DECEMBER 25TH 1862
Bethel Tennessee

I was Examined by Dr. Green this morning and recommended for the position of 2nd Asst Surg of the 49" Ills. Infty. The Doctor left for Corinth. I passed a very dull Christmas to day. am not very well. no news from the East, and no train from the North. The Railroad has been torn up by the rebels under Forrest north of Jackson~

FRIDAY DECEMBER 26TH 1862
Bethel Tennessee

I went to the commissary to draw rations, but found them without. Raining most all day. Hoss & Burrows down to the Hospital to spend the evening. I saw Capt. Wm P. Moore this P.M. in camp for the first time since his capture at Henderson on the 25th November 1862

SATURDAY DECEMBER 27TH 1862
Bethel Tennessee

I gave a darky a plug of tobaco to-day to wash my clothes. Add Ward Brought in two turkeys from the country to day. now for a roast. no train from the north Co. "D,, detailed and Sent up to the Fort on Tatum's Hill to stay to night~

SUNDAY DECEMBER 28TH 1862
Bethel Tennessee

Fine weather. Short of rations. A. Ward went out and brought in half a hog. we had baked turkey for dinner. Dr. Goslin of the 48" Ills dined with us. I got some dried fruit. foraging party brought in some Sheep, to be butchered & Issued. I read most all day~

MONDAY DECEMBER 29TH 1862
Bethel Tennessee

There was corn meal brought in for issue from the mills to day. we are on half rations by order, but on full feed by good foraging. there is plenty in the country and we know how to get it here~ The regiments are drilling again to day for the first for some time. Madam rumor says that Richmond and Vicksburg are both ours, but there is no-body in camp vain enough to Swallow it~

TUESDAY DECEMBER 30TH 1862
Bethel Tennessee

There is a party in contemplation to take place in our Hospital on the evening of new years. Dr. Marlow & I got an invitation to furnish the candles for the lights but no invitation to participate in the festivities.~ Col Morrison gone to Jackson Lt. Col. P. Pease in command of the Post. Maj. Bishop of the Reg't.

WEDNESDAY DECEMBER 31ST 1862
Bethel Tennessee

The train brought some provisions from Jackson. I drew a supply for the Hospital. The regiment mustered for pay again to day. Col. Wm R. Morrison going to Start for home to morrow. he made a little speech on dressparade this evening. Lt. Col. W.W. Sanford 48" Ills Comndg. Post. Lt. Harlan acting Post Adjt. Heavy canonading in the direction of Lexington. Great preparations being made for the party tomorrow evening. I helped Mrs. Goslin, Bishop, Haynie, and Drs. Goslin & Young to decorate the room with evergreens. I have now been in the capacity of a Soldier one year to day, and many and varied have been the scenes, circumstances, and vicissitudes of that short period of my life. perhaps there has been more of human nature learned in that year than the ballance of my life, I wrote to Lyde.~

THURSDAY JANUARY 1ST 1863
Bethel Tennessee

Col Wm R. Morrison having resigned his commission as Colonel, left this morning for home after one years Service in the field, to accept a Seat in Congress~

I was put on duty to day as Ass't Surg of the 49" Ills. Infty. by Lt. Col. P. Pease Comnd Reg't. we decorated the Hospital and had a ball at night, a good time. the boys fired into the Room, nobody hurt. I went to Purdy with an ambulance to take the girls home at midnight.

FRIDAY JANUARY 2ND 1863
Bethel Tennessee

The 49" had orders and marched at 4.A.M. via Purdy to Adamsville. Dr. Medcalf accompanied the Regt and left me in charge of the Hospital, though a very light charge as all were able to go to quarters during the ball Dr. Marlow was relieved from duty yesterday morning. a very dull day every thing very quiet, in camp

SATURDAY JANUARY 3RD 1863
Bethel Tennessee

Thos. O. Hoss returned for provisions, and brought in Six prisoners Gen'l Forrest has been defeated with a loss of Six pieces of Artillery, and 400 prisoners, and the ballance of his command Scattered. Lt. Col. Sanford 48" Ills. Comndg Post. sent dispatch to Col Pease to be on the alert and "gobble them up."

SUNDAY JANUARY 4" 1863
Bethel Tennessee

No news from the Reg't to day. The report of the Capture of Vicksburg and Richmond wants confirmation. I borrowed $.10.00 of Bridges Co. "I,, to day. Prospect of an attack 48" out in line at 11.P.M. but very few of our men left in camp just enough to take care of the camp for the time

MONDAY JANUARY 5" 1863
Bethel Tennessee

The 49" Ills returned at 1.P.M. after being sent for brought in some fresh pork with them been living pretty well during their absence I think. Lt. Harlan & F.J. Burrows eat Supper with me Adj't. Wm Martin on a drunk and did not get in. The Sutler, (Hoskins) came to day and brought some goods for sale. we have not had money for some time. I rec'd letter from J.F.B.

TUESDAY JANUARY 6" 1863
Bethel Tennessee

I made out a Voucher and drew $.17.70 Hospt. Fund. paid Dr. Marlow $.15.00 on a keg of butter we got from Ills. George E. Dillingham Co. "K,, detailed, and reported for duty as Hospt Steward. quite a revolution in the Medical Dep't lately. got my watch fixed $.3.00. wrote to J.F.B.

WEDNESDAY JANUARY 7" 1863
Bethel Tennessee

Reinforcements came into camp to the amount of two briggades on their way to Corinth. we finished our chimney to our cook tent to day. I drew 1. pr pants, 2. pr. drawers & .2. pr. Socks. Capt. Berry & Lt. Spiro returned yesterday evening from recruiting service in Ills. I rec'd a letter from F.M.A.

THURSDAY JANUARY 8" 1863
Bethel Tennessee

Gen'l Lawler's forces left to day some for Jackson and the ballance for Corinth. I went out and helped haul two loads of wood. Add. Ward went to the country for some chickens but did'nt return as he has to go out several miles now to find them, getting scarce.

FRIDAY JANUARY 9" 1863
Bethel Tennessee

Add Ward returned with a bountiful supply of Eggs Chickens, butter etc. I read gray's anatomy most all day I have very good opportunities for reading here. Lt. Harlan came up from Hd Qrs to see me. I went three times to the regiment to see the sick. I generally have to go in day time and always at night, as Dr Medcalf is apt to be sick if called at night.

SATURDAY JANUARY 10" 1863
Bethel Tennessee

Some of the battery-men went out to Purdy last night and broke into houses and stole some goods and tobaco. One of them whiped to day with a rope. The Sutler shut up and a general investigation being made to find the property, and the guilty parties.

SUNDAY JANUARY 11" 1863
Bethel Tennessee

Some troops stoped over night here on their way to Corinth. I went with Frank J. Burrows to spend the evening with Adj't Harlan at Post. Hd. Qrs. There is no reliable news from Vicksburg, nor from Gen'l Rosecrans Army at present. nothing of interes in camp to-day.~

MONDAY JANUARY 12" 1863
Bethel Tennessee

I moved into the room formerly occupied by Dr. Marlow. his things are still in it. Dr. Medcalf wants it for the old negress. (cook.) Col. Pease and Dr. Medcalf went to Purdy to day to take dinner I bought an I.O.O.F. pin to day for $.2.00 it is a right hand with a heart in--gold.

TUESDAY JANUARY 13" 1863
Bethel Tennessee

A lot of flour brought down from Jackson to day, replenishing the commissary here. a mail came also but none for me this time. We have Measles in camp, brough in by the contrabands, from the country. so much for their associations. While the Negroes are of some advantage, they also bring some inconviniences, and disadvantages.

WEDNESDAY JANUARY 14" 1863
Bethel Tennessee

Rained all day. I went up to camp, and eat dinner with the boys of Co. "D,, been a fine day for playing cards checkers etc. and has been spent that way by most of them, though there is but little or no gambling going on I think among them now I think

THURSDAY JANUARY 15" 1863
Bethel Tennessee

It snowed, and blew all day and we had no train in consequence I suppose of the inclemency of the weather. I spent the day in Quarters reading anatomy. The "Sunny South" is far from being all Sunshine, as we have endured some very disagreeable weather here.

FRIDAY JANUARY 16" 1863
Bethel Tennessee

Snow three inches deep. weather cloudy and cool. There is heavy log rolling among the Com officers in view of the future promotions. Bishop wants to be made Col. over Pease, and Capts Morgan, L.W. Moore, Berry, Laur, & Kurghoff, all want to be Majors. Morgan is the Sen Capt. and best officer

SATURDAY JANUARY 17" 1863
Bethel Tennessee

The Com. Officers held a meeting, in view of the promotions to be made. Capt Thos. W. Morgan informed them that they were a little to late, as he was Major, and the commission already forwarded.

The Serg't[s] of the Reg't met at Co. "D,, Quarters, and signified their prefrence in favor of Capt. Jacob E. Gauen Co. "H,, but it is all to late as Morgan had a fast friend in Col Morrison, ~

SUNDAY JANUARY 18" 1863
Bethel Tennessee

Preaching in the Hospital this afternoon by Chaplain Lockwood. The boys of the 48" & 49" Ills snowballing one Reg't against the other, on the drill ground between their respective camps. Camp dull no news. neither papers nor mail, since the 18" ult. [from the word ultimo: meaning of or occurring in the month preceding the present] (Forrest raid, on the Railroad)

MONDAY JANUARY 19" 1863
Bethel Tennessee

Rained most all day. weather very disagreeable Esq. J.B. Bozorth came from home yesterday, and brought me some letters from Wayne County. The train brought papers to day but not much news in them of interest. there is a blank in history to us. I rec'd letters from J.K., A.K.A. & A.F.A.

TUESDAY JANUARY 20" 1863
Bethel Tennessee

I repaired the roof of my shebang to day and built my chimney higher. A. Ward went out for butter & Eggs. Lieut. W.W. Bliss made Post Q.M. to day as Q.M. Haynie leaves to join the Gen'l. Lieut. A.S. Rowley made Regt'l Q.M. or rather detailed for duty as such. Jim Davis holds the position yet.~

WEDNESDAY JANUARY 21ST 1863
Bethel Tennessee

Capt. Wm P. Moore returned, no mail to day. Three pay-masters went by here going to Corinth to pay off the troops there. There is prospect of another attack on Vicksburg soon, the recent rumor of its capture together with that of Richmond both proved to be unfounded, before. I wrote and sent letter by the Sutler to J.F.B.

THURSDAY JANUARY 22" 1863
Bethel Tennessee

I commenced making an anual report of the Medical & Hosp't property, received, expended, and on hand for the year 1862, in our Reg't Dr. Marlow in camp today. he is out of a job~ I had some wood hauled to day. the weather warm and raining. more mud~

FRIDAY JANUARY 23" 1863
Bethel Tennessee

Working at the anual report find it a tedious job, papers are missing. I went down to see Lieut E Harlan his fair correspondent about to prove an enigma to him. he dont know what to think of her. Charley Burrows, Wiley, and George Cunningham wounded.~ Rec'd letter from Lyde.

SATURDAY JANUARY 24" 1863
Bethel Tennessee

It rained all day. I had some wood cut and hauled to day. it seems our luck to have to haul wood in the rain. F.J. Burrows came down and wrote some letters this evening. he is uneasy about Charlies being wounded I wrote to J.F.B. & R.H.~

SUNDAY JANUARY 25" 1863
Bethel Tennessee

Dr. Medcalf went to Cairo Ills. I am in charge of the Hospital. Thos O. Hoss & Frank J. Burrows came down and took dinner with me to day. The Payrolls came back to day prospect of our getting some money soon and it will not come amiss if it comes at all, as we have not been paid since last August, and have pay due us from June 30" 1862~

MONDAY JANUARY 26" 1863
Bethel Tennessee

I got a detail and had wood cut and hauled Col. Pease put Eph Williams in the ranks to day because he could not fife to do any good. Co. "D,, ordered to Fort Hooker to day six miles north of here on the railroad to forage for the Q.M. at Corinth for corn. It rained again to day.

TUESDAY JANUARY 27" 1863
Bethel Tennessee

Co. "D,, packed up and left for McNairy Station ("Ft Hooker") to forage to-day. Weather is pleasant. I was ordered by Col Pease to get a barrell of Whisky to day from the A.C.S. to be issued to the fatigue and guard details, and an excuse for the Com. Officers. I Rec'd a letter from E.M.

WEDNESDAY JANUARY 28" 1863
Bethel Tennessee

Companies signing the Payrolls preparatory to being paid off. I made requisition and drew a barrell of Whiskey. some of the Co. or Co. Officers are troubled with whisky on the brain. The rebels are threatning us again. said to be crossing the Tenn. river. I wrote to E.M.

THURSDAY JANUARY 29" 1863
Bethel Tennessee

I got the very desirable article Whisky to-day. Maj. Bishop & Lieut Kerr made a demand for some, for "Medical use," but they failed in their attemp, as Col Pease directed it should be issued upon his order for details and at the discretion of a Medical Officer for Medical purposes. and the Major's was a prescription of his own making~

FRIDAY JANUARY 30" 1863
Bethel Tennessee

Dr. Marlow in camp to get some money The Pay master in camp going to pay for two months only. (May & June. 62) Money scarce among soldiers as well as officers generally. I have been paid but once since I left Camp Butler. Mail & Papers came

SATURDAY JANUARY 31" 1863
Bethel Tennessee

I sent an Ambulance down to Post. Hd. Qrs. and brought the Pay master Maj._____ up to Col. Pease' Quarters and he paid off the 49" Ills. for two months. I rec'd $.34.00 only. Sergeant's pay. I had rec'd that on the company rolls supposing Stewards were paid like other Hospt attendants, but the Paymaster said he could not pay on two rolls, and owing to Maj. Bishops Official stupidity, Capt Cheney had rec'd no notice of my promotion and the rolls even failed to state the fact of it. I paid Lieut Wm Whaling $.9.00 on a note given to E.W. Charles for two books. I paid Peter Taylor $.5.00 borrowed money. Dr. Marlow got Ass't Surg's pay. I ruled out and made monthly return. Cheney drew Co. "D,, pay here. I rec'd letter from Lyde.

SUNDAY FEBRUARY 1" 1863
Bethel Tennessee

It rained in the forenoon. We are wanting for blanks to make monthly report of "Sick and Wounded. Frank J. Burrows went up to McNairy Station to see Co. "D,, boys on duty there. I was in camp all day. stole Tom Moore's works from Lt. Harlan to read. We have but few books in camp to read, aside from Army Regulations and Hardee's Tactics I rec'd a letter from E.M.

MONDAY FEBRUARY 2" 1863
Bethel Tennessee

I collected $.10.00 from Capt Cheney, $.10.00 from Lt. Harlan, and added $10.00 myself and Expressed the $.30.00 to Wm Holmes at

Kimmundy Ills. according to his direction. O.W. Brokaw did'nt pay any of his but said he would next time we were paid off.

TUESDAY FEBRUARY 3" 1863
Bethel Tennessee
Capt. T.W. Morgan ordered to be reported as Major and his successors in the Co. according to their respective promotions. I borrowed $.20.00 of Wm. E. Farrow to day to be returned when we are next paid. got a detail and hauled wood. no train to day.

WEDNESDAY FEBRUARY 4" 1863
Bethel Tennessee
I issued the last of my barrel of Whiskey to day details have been heavy on 'Tennessee tanglefoot.' T.O. Hoss down from McNairy. Dr. Marlow in camp snowed in the afternoon. I read anatomy all day. Train came from Jackson but brought neither papers nor mail. camp dull.

THURSDAY FEBRUARY 5" 1863
Bethel Tennessee
Col. Sanford gone to Jackson. Col. Pease Comndg Post. Maj. Bishop Comndg the Reg't. he came down to the Hospital and peremptoraly ordered me to get another barrell of Whiskey from the Post Hospital, pretending to take a deep interest in the mens welfare, when it is purely from his own love of the ardent. snow three inches deep weather disagreeable.

FRIDAY FEBRUARY 6" 1863
Bethel Tennessee
Got a detail and had wood hauled to-day I issued whiskey to the guards at the Hosp't and cut the commissioned officer out of theirs as they dont like to acknowledge before the men that they are fond of whiskey. A. Heese hauling logs [to] build a Commissary shebang.

SATURDAY FEBRUARY 7" 1863
Bethel Tennessee
I settled up with the Post Commissary and got $.21.65 for "Hospital fund." The train came at 9.P.M. Doctor Medcalf & Lady came, also Mrs. Pease and Mrs Bliss. I sent an ambulance to the depot for them Col. Pease and lady going to board with us until we establish another mess

SUNDAY FEBRUARY 8" 1863
Bethel Tennessee

Weather fine and drying up the mud. Lieut Harlan went to McNairy to day to see the boys. Albanus Bishop came down with a very bad looking arm. Some of the Officers of the 111" Ills said to be under arrest for treasonable language. I wrote to Lyde.~

MONDAY FEBRUARY 9" 1863
Bethel Tennessee

George E. Dillingham Hosp't Steward left for Memphis to procure Medical & Hospital supplies. I put R.A. Grunendike on duty as Wardmaster in the Hosp't to day, as he is unable for duty in the Co. since he was wounded at Shiloh, and since E.W. Charles left we need some one in the Hosp't at night. rained most all day I got a paper but not much news.

TUESDAY FEBRUARY 10" 1863
Bethel Tennessee

There is talk of a meeting being organized in camp to draft a Series of resolutions, to send home, to show the people there what the feeling of soldiers in regard to some of the questions of the day, and especially for the information of Copperheads. James Thompson returned. I got a Memphis paper.

WEDNESDAY FEBRUARY 11" 1863
Bethel Tennessee

Dillingham returned from Memphis Tenn. but brought no Medicines. Add Ward returned from the country and brought a fine lot of provisions. Chickens, Eggs, & butter are the staples of this country. The weather is quite pleasant. I got a pass to go to Jackson to-morrow.

THURSDAY FEBRUARY 12" 1863
Bethel Tennessee

I went to Jackson, and bought a pr boots $.8.00 also a brush & comb. I could get no coat nor vest. goods scarce and prices high. I left Jackson at 3.P.M. and arrived at 7.P.M. four hours coming had to forage along the road for the fuel we burned in coming.

FRIDAY FEBRUARY 13" 1863
Bethel Tennessee

The 10" Mo Cavalry with a battery of Mountain howitzers stoped here for dinner on their way to Corinth Miss. Sent Dillingham to Corinth to hunt up some lost Medicines Chaplain Lockwood is building a house for quarters, and to hold meeting in, in bad weather. has quite a number of the men helping him

FRIDAY [SATURDAY] FEBRUARY 14" 1863
Bethel Tennessee

Dillingham returned found four boxes of our medicines at Corinth. Lt. Rowley and F.J. Burrows returned from Ft. Hooker. O.W. Brokaw returned from home, to-day. Serg't S.C. Goshorn reduced to the ranks two weeks for drunkenness. I would make it permanent.

SATURDAY [SUNDAY] FEBRUARY 15" 1863
Bethel Tennessee

We got our Mess started to day. A. Heese presented us a fine turkey for the first meal Dr. A. Goslin & lady of 48" Ills dined with us. "Our Mess" comprises Dr. Medcalf and lady, Col. Pease and Lady George E. Dillingham & myself. I went over the creek to see a sick girl. (citizen)

SUNDAY [MONDAY] FEBRUARY 16" 1863
Bethel Tennessee

The Officers held a meeting, appointed a committee to draft resolutions expressing the views of the command in regard to some of the questions aggitated at the north. I rec'd a series of resolutions from the 111" Ills in refrence to the Advocate [Salem, Illinois, newspaper] & letter from J.F.B.

MONDAY [TUESDAY] FEBRUARY 17" 1863
Bethel Tennessee

The Officers re-assembled. the committee reported a series of resolutions which were adopted, then were submitted to the troops on dressparade, and were adopted by the 48" & 49" Ills. with but three dissenting voices in the former, and six in the latter Reg't. unanimously adopted by a battallion of the 11" & 12" Ills. Cavalry, and ordered to be published in St. Louis papers.

TUESDAY [WEDNESDAY] FEBRUARY 18"
1863

Bethel Tennessee

I made a requisition for Medical & Hosp't'l supplies. Clark came last night and brought me a letter from Frank. he is trying to settle up P.P. Hamilton's old sutler accts. for him. Capt Cheney in camp to day. Wm P. Blake sick. I rec'd a letter by mail from J.F.B.~

WEDNESDAY [THURSDAY] FEBRUARY 19"
1863

Bethel Tennessee

Very windy to-day. Capt. Cheney eat dinner with us. The Artillery out on the parad[e] ground drilling to-day. The Reg't on battalion drill not much interest manifested in it tho', except by the Col. himself. no news this evening. camp quiet and dull.~

THURSDAY [FRIDAY] FEBRUARY 20" 1863

Bethel Tennessee

F.J. Burrows went to Memphis Tenn. for blanks. I sent by him for a vest, wreath & shoulder straps. I got a copy of the resolutions adopted the other day, and transcribed them. Col Sanford gone to Memphis Resolutions sent by him for publication. Pease Comndg Post.

FRIDAY [SATURDAY] FEBRUARY 21" 1863

Bethel Tennessee

Dr. Brown, (citizen) reported killed in the country recently, in camp to day though unwell. he was considerably bruised up~ considerable disturbance in the country occasionally at a distance from camp. I dressed a Wound for a rebel by the name of Black to-day. It rained most all day and consequently quite disagreeable~

SATURDAY [SUNDAY] FEBRUARY 22" 1863

Bethel Tennessee

Batt."K,, 1st Mo. Arty. fired thirty four guns to day in commemoration of the birth day of Washington. The Reg't out on parade F.J. Burrows returned from Memphis brought me a pr. "Straps," vest & Wreath and $.1.00 worth of Stamps. I wrote to E.W.C.~

SUNDAY [MONDAY] FEBRUARY 23" 1863
Bethel Tennessee

Col Sanford returned from Memphis. he lost those resolutions he says, though it is believed he destroyed them. they did'nt suit him. I went riding with Lt Harlan to Purdy, the first horseback ride since in camp. The weather is very fine now. I rec'd letter from Lyde, & wrote to J.F.B.

MONDAY [TUESDAY] FEBRUARY 24" 1863
Bethel Tennessee

I called with Lt Harlan at Wilson's to day. I played checkers with Col. Pease, Medcalf, Harlan & Rowley. checkers is the game in camp now. I got $.5.00 worth of sutler tickets to day, as money is scarce. I bought a Diary of him for .50cts for 1863

TUESDAY [WEDNESDAY] FEBRUARY 25" 1863
Bethel Tennessee

It rained most all day I'm not very well have the head-ache. I played checkers with the boys. there is a fine lot of grain being foraged from the country and shiped to Corinth. Forrest's tearing up the railroad has not been very profitable to rebel sympathizers. I Met with the "Never Swet Society" at the depot. bought three Memphis papers. No mail scarcely.~

WEDNESDAY [THURSDAY] FEBRUARY 26" 1863
Bethel Tennessee

Still raining, camp dull. Lt Harlan's brother came to see him from Ohio. I read most all day. bought Democrat this evening with an account of the Union Meeting at Salem Ills. recently. a good omen from the citizens at home. but little mail this evening.

THURSDAY [FRIDAY] FEBRUARY 27" 1863
Bethel Tennessee

I got a detail and hauled wood for the Hosp't I played Euchre with Maj. Bishop and we beat Mrs. Bishop and Dr. Medcalf, though to the Major the praise is due, as I play a very poor game I beat Col. Pease playing at checkers to-day though cant play a very strong game. weather fine.

FRIDAY [SATURDAY] FEBRUARY 28" 1863
Bethel Tennessee

Reg't mustered for pay. field and Staff mustered proper for the first time in the service to-day. I made Monthly report, Dr. Medcalf muster rolls. Ward returned with chickens etc. we had a Miss Brown with us for dinner. a De't. [Detachment] of 49" went to Purdy relieved De't 48" had a letter from Wm Holmes acknowledging the receipt of money sent. says collect the ballance. Wm Holmes

SUNDAY MARCH 1ST 1863
Bethel Tennessee

I went with Dr. A. Goslin to see him make a post Mortem examination on a negro who died of Pleuricy in the Cavalry camp, yesterday. We experimented on him then I ligated the femoral artery. Lt Harlan and his brother gone to Corinth A detachment of Cavalry sent out yesterday to Hamburg to capture some guerrillas who are secreted in houses in that country.~

MONDAY MARCH 2" 1863
Bethel Tennessee

Capt Cheney brought in Julius Jones, to-day. noted guerrilla chief, who escaped from the guard house here recently also, from Cheney, the other night. Capts father came. A Tennessean sworn into Co. "D,, to-day, by Col. Pease, by the name of Abner Whit, from about McNairy station

TUESDAY MARCH 3" 1863
Bethel Tennessee

Lt. Harlan returned from Corinth. I had a little jaw with him about a paper which came in the mail for him, and got by Col. Pease to read. Co. "B,, returned this evening from Illinois, the first since their capture. Mr. Cheney left. Rec'd Invoices of our Medicines.

WEDNESDAY MARCH 4" 1863
Bethel Tennessee
Dr. Medcalf took dinner with Major Bishop An Artillery man run over to day while drilling. A man accidently shot on picket to day of the 48" Ills. in the side of the neck I went with Dr Medcalf to see him Dr. Goslin absent. I settled with the commissary, and reported the "Hospt Fund"

THURSDAY MARCH 5" 1863
Bethel Tennessee

Xenia

W.W. Willard and Dr. Sherly of Xenia in camp to day we went over to Dr. Goslin's to spend the evening. had Egg-nog, and had toasts from several very nicely chosen for the occassion Dr. Mercer is to be at Jackson in a few days. Willard is down to defend Dr. Lakon's son of the 62" Ills at Jackson charged with desertion and in the guard house there at this time. the old man, (Lakon) is responsible for it.

FRIDAY MARCH 6" 1863
Bethel Tennessee
Willard left for Jackson. Artillery firing heard the 48" Ills on the alert. Commissions came to day for P. Pease as Col., W.W. Bishop Lt. Col., T. W. Morgan Major, Wm Cogan Capt. of Co. "A,, A.K. Dement 1st Lt. Co. "A,, A.S. Chalfin 2" Lt. Co. "A,, and mine as 2" Ass't Surg. dated Nov 17" 1862. made Jany. 17" 1863. I rec'd a letter from J.F.B.

SATURDAY MARCH 7" 1863
Bethel Tennessee
We received orders to march to Bolivar Tenn to morrow morning. Dr. Mercer & Willard came from Jackson. Co.s "D,, "F,, & "H,, returned from the outposts to day preparations makink [making] for the move. a lot of us went out to a Mr Stiles at night to a shindig. Dr. Sherly went with us.

SUNDAY MARCH 8" 1863
Bethel Tennessee
I went down to Hd Qrs and got a Gov. hors and rig of the Q.M. to be used until called for, by the Q.M. Rowley got one for himself, and one for Edd. Nixon Teams, Wagons, harness, saddles, etc being turned

in and reissued. we didn't get off to day everybody busy getting ready to go to-morrow.~

MONDAY MARCH 9" 1863
Bethel Tennessee

We moved our goods to the depot. an enormous quantity of them there was too. three companies of each Reg't were put on one train and left. I accompanied them. we went to Jackson there took the other road passed Bolliver and went on to La-Grange. stoped there and were put into two churches to await the arrival of the ballance of the Command~

TUESDAY MARCH 10" 1863
La-Grange Tennessee

We were ordered to re load our tro[o]ps for another move, to Germantown this time the ballance of the command past us. we have a big job and there seems to be no one in command of our Det's, many men drunk. Lt. Chalfin and I sewed on <u>each</u> others Straps.

WEDNESDAY MARCH 11" 1863
La-Grange Tennessee

We left at 6.A.M. for Germantown. three Co's of the 48" Ills were left behind because they would not get ready. we arrived, unloaded our plunder and then Rec'd orders to march on to White's Station to-morrow. we have had a lively time since we left Bethel with drunk men & rain

THURSDAY MARCH 12" 1863
Germantown Tennessee

We re loaded our goods and moved on to White's Station. we relieved the 72nd Ohio, on duty here found a fine church for a Hospital close to camp. We left Mrs Pease & Mrs Medcalf at Germantown until things could be put in order and a camp established

FRIDAY MARCH 13" 1863
White's Station Tennessee

The 72" Ohio left. they tried to burn their quarters and a school-house used as kitchen to the Hospital, here. we went to work putting things in order, started our Mess agoing. cleaned out the church and put our sick in. Mrs Pease & Mrs Medcalf came from Germantown. Major

T.W. Morgan came to camp. we are situated the best we have been since in the field.~

SATURDAY MARCH 14" 1863
White's Station Tennessee
I went back to Ridgeway station to see the sick of the co.s left there, sent back to Germantown and drew rations. Three co.s of the 119" Ills Inft stoped here to day. The 28" Ills left here and the 12" Mich. past here. Dr. Medcalf talking of going back to Germantown, to be sen Surg of the Briggade.

SUNDAY MARCH 15" 1863
White's Station Tennessee
Col. Sanford and Lt. Green Batt "K,, down here to day. Capt. Wm P. Moore detailed for provost Marshal of this place. Frank J. Burrows appeared on dressparade for the first time as adjutant this evening. he made no mistake except in bout facing to the Col. he turned to the left instead of the right

MONDAY MARCH 16" 1863
White's Station Tennessee
I went to Ridgeway found Serg't Pickett Co. "B,, very sick and sent an Ambulance for him. I moved to Ridgeway, took a field tent and a few medicines with me found it a dull dry place. no shade. no water close at hand, and no shelter for my horse and only a stockade for fortifications.~

TUESDAY MARCH 17" 1863
Ridgeway Station Tennessee
I went into Paddy Burns' Mess to board. all the officers of the Det. board there except Col Bishop & Lt. Barbee of Co. "K,, We have half the Reg't here Companies "D,, "E,, "K,, "G,, & "B,, with the Co. officers, except Capt. Wm P. Moore I made a temporary table for me [my] Medicines, and fixed up things generally, as well as I could. Weather very fine~

WEDNESDAY MARCH 18" 1863
Ridgeway Station Tennessee

I rode around the Picket lines with Capt Cheney. Picket firing in the night we were up and in the stockade, some one said to be crawling up to one of the posts, no farther alarm. perhaps an imaginary object seen. We went back to bed.

THURSDAY MARCH 19" 1863
Ridgeway Station Tennessee

I went with Thos O. Hoss to Germantown~ Saw the Pay master working on the pay rolls going to pay us soon I suppose. Lt Rowley eat dinner with us he is going to have some tents soon to issue to the officers. I am to have one of them.~

FRIDAY MARCH 20" 1863
Ridgeway Station Tennessee

I sent to White's Station for an Ambulance and sent two Co. "B,, [men] to Hospital. Capt Lockwood stoped with us to night. the boys playing poker most of the time now, gambling considerably. I rec'd a letter from Fort. Heiman from J.F.B.

SATURDAY MARCH 21ST 1863
Ridgeway Tennessee

I went with Capt Cheney to White's Station and got tents for the Reg't. there was not tents enough for all the officers but I was fortunate enough to get one, (a wall tent) but it is to low at the sides and of awkward shape We returned and put them up. they mak much better shelter than the old things we did have Lt. Stanley sent out with a Det. on a reconnaisance

SUNDAY MARCH 22" 1863
Ridgeway Tennessee

Lt. Harlan came by, and stoped on his way from Germantown to White's Station, those two places are five miles apart and we are half way between. Chaplain Lockwood came down, and preached in the Stockade to day. The Cavalry heard we were attacked and came to assist us, but all a mistake.

MONDAY MARCH 23" 1863
Ridgeway Tennessee

The team went out and brought in some lumber and I floored my tent with some of it to-day. Rained most of the day. We got four barrells of unions [onions] for the detachment. vegatable are very sparsely issued to the men now, & here. Dickson & Wife came. In line of battle at day light.

TUESDAY MARCH 24" 1863
Ridgeway Tennessee

I got a pass and went to White's Station for my boots. Col. Pease gave Lt. Dement and Caldwell a raking for meddling with the affairs of the staff mess. he talked pretty rough to them. they tried to deny the offence. Mrs. Pease and Mrs Medcalf going to start for home to-morrow. I rec'd a letter from Lyde.

WEDNESDAY MARCH 25" 1863
Ridgeway Tennessee

Pay master came preparing the rolls. for four months. going to pay to-morrow. he went back to Memphis to night Commissioned Officers who have been promoted recently have to be mustered, by regular mustering officer before they will be paid so I will not be able to get mine this time, in consequence, and no mustering officer nearer than Memphis.

THURSDAY MARCH 26" 1863
Ridgeway Tennessee

The Det. was paid four months pay. I did'nt get any. am going to be mustered first opportunity, and try to get straight on the rolls. I have had trouble ever since last august on account of promotion and not having been mustered.~

FRIDAY MARCH 27" 1863
Ridgeway Tennessee

I borrowed $.40.00 of Steve Frump and $.60.00 from Harrison Burt, both of Co. "D,, until paid off myself. Dr. Medcalf came along going to Germantown to see Lt. McClure Co. "I,, he sent me to White's Station to stay at the Hospital with the sick there until morning.~

SATURDAY MARCH 28" 1863
Ridgeway Tennessee

I returned from White's Station. Lt. McClure died this morning. I saw Dr. Tom Williams on the train this morning with his wife. Dr. Marlow was on also. the train was captured east of here to-day, this morning, and passengers robed of their valuables. I paid Henry Bridges Co."I,, $.10.00

SUNDAY MARCH 29" 1863
Ridgeway Tennessee

Capt Cheney returned from Memphis Tenn. and brought the boys two dozen cans of Oysters, and a box of cigars, for catching Julius Jones, building him a house, and merittorious services generally. it is a treat highly appreciated by the boys. Cheney will be the best Officer in the company now for a while at least. especially while the others are absent.~

MONDAY MARCH 30" 1863
Ridgeway Tennessee

I got a pass and went with Thos. O. Hoss to Memphis. and bought a suit of clothes for $.57.00 Coat, pants, & vest. I saw Lt. J. B. Houston there with the body of Lt. McClure on his way home. everything lively in Memphis, full of trade We went to the theatre at night.~

TUESDAY MARCH 31ST 1863
Memphis Tennessee

I bought a gold pen for $.3.00, and a valise for $.12.50 We stoped at the Gayoso house paid $2.00 for supper lodging and breakfast. Went to the Bullitin office. bought a book entitled Les-Miserables, by Victor Hugo. Hoss bought a Doz. oil clothes for the Company. Saw Major Morgan & Capt Kurghoff & a numbr of men from the 49" Ills at Memphis. We went to the provost Marshal and got a pass and left on the noon train for White's Station. I walked from there to Ridgeway, and let Hoss ride my horse and cary my valise, and his oil cloths. Prospect of an attack some where along the line an order for 20. men to patroll the road both ways during the night, like patrolls from other posts on the line. I rec'd a letter from E.M.

WEDNESDAY APRIL 1" 1863
Ridgeway Tennessee

In camp all day reading Les-Miserables by Victor Hugo. The road is being patroled each way every night by forty men or rather by twenty each way, and a commissioned Officer Chaplain Lockwood up from White's Station The officers are going to have a meeting to pass resolutions, in commemoration of Lieut McClure.   I wrote to E.M.

THURSDAY APRIL 2" 1863
Ridgeway Tennessee

I was called to see a young lady at Mr Hall's with a sore Eye. had an invitation to call again. The health of our men is not very good, owing to the inclemency of the weather and the excessive guard duty, since the patrols have been on the road at night

FRIDAY APRIL 3" 1863
Ridgeway Tennessee

Lt. E.B. Harlan came down and took supper with us. he has got another horse. he lost one the other evening while visiting Miss Tubbyville. his present one is not so good I spent the day in camp reading. it is a dull place no neighbors except rebels.

SATURDAY APRIL 4" 1863
Ridgeway Tennessee

I got a pass and went with T.O. Hoss to Germantown I collected $.2.00 from Noah Middleton and bought a halter. We went out into the country, to Wolf-Creek. Capt. L.W. Moore returned from home. O.W. Brokaw, Noah Byrum and Thos Farro on a big drunk.

SUNDAY APRIL 5" 1863
Ridgeway Tennessee

I got a pass and went to White's Station with Capt. Cheney. Dr. Medcalf has received a circular making him brigade Surgeon, and he is considerably elated over it. Dr. A. Goslin Surg. 48" Ills. was down to White's Station. I eat dinner with Frank J. Burrows and the Non-Com's Mess. they have possession of a house belonging to the premises.~

MONDAY APRIL 6" 1863
Ridgeway Tennessee

Capt. John G. Berry Co. "E,, 49" Ills went out on a Scout with some of the boys across Wolf River. they saw a guerrilla and fired at him but he escaped. A salute fired at Memphis and La-Grange in commemoration of the battle of Shiloh.

TUESDAY APRIL 7" 1863
Ridgeway Tennessee

I went out on a Scout with Lt. H.W. Kerr, Co. "E,, 49" Ills. and 35. men T.O. Hoss and I went with the advance guard. we went 6 miles South of the Railroad. we saw no rebels "Subsisted upon the country." and returned at dark quite tired of walking.~

WEDNESDAY APRIL 8" 1863
Ridgeway Tennessee

I went out on an other scout to day with Capt. Cheney. We crossed Wolf river, struct the trail of and captured R.W. Terry & Massey, two of Richardson's Men, with three revolvers two hoster pistols carbine & Shotgun. we got dinner at Galaway's. brought our men to Germantown.

THURSDAY APRIL 9" 1863
Ridgeway Tennessee

I gave a memorandum receipt for a pair of Holster pistols. Col. Pease and Dr. Medcalf in camp. Lieut. A.S. Rowley came up with teams and went out to Mr. Brooks and got some corn and brought in for us to feed with. there seems to be plenty of corn in the neighborhood in the hands of rebel sympathizers.

FRIDAY APRIL 10" 1863
Ridgeway Tennessee

I went with Capt Cheney out to a Mr. Thompsons and introduced ourselves. saw and heard the girls sing and play on the piano they are rabbid rebels. Major Thos W. Morgan & Capt Redden of the 48" Ills. took supper with us. Lieut. Barbee is sick and moved to Mr. Brooks.

SATURDAY APRIL 11" 1863
Ridgeway Tennessee

I went to White's Station and stayed while Dr. Medcalf went to Memphis in an ambulance it rained and hailed to day. The rebels are threatning to attack our lines some where soon from the north side of the railroad, Richardson's Men~

SUNDAY APRIL 12" 1863
Ridgeway Tennessee

I got a pass to go to the country, but went to White's Station for muster rolls for a special muster, ordered with a view of catching officers and men who are absent with out leave. The weather is pleasant & clear I wrote to Jas. S. Moody.

MONDAY APRIL 13" 1863
Ridgeway Tennessee

I got a pass and went with Capt Cheney out to Massey's and got our dinner with them. found a pleasant family. then we went over to Mr. Thompson's and chated the girls and heard them sing and play. Thompson's & Massey's each live about one mile north of camp. I think we will visit them often. I rec'd a letter from, and wrote J.F.B.

TUESDAY APRIL 14" 1863
Ridgeway Tennessee

The weather cool raining and wind blowing. In camp all day reading. Wm Flake returned from Illinois. camp dull. a great want of events to make Time more interesting it drags a perfect monotony. nothing of interest in the lines, nor without.

WEDNESDAY APRIL 15" 1863
Ridgeway Tennessee

The Pay-master at White's Station paying off three companies of the 119" Ills. that are there. My horse run off. and I found him at a Mr. Patten's. (a Union Man) I went out and did'nt get in until after night, one & half miles N.E. I wrote to Lyde.

THURSDAY APRIL 16" 1863
Ridgeway Tennessee

Lieut Rowley came up, and, we went with the boys to Wolf river and saw them Swim. We stoped at Mr Massey's as we returned Brokaw & Musgrave had a fight. The bridges on Wolf river have all been destroyed so the[that] there is no crossing except on logs.

FRIDAY APRIL 17" 1863
Ridgeway Tennessee

I went with Lt. Kerr out to Mr Thompson's then went on to the creek with the boys of Co. "E,, to Swim, I had a spree with Capt Cheney & Washburn t[h]rowing water on one another. I broke Capts bed down, in the romp, and I got a pair of pants spoilt with greesey water. Lt. Houston Co. "I,, returned from home.~

SATURDAY APRIL 18" 1863
Ridgeway Tennessee

In camp all day. It is reported that Vicksburg has fallen again but it wants confirmations, it, and Richmond has been reported captured to often to be believed now without positive evidence. prospect of a thunder shower to night. I rec'd a letter from E.M.

SUNDAY APRIL 19" 1863
Ridgeway Tennessee

Frank J. Burrows came up, and I went with him out to Mr Patten's and took dinner pr. invitation. Then went to Mr Thompson's found Lt. J.L. Stanley & Capt. L.W. Moore there. we spent an hour there and returned. Lt. E.B. Harlan came and went with us to Wolf river. I wrote to E.M.

MONDAY APRIL 20" 1863
Ridgeway Tennessee

I was in camp all day, rather dull just now. Pay master at White's Station paying up to Feb. 28". Not paying those who have not been regularly mustered in by a mustering officer and no provision made that we may be mustered in here.

TUESDAY APRIL 21ST 1863
Ridgeway Tennessee

I got a pass and went with Thos O. Hoss to White's Station to draw some clothing I bought 4 pr of sock of Hoss at 32cts. = $1.28. I saw Dr. Woods Ass't Surg. 119" Ills. Dr. Medcalf has him at the Hospital to do the work that he may give his undivided attention to the duties of his office as brigade Surgeon. anything will serve him for an excuse, to keep from duty

WEDNESDAY APRIL 22ND 1863
Ridgeway Tennessee

Weather fine, and the season as far advanced as it will be in Illinois on the 1st of June, it is most a month and a half in advance here. Health good in camp. a few intermittants, and some Diarrhoeas from exposure while on guard. the nights are very cool.

THURSDAY APRIL 23RD 1863
Ridgeway Tennessee

Pay-master came and paid off Co. "E,, and then went back to Memphis for his Stopages, against the regiment. forgot his business Lts Harlan and Rowley were both here for pay but they could not get the extra pay for being detached Harlan as A.A.A. Gen'l. & Rowley as Reg't Q.M.

FRIDAY APRIL 24" 1863
Ridgeway Tennessee

Pay master returned and paid all except those who had been promoted and had not be[en] mustered into the new grade. I got no pay. Capt. Cheney wrote Capt Berry a letter in refrence to furnishing Old Mosby, (a rebel,) with provisions from Memphis.~

SATURDAY APRIL 25" 1863
Ridgeway Tennessee

Dr. S.F. Mercer came from home, and joined the Regiment for duty. he brought me Shirt & drawers and a needle cussion. I went to White's Station. Went out to Mr Thompson's to spend the evening~ I borrowed $.30.00 of Capt. J.W. Cheney, to be returned when I get pay. which will not be until I get Mustered as Ass't Surg. and have an opportunity to be paid. letter from Lyde

SUNDAY APRIL 26" 1863
Ridgeway Tennessee
Lt. Wm Whaling opened a Bbl of beer sent up by the sutler, and he has got a lot of the boys drunk on it. I think keeping a grocery would just suit him. F.J. Burrows & Edd. Nixon in Camp. T.O. Hoss rec'd a box of provisions from home. gave me ap[p]les & Mapl Sugar. I wrote Lyde.

MONDAY APRIL 27" 1863
Ridgeway Tennessee
Capt. Cheney went to Memphis Tenn. Lieut Jas Lemmon Co. "K,, returned Silas Dickson and his Wife came down from Germantown. It rained to day. the boys gambling in the stockade most of their leisur time since they were paid off.

TUESDAY APRIL 28" 1863
Ridgeway Tennessee
The boys gambling heavy Co. "D,, against Co. "K,, another Bbl. of beer opened, and another big drunk. I went to Mr. Halls to day and lanced a Whitlow for a young lady. some more citizens brought in by Sergt Joe Lucas "The rebellion must be suppressed"

WEDNESDAY APRIL 29" 1863
Ridgeway Tennessee
I went to Germantown and got a picture taken, (Ambrotype,) to Send home by Frank J. Burrows as he expects to go soon I bought a Harper's Weekly to send off, to day. The weather is very pleasant. fine for planting cotton and the citizens are availing themselves of the opportunity. there is being considerable cotton and corn planted about here.

THURSDAY APRIL 30" 1863
Ridgeway Tennessee
I got a pass and went to White's Station to be mustered for pay. I came back and accompanied Capt. Cheney to Germantown he went pr. order of Col Sanford, Comndg Post. Sanford ordered Cheney to exemp[t] some horses and Mules, some time since, and the owners

made complaint to Gen'l S.A. Hurlbut and he has taken notice of it, and called Col Sanford to account for it. We are now brigaded with the 48" Ills and 119" Ills. the former is on duty at Germantown. the latter is divided three Co's at White's Station, and the other seven at Buntin [Buntyn] Station, five miles west of there on the Railroad. five Co's of our Regt. (49" Ills.) are at White's Station (Co's, "A,, "F,, "I,, "C,, & "H,, and the other five, (Co's, "D,, "E,, "K,, "G,, & "B,, are on duty at this place. Col Sanford of the 48" Ills Commands the Post of Germantown, and the brigade. Dr. Medcalf is brigade Surgeon. Lt. W.W. Bliss of Co. "G,, 49" Ills. is brigade Quartermaster. Lt. E.B. Harlan A.A.A. Gen'l., and a Lt. Reed of a cavalry Reg't is A.C.S. in all there is perhaps 1600 men for duty. there are many absent from most, of the regiment that have been long in the service

FRIDAY MAY 1ST 1863
Ridgeway Tennessee

Thos. O. Hoss and Frank J. Burrows left for home. I got a pass and [went] with Capt. Joe Laur to hunt his horse, which he turned out to eat grass, and has stragled off. I stoped with Capt Cheney at Mr Pattens Capt. L.W. Moore Comnd'g Post. Col Bishop gone to Memphis Tenn. Things run at loose ends at this post under Col Bishop.

SATURDAY MAY 2" 1863
Ridgeway Tennessee

I got a pass and went with Capt. Cheney to Wolf river fishing. through the rain we caught no fish, didn't even get a bite. except Musquito bites which were more numerous than agreeable. We got some bushes with red flowers and brought to camp.

SUNDAY MAY 3" 1863
Ridgeway Tennessee

Chaplain Lockwood came up and preached to the Detachment in the afternoon in the camp. I was in camp all day. quite dull, not much news. and nothing of interest in camp or the country I wrote letters to A.K.A., J.F.B., & E.M.

MONDAY MAY 4" 1863
Ridgeway Tennessee

Capt. L. Kurghoff Co. " C, came up and went with Lt. Stanley & I to Mr. Duke's Mr Patten's and Mr. thompson's saw the girls and heard them sing, and play, various pieces of music. We saw Miss. Duke & Miss Stendman at Patten's. I rec'd a letter form & wrote E.M

TUESDAY MAY 5" 1863
Ridgeway Tennessee

Capt. Jacob E Gauen Co. "H,, came up and took command of the post, relieving Capt. L.W. Moore by order of Col. Pease. there is some jealousy existing somewhere which led to the change. Serg't S.C. Goshorn's furlough came back approved, and he will leave soon for home Serg't. F.A. Niles was at Mr. Thompson's to day it is getting to be a place of general resort.

WEDNESDAY MAY 6" 1863
Ridgeway Tennessee

Saml C. Goshorn Co."D,, Sergt Levi Stewart and Dobbs of Co."K,, left for home on furlough also some from each of the other companies the[re] is a gen'l Order now permitting furloughs to five per cent of the command present for duty."To the Merittorious."

THURSDAY MAY 7" 1863
Ridgeway Tennessee

The papers states that Gen'l Hooker is on the move, crossing the Rapahannock on pontoons in force, skirmishing with Lee's advance briskly. something going to be done. everybody confident of success. all is quiet in this part, and all eyes are turned Eastward.

FRIDAY MAY 8" 1863
Ridgeway Tennessee

John J. Rinck Co."D,, went to Memphis. The news from the East is encouraging. Gen'l Hooker has taken 6'000 prisoners. Gen'l Stoneman's cavalry in two miles of Richmond tearing up railroad. The prospect of success looks more flattering East than ever before, during the war.

SATURDAY MAY 9" 1863
Ridgeway Tennessee

I got a pass and went with some of the boys to Wolf river swiming Capt. J.G. Berry Co. "E,, was taken very sick with Colic and sent to White's Station for Dr. Mercer I returned before he came and had the Capt better before he got here, though. Col. Bishop returned from Memphis. he has been on a Military commission or Court Martial there for some time past.

SUNDAY MAY 10" 1863
Ridgeway Tennessee

Capt. J.E. Gauen returned and took command of the Post again. There was a telegram or note thrown of[f] the train this morning stating that Richmond was ours, but it wants confirmation It is thought generally that if it was it would be anounced by telegraph officially

MONDAY MAY 11" 1863
Ridgeway Tennessee

I went with Capt Cheney Lt Stanley and a Squad of men to Mr Gallaway's and took dinner. I met with Lt. Harlan over there and went with him to Mr Pattens he had "confisticutull" a horse over the river and borrowed a saddle at Gallaways to ride home

TUESDAY MAY 12 1863
Ridgeway Tennessee

I went with F.A. Niles and H. Burt Co. "D,, over to Mr Gallaways for some butter for Paddy's mess. Capt. L.W. Moore Capt Cheney and Lt. Stanley went out to Mr. Thompsons and didn't get back until after tatoo. we were uneasy as Cheney never staid out so late before~

WEDNESDAY MAY 13" 1863
Ridgeway Tennessee

In camp all day. Troops are passing going to-wards Memphis, perhaps to go down the river The fall of Richmond is still in want of confirmation. Gen'l Grant Sent up a lot of prisoners from his dep't. he probably holds Jackson Mississippi by this time he has been fighting in the rear of Vicksburg and in the direction of Jackson Miss.

THURSDAY MAY 14" 1863
Ridgeway Tennessee

Camp dull. a great want of events to make time pass, and relieve the monotony of camp after the recent excitement in regard to the fall of Richmond. We bought some buttermilk at Mr Mosby's and drank for supper in the mess.   I rec'd a letter from and wrote to J.F.B.

FRIDAY MAY 15" 1863
Ridgeway Tennessee

I went to White's Station and bought a Shirt $.4.00 a hat $.4.50 from the Sutler (Mr Hoskinson) Chaplain Lockwood has gone to La-Grange, to be mustered into the Service of the U. States as that is required now before an Officer can get his pay. Pay masters are getting more particular

SATURDAY MAY 16" 1863
Ridgeway Tennessee

I got a pass and went across Wolf river with a Squad of men. two of the 48" Ills shot by guerrilla in about a half mile of us. I hurried on but the rebels had left when we arrived. I dressed the wound and sent for an ambulance. I got ten lbs of butter & some Eggs and returned.~   I rec'd letter from E.M.

SUNDAY MAY 17" 1863
Ridgeway Tennessee

Some of the boys Sending in applications for commissions in colored regiments and they are generally made by men who are known to be unworthy of positions, by their comrades and they seek a shorter road to glory. there are some honorable exceptions. There was some houses burned across Wolf River to day I suppose, by the boys of the 48" Ills. in retaliation. I wrote to E.M.

MONDAY MAY 18" 1863
Ridgeway Tennessee

Capt. Cheney went to Union depot to day with 28. men he surrounded the town and some rebels made a rush to escape, and were fired upon by the boys, and two were wounded one mortally. Mrs. Bishop left for home. there is said to be 8'000 rebels, 8. miles south of here.

TUESDAY MAY 19" 1863
Ridgeway Tennessee

Prospect of an attack. twenty rebels passed on the other side of Nonconna Mr. Duke said to be with them. I took two or three men and went out to his house, and found him at home. I think it is his brother. We rec'd orders at midnight for one hundred men

WEDNESDAY MAY 20" 1863
Ridgeway Tennessee

100 men left at 3.A.M. for Germantown they went with a part of the 48" Ills to-wards Cold-Water. Col. Pease sent up Co's "A,, & "H,, to relieve our guards. We heard firing in the afternoon and prepared to repell an attack, but it turned out to be the cavalry firing off their Carbines.

THURSDAY MAY 21ST 1863
Ridgeway Tennessee

Co's "A,, & "H,, returned to White's Station. The Excitement has subsided I went with Capt Cheney around the Picket-lines his pony fell through a bridge with him but nobody hurt by it. The 100. men returned after a bloodless tramp they found no enemy and returned very tired many of the men with sore feet. The 8'000 men said to be near turns out a hoax.~

FRIDAY MAY 22" 1863
Ridgeway Tennessee

I went to the river and had a Swim stoped at Mr. Masseys. Lt. Kerr and I stoped at Mr Thompsons and had some Music. Capt. J.E. Gauen relieved from the command of the post by Capt. L.W. Moore again, by order of Col. Pease I rec'd a letter from Columbus Ky from J.F.B.

SATURDAY MAY 23" 1863
Ridgeway Tennessee

I went with Lt. Kerr and 30 men across Wolf river I called upon Dr. Shore with 14. men for dinner for his services the other day. Lt. Kerr and the rest of the men went to Mr. Munson's for dinner. we had a swim. stoped at Mr. Thompson, saw Cheney & Harlan there. saw the rebel Capt Price, returning.

SUNDAY MAY 24" 1863
Ridgeway Tennessee

We received orders to be ready to march at noon. The ballance of the regiment came along and we moved to Germantown and went into camp out east of town. there is a prospect of an attack here now. at least that seems to be the calculation of Col. Sanford

MONDAY MAY 25" 1863
Germantown Tennessee

We were up at 3. A.M. and in line of battle but no attack. our cavalry returned having driven the rebels beyond the Hatchie no fight this time. there are three regiments of Infty here the 48" Ills 49" Ills & 119" Ills. Infty and a part of the 3" Ills & 9" Ills cavalry and Bat. "K,, 1st Mo. The news is interesting from Vicksburg Miss.

TUESDAY MAY 26" 1863
Germantown Tennessee

Col. Sanford had brigade drill to day. there was a little fuss on the drill ground between Lt. Col. Taylor of 119" Ills & Lt. Col. Greathouse of 48" Ills. in regard to a certain movement in the drill The[y] drilled in front of Mr Raguise. I took a ride with Lt. Harlan. I rec'd a letter from Lyde.

WEDNESDAY MAY 27" 1863
Germantown Tennessee

I sent to White's Station and got a cott, and put up a table in my tent. then went with Capt Cheney to hunt his pony. he got away and has gone off somewhere, or the cavalry has taken him up and are using him somewhere. Weather dry. I wrote to J.F.B.

THURSDAY MAY 28" 1863
Germantown Tennessee

I made out certificate of disability for a man of Co. "E,,. I went with Lt Harlan out to Mr. Pattens, Massey's & Thompsons. had a fine visit and some music and returned. I saw W.C. Pittner to day he belongs to Co. "C,, 119" Ills Infty

FRIDAY MAY 29" 1863
Germantown Tennessee

We rec'd orders to strike tents, and be ready to march at noon. We left in the afternoon and marched as far as White's Station and camped for the night. I rode out with Capt. Lockwood to a Mr. Hains' and stoped for an hour or so. Some of the officers went to Mr. Thompson's, as we are probably leaving for good I slept in the Provost Marshalls office

SATURDAY MAY 30" 1863
White's Station Tennessee

We moved at 3.A.M. the drumers filled up the a[m]bulances with their drums, and I left them at the Hospital to be brought on the train. Col. Pease sent back for some of them. We arrived at Memphis at 8.A.M. and stoped out on the S.E. part of the city it rained this morning. I went to the river to see the big swim.

SUNDAY MAY 31" 1863
Memphis Tennessee

All quiet in camp. many conjectures as to our destination. probabilities favorable for our going to Vicksburg Miss. I went with Lt. A.S. Rowley to the river he went swiming. We went to Gen'l Veatch's and got a pass and went into Fort Pickering. saw a strong fortification and many heavy guns mounted on the works I saw some Colored troops on duty in there, the first I have seen. they seem to make Efficient guards, and appear to handle their pieces as though they had been well drilled. We returned to camp and found it full of Peddlers of evry description. The 119" Ills Infty is cam[p]ed close to us. F.J. Burrows & T.O. Hoss returned. I made personal report, and wrote to Lyde.

MONDAY JUNE 1ST 1863
Memphis Tennessee

We sent to White's Station for the Hospital property, and put up the tents here. Troops are going down the river destination Vicksburg I suppose. Capt Hayes Co. "I,, 11th Ills Cavalry was in camp to day. he has been dismissed [from] the Service for being captured East of the O.&M. R.R. We signed a petition to have him reinstated. he was a good officer

TUESDAY JUNE 2" 1863
Memphis Tennessee

The Officers drew some wall tents to day. the 119" Ills Infty drew Enfield Rifles to day. I went with Dr. Mercer to see Mr. W.C. Pitner Co. "C,, 119" Ills he is looking bad, not physically able for a soldier. he cant stand the exposure I rec'd letters yesterday from Cephline Lyde & E.M.

WEDNESDAY JUNE 3" 1863
Memphis Tennesse

I went with Col Pease and Dr. Mercer to Lt Falay's office in town and was mustered into the service as 2nd Ass't Surg. 49" Ills Inft. Muster to date from this inst. [from the word instant: occurring in the present or current month] rank from March 6" 1863. Mercer's muster dates the same his rank from a later period. I wrote to Cephline & E.M.

THURSDAY JUNE 4" 1863
Memphis Tennessee

I made a requisition and Dr. Medcalf drew a pannier, and a pocket-case for Dr. Mercer I borrowed $.20.00 of Lt. Wm. Whaling. it rained to day Col. Barnhill of the 40" Ills Infty was in camp to day he has been Provost Marshall at Corinth. transports returned from below to day

FRIDAY JUNE 5 1863
Memphis Tennessee

There was 200 Prisoners brought up from Vicksburg to day. S.C. Goshorn returned from home to day. I have been Sick with Dysentery and not able to stir around much. I settled up my board in the mess for last month. Our Regiment furnished men for Picket to day. the first duty they have done since we have been here. I suppose our destination has been fixed at this place.~

SATURDAY JUNE 6" 1863
Memphis Tennessee

I got up at 3.A.M. and found the regiment had marching orders. We left at 6.A.M. for Germantown An old man living by the roadside asked the Col. to halt and let the band play Yankee Doodle for him. 'twas granted. we arrived at 4.P.M. Saw the 40" Ills on their way to Memphis. The 48" Ills have marching orders.

SUNDAY JUNE 7" 1863
Germantown Tennessee

To day Six or Eight Reg'ts of Infty and three or four Batts. of Artillery past going towards Memphis The 48" Ills, and Batt. "K,, 1st Mo left to day for Memphis. Col. Sanfords brigade has played out. Their destination is very probably Vicksburg. We moved into the 48" Ills' old quarters

MONDAY JUNE 8" 1863
Germantown Tennessee

Camp quiet. beginning to feel like we were at home again. I carried some lumber and floored my tent. preparing to stay any way. Lt. Jas Lemmon, and Lt. Barbee went to Memphis to be mustered into the U.S. Service no mustering officer this side. We had showers of rain to day

TUESDAY JUNE 9" 1863
Germantown Tennessee

Capt Cheney went to Memphis to day I sent my coat by him to Isaac Isaacs, to have it cleaned up. Lt Harlan returned from Memphis Capt. Vaughn's Battery, ("A,,) 3rd Ills. came here to day for duty and went into the fort, north West of town, where "K,, batter[y] has been. It rained to day. all quiet in camp I wrote to Missouri and Lyde~

WEDNESDAY JUNE 10" 1863
Germantown Tennessee

I got a pass and went with Capt Berry and Lieut Stanley to the country we called at Mr Woods Mr Thompson's & Mr. Harrison's. we got some buttermilk at Mr. Woods and got berries. Col. Pease and Lt. Harlan went to La Grange Harlan is trying to get a leave of absence

THURSDAY JUNE 11" 1863
Germantown Tennessee

Orderly Serg't. Thos O. Hoss Co. "D,, went to La Grange and got an order to recruit a company of negroes. Orderly Serg't Stuth, Co. "C,, and the Lofink boys are making up a company here, of negroes Camp is dull nothing of interest going on. Events of importance are scarce here.

FRIDAY JUNE 12" 1863
Germantown Tennessee

I bought a clothes brush, pens, paper, and collars. Geo. E. Dillingham returned from home also Capt Joe. Laur bridges were burned this morning by guerrillas east of here they still hovering around availing themselves of opportunities to do mischief. I visited the picket with Cheney

SATURDAY JUNE 13" 1863
Germantown Tennesse

I had the men to clean up quarters for to-morrow. Two Co's of Cavalry past here to day going to La-Grange for duty. I went over to Co. "D,, and Vaccinnated some of the boys. Co's "D,, & "K,, are quartered over near the fort, in order to support the battery in case of a sudden attack there I got my coat from Memphis pretty well cleaned up.   I rec'd a letter from J.F.B.

SUNDAY JUNE 14" 1863
Germantown Tennessee

I went with Frank J. Burrows out to Mr. Pattens Mr Thompson's and Mr. Massey's returned about dark. I went with Capt Cheney and about thirty men out S.E. of town and searched some houses for some rebels but did'nt find any. We tramped about ten miles, and returned at 2.A.M.

MONDAY JUNE 15" 1863
Germantown Tennessee

Lt. E.B. Harlan started home on leave of absence I went with Frank J. Burrows out to Mr Rodgers' to spend the evening. We met Major T.W. Morgan out there. We had a pleasant visit. the girls are quite fond of Yankees, notwithstanding they have a brother in the rebel army.   I wrote to Lyde.

TUESDAY JUNE 16" 1863
Germantown Tennessee

I went with Lt. Kerr and a squad of men to the river swiming. we stoped at Mr Pattens awhile. I saw Mrs Gallaway in camp hunting a horse that somebody has taken off. Thos O. Hoss is out hunting up darkies for his company. Contrabands are in demand about here just now.

WEDNESDAY JUNE 17" 1863
Germantown Tennessee

I rode out with Dr. Medcalf to see some cases of Smallpox. saw three casses two Cavalrymen and one darkey, in different stages of the disease. We gathered and eat some wild plums The Tennessee deserters of our regiment returned to day. their part of the country is not a good place for men who have been in our army. Capt Cheney gone to Memphis.

THURSDAY JUNE 18" 1863
Germantown Tennessee

In camp until evening then went with Frank J. Burrows to Mr. Rodgers' to spend an hour or so. I paid one months board to day $.10.00 settling it up to July 15". we are living very cheap now, and set a good table too provisions are very cheap in the country, and in the commissarys.

FRIDAY JUNE 19" 1863
Germantown Tennessee

The citizens are coming in and taking the oath of allegience Mrs. Gallaway and Miss Fanny Brown both took it to day. Capt Wm. P. Moore is Provost Marshall Capt Cheney ordered to Memphis by Gen'l Hurlbut, on account of some horses taken by him by order of Col. Sanford.~ I rec'd letter from J.F.B.

SATURDAY JUNE 20" 1863
Germantown Tennessee

I got a pass and went out to Mr Thompson's and Mr. Masseys. Capt Berry & F.J. Burrows were with me. we had some berries and plums. we stoped at Mr. Woods and got some buttermilk. The Regt'l teamsters out also on their mules We had a good time~ I wrote to E.M.

SUNDAY JUNE 21ST 1863
Germantown Tennessee

The Cavalry returned from their Scout T.O. Hoss with them. they have been out several days. they went down in a southeasterly direction Hoss got some darkies for his company. some of us went to Wolf River and found a place where somebody had been crossing with horses, recently Notwithstanding citizens have been telling us there was no place where it could be forded.

MONDAY JUNE 22" 1863
Germantown Tennessee

I left camp at 2.A.M. with Capt. Wm P. Moore and forty men. we went accross Wolf River. we searched several houses and caught two of Richardsons men and returned at 11.A.M. Lt. Stanley and patrols were fired into last night by the cavalry patrols near White's Station, no body hurt.~

TUESDAY JUNE 23" 1863
Germantown Tennessee

I went with Col. Pease and Capt Laur to White's Station and took dinner there with Capt. J.E. Gauen. Co. "H,, is on duty there. then we returned by Mr Brooks', & Messers[Messieurs] Benson's & Thompson's and had some music at each of the latter places. The Benson family are all musicians and good ones too.

WEDNESDAY JUNE 24" 1863
Germantown Tennessee

We received orders to be ready to March at a Moments warning to La Grange the rebels are said to be near and threatning an attack we had the teams harnessed and ready but did'nt rec'd the orders to march. It rained all day and would have been disagreeable marching.~

THURSDAY JUNE 25" 1863
Germantown Tennessee

The hands working on the Railroad got frightened and run in from the west, to day. I went out with Lt. Kerr and some of the teamsters, to Ridgeway and below there but we saw no one and could hear of no enemy, and we returned and they went back to their work. camp is quite dull nothing of interest going. hence I run about the country to pass the time.~ I wrote to M.W.

FRIDAY JUNE 26" 1863
Germantown Tennessee

I went to White's Stations with Lt. Jas. Mitchell to see the sick of Co.. "H,, We had a shooting Match with Capt. Gauen and Lt. Jacob Fischer Co. "H,, we eat dinner with them. We had lots of blackberries and plums, on the road. Frank & Capt & I Advertised for corespondents in the Commercial~

[Newspaper clipping found in diary:]

WANTED - CORRESPONDENCE - By three young soldiers, of good character, with an equal number of respectable and handsome young ladies. Inclose photographs if convenient. Addreess WILDRAKE, WILLIE HARTLEY or JAS C. COVINGTON, 49th Regiment Illinois Infantry, Germantown, Tenn., via Cairo, Ill.

SATURDAY JUNE 27" 1863
Germantown Tennessee

It is still raining almost every day now. camp is exceedingly dull. Frank J. Burrows and I concluded that the wants of the service required us to go out to Mr. Pattens visiting and we obeyed the dictates of our better judgement and went.~ I wrote to Minnitte Seymore

SUNDAY JUNE 28" 1863
Germantown Tennessee

I went with Frank J. Burrows out to a Mr Reasonouers and took dinner. we went to see the girls but they were not at home. it is still raining. The papers report that Port Hudson has fallen, and it seems to be generally credited as true.~

MONDAY JUNE 29" 1863
Germantown Tennessee

I went to White's Station to see and prescribe for the sick of Co. "H,,. I came back by Mr. Thompson's and found some of Co. "D,, there pressing Negroes they say to work on fortifications at Germantown I had a high time with the women they were very mad, particularly the old lady. I quarreled with her awhile and left. I stoped at Mr Massey's and Found Capt Cheney and Lt Stanley there.~

TUESDAY JUNE 30" 1863
Germantown Tennessee

I was in camp all day, with sore Eyes. I made Personal Report. The Reg't mustered for pay, at 8.P.M. a Detachment of 100 Cavalry under command of a Major Bishop of the Cavalry was going out on a scout towards Coldwater. Capt Wm P. Moore Lt. Rowley Frank J. Burrows, Twenty Infty. & I accompanied them. they were going down into the rebel teritory to see if they could not surprise and capture some rebels, that were in the habit of coming up and doing mischief when an opportunity offered. and then, returning and throwing off the habiliments of war, and claiming the protection due to peacefull citizens. a specie of men that infest this country and have the advantage of our cavalry in playin[g] their two characters, as circumstances happen to suit their preferences. they have nothing in the country to defend more than the wild beasts, merely an abiding place; not a home. if they had they might be compelled to abide the rules of an honorable warfare. neither have they principle involved further than their opportunities for plunder. We road most all night and stoped at a little place called Pleasant Hill in Miss.~

WEDNESDAY JULY 1ST 1863
Pleasant Hill Mississippi

We caught three rebels only. The Major in command is a perfect nonentity. The cavalry broke into houses, then into a Safe with axes and hammers. they broke open the Odd Fellows Hall and scattered the regalia and cords evrywhere. We returned to camp, not very proud of our acchievements. Our cavalry are a humbug. they only seek to plunder when they go out.

THURSDAY JULY 2" 1863
Germantown Tennessee

Co. "G,, detailed to guard prisoners to Alton Ills. through the instrumentalities and begging of Capt L.W. Moore. all the detached and detailed men rejoined the company for the trip home. It rained in the P.M., too wet for the farmers plow.~ I rec'd a letter from E.M.

FRIDAY JULY 3" 1863
Germantown Tennessee

The Cavalry Officers had a ball at the Masonic Hall. the Enlisted dissatisfied about it, and are shooting and making considerable noise Col Pease sent Co. "C,, to stop it, which they accomplished directly. Not many ladies in from the country. Not a very interesting ball.

SATURDAY JULY 4" 1863
Germantown Tennessee

A dinner at Mrs. Burnby's. most of the officers went A National Salute fired. Mr Thompson in and eat dinner with us F.J. Burrows & I went home with him We stoped at Mr Pattens on our return to camp. Corpl. M.R. Kell, Pri John Mason, John C. Wilson & Ephraim Williams Co. "D,, went out the lines, and did nt return

SUNDAY JULY 5" 1863
Germantown Tennessee

Capt. Cheney, Frank J. Burrows & I, took ten men and went in search of Kell, Mason, Wilson & Williams, who went out yesterday to gather blackberries and did'nt return. We learned that they were captured yesterday and carried off in a Southerly direction by a party of rebel cavalry. We stoped with a Mr. Ellis and got dinner. We heard of a party of rebels in the vicinity to day, but saw none.~

MONDAY JULY 6" 1863
Germantown Tennessee

We received a dispatch anouncing the fall of Vicksburg, and a Victory at Helena by Gen'l Prentiss with an order to fire a salute of 13. guns to morrow On dressparade we had three cheers for the Army of the Tennessee, three cheers for Gen'l Prentiss and three Cheers for the Union.~

TUESDAY JULY 7" 1863
Germantown Tennessee

A Salute of 13. Guns fired in honor of the success at Vicksburg and Helena Ark. artilery firing heard in the direction of Memphis. I went with Capt Cheney and F.J. Burrows out to Mr Patten's and Mr

Thompson's to tell them the news, the latter pretend they dont believe it.~ I wrote to E.M.~

WEDNESDAY JULY 8" 1863
Germantown Tennessee

Capt. Cheney, Capt. Houston & I took some men and [went] to Mr. Brooks last night and tried to *sutch* him by making him believe we were rebels but we had Goshorn along drunk and he betrayed us. We have good news from the East. Pennsylvania a victory there.~ I wrote to E.M.

THURSDAY JULY 9" 1863
Germantown Tennessee

Co. "H,, relieved from duty at White's Station by Co. "I,,. I got a pass and went with Capt L. Kurghoff & Lt. S. Spiro Co. "C,, out to Mr Pattens Mr Thompson's and Mr. Massey's to spend the Evening. Pattens were well pleased with them but Thompson's were not. Rebels dont like Germans. Major T. W. Morgan went to Memphis to day.~ I wrote to J.F.B.

FRIDAY JULY 10" 1863
Germantown Tennessee

I pulled up stakes and moved into a Mr. Bliss' yard near the depot & stockade the Regt moved up near the Stockade. We had general inspection by a Capt. True, of the 62" Ills. to day. he was well pleased with the efficiency of the Reg't Charlie Grazier Co. "K,, died in Hospital to day.

SATURDAY JULY 11" 1863
Germantown Tennessee

The rebels across Wolf River said to be organizing, and threatning an attack somewhere. I went to the river swiming with Col. Pease Major Morgan; Capt. W.P. Moore; & Capt Cheney The mosquitoes were very bad, and the weather quite warm

SUNDAY JULY 12" 1863
Germantown Tennessee

I went with Capt. W.P. Moore & Capt Berry to White's Station. We called upon the Misses Moore. found them agreeable and interesting. We returned by Mr Thompson's but the girls were not at home. We called at Mr. Massey's and paid them a visit.

MONDAY JULY 13" 1863
Germantown Tennessee

Lt E.B. Harlan returned from home to day. Col Wm R. Morrison is in Memphis on his way to Vicksburg Miss. with sanitaries for the Army Major Morgan and Capt. Moore went to Memphis to see him. Lt. A.S. Rowley went to La-Grange Camp dull, and the weathr cloudy. nothing of interest going on. have to go to the country to pass off the time agreeably~

TUESDAY JULY 14" 1863
Germantown Tennessee

Payrolls being prepaired. some prospect of our getting pay soon. Weather clear and fine. I went with Col. Pease out to Mr Pattens to spend the evening. had a pleasant visit and the Col enjoyed it firstrate the old man played the agreeable.~ I wrote to Lyde.~

WEDNESDAY JULY 15" 1863
Germantown Tennessee

Lt. Harlan out on dressparade with Co."D,, the first time in a year.~ I went with Lt. Harlan and Lt. Kerr out riding. We called at Mr. Tubbyville to see Miss Jennie. Lt. Kerr acted the part of a paltroon[probably a noun formed from the adjective paltry] or blackguard. it is the last time I will call upon ladies with him. Weather clear and cool.

THURSDAY JULY 16" 1863
Germantown Tennessee

I went with Col. Pease and Lt. Harlan to White's Station then on to Mr White's for dinner three miles beyond. we had a very pleasant visit. had some blackberry wine. we called at several places on our return and had a general good time. Dr. S.F. Mercer sick again with the fever at Mrs. Burnby's.~

FRIDAY JULY 17" 1863
Germantown Tennessee

Col Pease went to La-Grange to day. I saw Dr. Gay (Med. Director) on the train going west I went with Lt. Harlan out to Mr. Reasonouer's we stoped at Mr. Thurmans, and at Mr Rodgers and took supper we found F.J. Burrows there and Spent a very pleasant evening Frank spends most of the evenings he [is] out of camp up at Mr. Rodgers'

SATURDAY JULY 18" 1863
Germantown Tennessee

An attack threatened. three of the cavalry and some road hands were captured. Capt. Cheney went out with some Inft. and a Squad of Cavalry followed and re-captured them with four rebels and brought them in and lodged them in the guardhouse.

SUNDAY JULY 19" 1863
Germantown Tennessee

The Cavalry returned with Eight prisoners We now have twelve rebels in the prison Col. Pease in command of the regiment. The Port of Germantown has played out. The cavalry and Infty dont get along well together. both Cols went to give posies to citizens

MONDAY JULY 20" 1863
Germantown Tennessee

I went to White's Station with Maj. Morgan he went on to Mr. White's. I returned and went with Capt. Cheney and Lt Rowley to Wolf River swiming. on our return Lieut A.S. Rowley and I stoped at Mr. Pattens and paid them a visit.~

TUESDAY JULY 21ST 1863
Germantown Tennessee

Lieuts. Harlan and Rowley went to Memphis to get their pay. Officers can get pay on orders or leaves of Absence. I thing[k] they just had orders to proceed to Memphis Dr. S.F. Mercer is very sick. a relapse, from stiring around too early after his recent illness. Dr. Medcalf has to take charge of the Hospital while Dr. Mercer is sick.

WEDNESDAY JULY 22" 1863
Germantown Tennessee

~~Lt. Harlan and Lt. Rowley left Memphis for Vicksburg~~ Harlan to join Col. Sanford as A.A.A. Gen'l and Rowley to recover the dead body of his brother who was killed there recently. Dr. Gay was here to day. Corpl. Jas White Co. "F,, accidently Shot, by a man of Co. "H,, to day though not dangerously, in the back. ~

THURSDAY JULY 23" 1863
Germantown Tennessee

I went to White's Station in an Ambulance J.G. Burggraf and his wife went along. and we stoped and gathered some apples off some trees growing outside, in front of Mr Brooks' I borrowed $.10.00 of Capt. Cheney and paid Lt. Lemmon $.5.00 Co. "G,, returned from Alton Ills.

FRIDAY JULY 24" 1863
Germantown Tennessee

Another day without events of importance in our camp, or vicinity, that I am aware of There is some talk of the Pay master's coming but we sometimes have a great many rumors of his coming before he arrives. money is generaly very scarce. ~ I rec'd a letter from E.M.

SATURDAY JULY 25" 1863
Germantown Tennessee

Some more of the boys furloughs came Capt. Cheney went with them to Memphis to try to get them paid off, but failed to accomplish it. I rec'd a kind of an offer of the place of Ass't Surg. in the 111" Ills in case I ~~resigned my present position in the 49" Ills.,~~ which I have been thinking ~~of doing.~~ ~ I rec'd a letter from J.F.B. ~

SUNDAY JULY 26" 1863
Germantown Tennessee

My application for discharge from Service as Hosp't Steward returned Col True, Comdg Brig. I went to church with Col Pease to night. Two cavalrymen were captured up at Mr. Rodgers this evening inside the Cavalry Pickets, half mile Dr. Mercer is very low, with fever ~

MONDAY JULY 27" 1863

Germantown Tennessee

I went to White's Station, then on a Scout below Raleigh but caught no one this time. Col. Pease's brother came. he is a Naval Officer and was on one of the gun boats up Red river. Jim Morrison came also. I think he is a kind of gentleman loafer~ Weather warm

TUESDAY JULY 28" 1863

Germantown Tennessee

I went with Ward to the country for a chicken for Dr. Mercer. we eat dinner at Mr. Pattens The cavalrymen who were captured the other evening were returned under flag of truce by rebels I took a lesson in Sword Exercises this P.M. Capt Cheney went on a scout to night

WEDNESDAY JULY 29" 1863

Germantown Tennessee

Capt. Cheney returned without making any discovery. Jim Morrison left for home to day I had a fuss with Pat. Marren Co. "A,, at sick call Camp dull another monotonous day with out events. we have nothing of interest here only capturing rebels occasionaly. and in turn loosing some of our men by ther being captured.~ I wrote to J.F.B.~

THURSDAY JULY 30" 1863

Three of Richardson's men brought in to day. they captured one of our men and three horses to day, but were all retaken. the Rebels are getting to be very bold. they are very anxious to get us away from this line between Memphis and Corinth. they have some teritory north of here that is not easy of access with us here.

FRIDAY JULY 31" 1863

Germantown Tennessee

Capt. True, Brigade Inspector was here and inspected the arms of the Reg't. with a view to having them condemned. Dr. Davis Surg. 18" Ills act Inspector of the 16" A.C. visited our camp to day The Rebels captured a Cavalry picket post to day and carri[e]d them off. With to day ends one of the sickly months of the season. we have had but one death in the Reg't. for three months The health is good. Col Pease went to Memphis this P.M. four guerrillas seen at Ridgeway to day. the hand car run in from below, in consequence. To day I have Eleven months pay due me and not much prospect of the Pay master at the present. I have not seen a pay master since I was mustered June 3" 1863. Weather warm.~

SATURDAY AUGUST 1" 1863
Germantown Tennessee

I went to White's Station with Maj Morgan Capt. Vaughn and others. Saw Dr. Bozorth. heard of two rebels, and we gave chase but couldn't catch them, and after following several miles we returned to camp. Col Bishop and wife came out from Memphis to day. he is still there on duty as a Member of a Court-Martial. It rained to night.~

SUNDAY AUGUST 2" 1863
Germantown Tennessee

Preaching at the church to day. one of Uncle Sam's boys gallanted a rebel lady home from church there is yet hope of compromising our National dificulties, with the ladies of the south, if not with the sterner Sex. Col Bishop and family returned to Memphis. Weather warm.

MONDAY AUGUST 3" 1863
Germantown Tennessee

Co. Wm R. Morrison came out from Memphis, and gave the boys a treat to beer, and the officers of the Reg't an Oyster Supper and we had a good time generaly. he was called out for a speech, and made a few remarks and promised to make a speech to morrow evening.

TUESDAY AUGUST 4" 1863
Germantown Tennessee

This has been a dull day. The Regt called out and Search made for stolen revolver in quarters. Col. Morrison made a speech at night he was not decisive enough to suit the Reg't. generaly though frail humanity differs Widely in matters of policy. he is tender footed~

WEDNESDAY AUGUST 5" 1863
Germantown Tennessee

Col. Wm. R. Morrison left for home. I received and read a speech of Gen'l. John A. Logans delivered at Duquoin Ills. it was very good.

he is Square on the war question. "The Special Artist," (Mathews) is putting up a picture tent. Dr. S.F.F. Mercer is improving again after a long and Serious illness It rained at night, and the weather is cool and pleasant I wrote to Dr. J.W.B. & J.K. Jr

THURSDAY AUGUST 6" 1863
Germantown Tennessee
This is 'thanksgiving day' We had an Oyster dinner. I went with Lt. Jas. Mitchell to Mr. Thompson on a visit. then I went out Squirel hunting to day. and I went to church at night. have had a stiring day though not an eventful day. A rain storm coming

FRIDAY AUGUST 7" 1863
Germantown Tennessee
A collission between Capt. Wm P. Moore Provost Marshall, and Col. McCrillis in refrence to Mrs Matlock and Mrs. Jordan. I rode out to see the Reg't drill, caught in a shower. A Wedding at Mr. Malliters a rebel lady climbed out of an uper window at night and went to a cavalry camp to Marry a Yankee Officer.

SATURDAY AUGUST 8" 1863
Germantown Tennessee
Mr. Massey in camp. I borrowed Dr. Mercer's saddle and got a bridle from Nick Burns The Q.M. brought in a load of corn. we have been without feed for a day or so. We miss Lt. A.S. Rowley now in that Dept. he is still absent taking the remains of his brother home for interment.

SUNDAY AUGUST 9" 1863
Germantown Tennessee
I went to White's Station with Major Morgan & Capt Moore. returned and went [with] F.J. Burrows to Mr Rodgers to spend the evenig had a pleasant visit but were careful to return before dark. since the rebels come in there and make captures we are a little more particular about getting in, in Season, [at the right time] though Mr Rodgers are inside the cavalry pickets.

MONDAY AUGUST 10" 1863
Germantown Tennessee
I was not well to day, in camp all day. the Reg't was out on battallion drill in the P.M. Capt. Wm P. Moore releived from duty as Provost Marshall. The provost guards taken off Col. McCrillis of the Cavalry is commanding Post now. I think he went to Memphis for it.~ I wrote to J.F.B.

TUESDAY AUGUST 11" 1863
Germantown Tennessee
I went with F.J. Burrows out to Mr Thurman's and eat watermellon's. No citizens permitted to come into camp now. rained this P.M. Dr. S.F.F. Mercer got a leave of Absence to day he is still very weak. he is going home to try to regain his health, and strenght.~

WEDNESDAY AUGUST 12" 1863
Germantown Tennessee
I went to Memphis with Capt Lockwood to help Dr. Mercer get off home. we took him to the Officer's Hosp't., and drew his pay for him. I didn't get mine. Major Morgan was at Memphis and helped us. we stayed at the Gayosa house. Capt Vaughn was with us, he was drunk

THURSDAY AUGUST 13" 1863
Memphis Tennessee
I was left by the train. We got Dr. Mercer aboard the Hilman Chaplain with him. We found Col Greathouse Dr. Gaslin and others aboard. Capt. Alexander Co."I,, was killed, and Capt. Berry, and Co."C,, man and a citizen were wounded by guerrillas near Ridgeway to day. our men were on a hand car running on the railroad from White's Station to Germantown.~ I boght linnen coat & pr of Shoes.

FRIDAY AUGUST 14" 1863
Memphis Tennessee
I returned and found the wounded easy.~ Went to the funeral of Capt Alexande[r] at 10.A.M. Then went with Col. Pease to see some of the citizens in the neighborhood of Ridgeway to inform them that they must give notice of the apprch of rebels in the future, failing at their peril.

SATURDAY AUGUST 15" 1863
Germantown Tennessee

I helped dress Capt. Berry's leg. the wound was in the head of the Tibia. Dr. Bozorth started home to day. I took a lesson in sword exercise this P.M. under the tudor ship of a Sergt of the 3rd Ills Art. Capt Moore returned from Memphis. I rec'd letters from Lyde Lawrence & E.M.

SUNDAY AUGUST 16" 1863
Germantown Tennessee

Officers held a meeting and adopted a series of resolutions in regard to the death of Capt. Alexander, I wrote a communication & sent a copy of the proceedings to the Salem Advocate for publication. other officers sent to other papers.   I wrote to E.M.

MONDAY AUGUST 17" 1863
Germantown Tennessee

Dr. Medcalf went to Memphis to day. I copied the resolutions passed yesterday and sent them off for publication in the Advocate. I have been taking it as there is no other paper published in Salem but will not take it another year. I called in to see Mrs. Burnby.(sick) I took a lesson in Sword exercises at 9.A.M.

TUESDAY AUGUST 18" 1863
Germantown Tennessee

I went to White's Station with Col Pease to see Co. "K,, on duty there, at this time. We received orders to be ready to march at moments warning. prospect of our leaving here soon. hope we may leave the state of Tennesse this time.~

WEDNESDAY AUGUST 19" 1863
Germantown Tennessee

We recived orders to day to be ready to march Friday. The 52nd Ills Infty have come already to relieve us here. I packed up a part of my things. Sent Benton, (the citizen who was wounded) home. The citizens here regret our having to leave.~ I wrote to Lyde & R.H.

THURSDAY AUGUST 20" 1863
Germantown Tennessee

I went with the Sick to Memphis Capt Berry and Lt. W. Moore & 18 Men.~ took them to Hospt's Lt Stanley & Major Morgan [and I] stoped at the Worshorn house. Went to the circus. there is prospect of our getting pay before we leave Tenn I am now Ten Months behind~

FRIDAY AUGUST 21" 1863
Memphis Tennessee

I returned to Germantown and found the regiment ready to March. the briggade came in last night. and will all move together. I find the brigade comprises the 27" Iowa Infty 49" Ills Infty 50" Ind Inft & 62" Ills Inft. and Batt "A,, 3rd Ills Art. Commded by Col. J.M. True of the 62" Ills Infty. I went over to Mr. Rhoade's and bade the girls goodbye. We camped at White's Station

SATURDAY AUGUST 22" 1863
White's Station Tennessee

We marched at 4.A.M. and arrived at Memphis at 8.A.M. we moved one & half miles north of town and put up tents. Sergt. O.W. Brokaw Co. "D,, reduced to the ranks for disobedience of orders he left the Co. and came in on the train. The boys drinking. Serg't of the battery very sick with Colic.

SUNDAY AUGUST 23" 1863
Memphis Tennessee

I went with Dr. Medcalf to visit Adam's Hospital and Officer's Hospt. The Pay master came and paid off[f] the Reg't didn't pay me for want of Muster in roll The Regt drew Enfield Rifles to day turned over the old guns. I returned my horse to the Quartermaster according to agreement.~

MONDAY AUGUST 24" 1863
Memphis Tennessee

I went to Major Fenney's office and drew ten months pay $.621.84. I bought a Sword $.18.00 Sash $.15.00, gloves, [&] 1/2 Dozen shirts $.21.00 had a negative taken, paid Capt Cheney $.40.00 and Sent

$.200.00 home by him. paid the Sutler $.20.00 The Reg't went on board the Str. Courier and started at Midnight. many of the men very drunk.

TUESDAY AUGUST 25" 1863
Harkle Roads Arkansas

The Courier Colided with the Str Des Arch and sunk the former at 3.A.M. We lost Several mules, and considerable other property including tents company records etc. The Courier sunk near the shore the Starboard to the herican [hurricane] deck. Col Pease went back to Memphis for anothr boat. I paid Lt. Wm Whaling $.20.00 We found lots of Watermelons. I rec'd letter from Lyde & Lute

WEDNESDAY AUGUST 26" 1863
Harkle Roads Arkansas

The crew of the Courier left us to day for Memphis Col Pease returned and, we went aboard the Str. Madison which took us down the river we started at 8.P.M. had a pleasant trip and reached Helena at 4.A.M. the next morning, all safe & sound.

THURSDAY AUGUST 27" 1863
Helena Arkansas

We disembarked and went into camp west of town. The Quartermaster is getting some more mules, and harness, and wagons. The Colonel some accoutrements, bayonets etc preparing for another move soon. I took some sick men to the Hospital here to be left.

FRIDAY AUGUST 28" 1863
Helena Arkansas

The Act. Adj't (Lt Spiro) issued some new accoutrements to the Regt. and we marched this morning at an early hour. I had to foot it as I have no horse of my own and returned the one I had to the Q.M. We found the roads muddy, and it rained on us to day.~

SATURDAY AUGUST 29" 1863
Big-Creek Arkansas

We marched at 4.A.M. We were up at 2.A.M. by mistake of the drummers. We find a level country, rich in Soil, but none of the inhabitants at home to work it. the cultivated lands of other years, yields a luxuriant crop of weeds this season. We have fine weather for marching. though good water is scarce along the road at this Season.~

SUNDAY AUGUST 30" 1863
Cypriss-Creek Arkansas

We marched at day-light in the advance of the Bigade over a level country. we reached Clarendon a little town on the East bank of White River at noon. a gun boat came up with orders. I paid $.20.00 into the Mess to day preparations being made to muster for pay to-morrow

MONDAY AUGUST 31" 1863
Clarendon Arkansas

Some boats came down the river, and set the Brigade accross. several boats went down the river, came from Duballs bluff I suppose White River is a very pretty stream deep & narrow, of very clear water, but quite crooked. it runs through a rich and fertile country, though the inhabitants suffer from Ague & Fever. they are a cadaverous looking set of people. Our Reg't is in good health at present except fatigue from hard marching the weather has been excellent since we left Helena. Our boys have caught some very nice fish here, and there is a cane brake here on the west side of the river the first I ever saw. I think this would be a fine country for game. I wrote to J.F.B.

TUESDAY SEPTEMBER 1ST 1863
Clarendon Arkansas

We marched at 5.A.M. The 49" Ills. in the rear. we past through a bottom of cane-brake, and at the bluff we passed Fort Hindman, and soon afterwards we came to a prairie, level, but a very thin soil. We found water very scarce and bad. there was many of the men 'gave out,' and we had to haul them in the train. We had Eight or Nine wagons to the Reg't. we turned off the road and stoped at Dead Man's Lake

WEDNESDAY SEPTEMBER 2" 1863
Dead-Man's Lake Arkansas

We marched at day-light. traveled through prairie all day. it was very hot. water very scarce and the roads dusty. in the afternoon our men droped down by scores, and I had the train and Ambulances full. Dr.

Medcalf was sick in the evenig and got into the ambulance. we reached Brownsvile at dark.

THURSDAY SEPTEMBER 3" 1863
Brownville Arkansas

I had 46. men at Sick-call. great many with Intermittants, some Diarrhoeas. I saw Capt Joe. Thorp of the 126" Ills Infty. also Capt Fish of Batt."K,, 1st Mo. Arty. no news from the front. We are camped about a mile south of the town in the woods. water very scarce here.

FRIDAY SEPTEMBER 4" 1863
Brownville Arkansas

I gave up a horse the Q.M. let me have the day we left Helena. we have papers in camp of Aug. 25. I received a dozen photographs from J.S. Armstrong, over S. Mansfield's Drug Store, No. 281. Main St. Memphis Tenn. I was in camp all day we rec'd a mail to day. I rec'd letter from A.K.A.

SATURDAY SEPTEMBER 5" 1863
Brownville Arkansas

No mail. and no news from the front to day. I had 24 cases of Intermittents this morning in the Reg't. I was in camp all day. I gave Col. Pease one of my Photographs. sent one to A.K.A. Brownsville is a small place of perhaps 200 inhabitants in times of peace. situated in a poor country. poorly watered and 'out of the way' kind of place.   I wrote to A.K.A.

SUNDAY SEPTEMBER 6" 1863
Brownville Arkansas

The whole command moved at 6.A.M. towards Little Rock. but our Bigade camped when they got out North of town a way. we camped in a hollow Square, with Brig Hd Qrs in the centre We received Ammunition here. Caldwell rejoined the Reg't. Weather warm and dry.~

MONDAY SEPTEMBER 7" 1863
Brownville Arkansas

I was in camp most of the day. had several very sick men in the Reg't. Lt. Kerr is sick. Capt. Cogan is getting better. water is scarce here and the place stinks with caron [carrion], it has been a kind of slaughter pen for Gen'l Steele's Army. we received orders to March to-morrow.~

TUESDAY SEPTEMBER 8" 1863
Brownville Arkansas
Marched at 7.A.M. with the Brig. Jacob Hof Co. "C,, died in the ambulance, while on the march to day. he was burried at noon. I left Dillingham with some sick men, at a Slough by the roadside. we reached camp at dark, and sent back the ambulances for the "Sick men" some of the Wagons broke down on the road.~

WEDNESDAY SEPTEMBER 9" 1863
Bear-Skin-Lake Arkansas
The Reg't marched at 7.A.M. three miles to Ashley's Mills, and left me behind with the sick I sent the Ambulances back after yesterday's sick the roads were so narrow, and so many wagons on them, with some broke down that they could not make it last night. after they returned I moved forward and found the regiment at 6.P.M. after a hard day's work, and fatigue.~

THURSDAY SEPTEMBER 10" 1863
Ashley's-Mills Arkansas
We left the "Sick, lame, & layzy" behind and marched at 9.A.M. put a pontoon across the river, and the cavalry crossed. artillery commenced fighting at noon & drove the rebels. The cavalry had considerable fighting south of the river. Two of Vaughn's men wounded by the bursting of their own shell. Price skedadled and we took possession of Little Rock. Our Brig camped north of the river.

FRIDAY SEPTEMBER 11" 1863
Little-Rock Arkansas
Our sick arrived, put them in a house near at hand Edd McLoughlin Co. "G,, died at 7.P.M. the Infantry are crossing the river on a bridge made of flatboats. Gen'l Davidson's Cavalry still in pursuit of Price the battery men who were wounded yesterday were brought to camp to day and put in Hosp't, still alive.~

SATURDAY SEPTEMBER 12" 1863
Little-Rock Arkansas

The wounds of the artillery men were not dressed until this morning. Dr. Medcalf removed the pieces of shell (weighing nine ounces) from Vlict's back. Dr's Cameran & Flack were present and assisted It was not supposed when they were wounded that either of them would survive three hours.

SUNDAY SEPTEMBER 13" 1863
Little-Rock Arkansas

I got a pass from Col. Pease and went over to the city I visited the State house, and Arsenal, and came near getting picked up by the patrols for not having my pass approved by the brigade commander. Little Rock is smaller than I had supposed it has only about 5,000 inhabitants, and is situated on the first Rocky bluff on the river. There is a detail working on the pontoon Reg't rec'd a mail. I rec'd letters from R.M.L. & E.M.

MONDAY SEPTEMBER 14" 1863
Little Rock Arkansas

Our Brig moved near one mile up the river and put up tents. I went to the Reg't. in the evening. found them in the weeds. not a very desirable location except we work considerably on it. Lt. J.L. Stanley moved to a citizen's house. Sick with Intermittent Fever. Capt Cogan & F.J. Burrows are on the sick list.

TUESDAY SEPTEMBER 15" 1863
Little Rock Arkansas

I was in camp all day and paid H. Burt $.20.00 Some of the boys went foraging. brought in some ducks. We had a wind-storm which blew away the Pontoon bridge so we will have no more crossing to day. Gen'l F. Steele is having a new one built here.~

I wrot to R.M.L. sent Photograph.~

WEDNESDAY SEPTEMBER 16" 1863
Little-Rock Arkansas

In camp all day. Col. Pease had the boys pull the weeds in camp. We are getting but half rations from the A.C.S. and forage for the other half, which was the largest. The Men are without tents and the weather disagreeable it rained and blew at night. and we are in an open field on the bank of the river.~

THURSDAY SEPTEMBER 17" 1863
Little Rock Arkansas

The weather is still cool. I went across the river in a Skift [Skiff] to the mill for some corn meal with Mike Colgan. The boys are firing off their guns to day I went up to the Hospital and saw a man (Dan'l Wilt of Co."A,,) with Smallpox. The first case we have had in our Reg't since I have been Asst Surg. contracted I suppose at Memphis or Helena Ark. Dr. Medcalf is keeping a sort of Brig Hospital.~

FRIDAY SEPTEMBER 18" 1863
Little-Rock Arkansas

Our Brig. was assigned to Gen'l Kimball's provisional Division. Col. True had Brigade drill in an open field about a mile from camp Chaplain Lockwood returned to day from home. I paid him $.20.00 borrowed money. The Regt was out on dressparade. I wrote to E.M. with Photo.

SATURDAY SEPTEMBER 19" 1863
Little-Rock Arkansas

There is a paper published in Little Rock called the National Union. a detail went foraging to day and got a load of Sweet Potatoes & pumpkins Cal. Sappington brought in a hog for our Mess. We board him for his forage. R. Higgins rejoined the Co. I wrote to Lyde-with Photograph.

SUNDAY SEPTEMBER 20" 1863
Little Rock Arkansas

I went with F.J. Burrows to town to church at 10.A.M. and heard a citizen preach. went again at night with Col. Pease & Capt Lockwood. a large audience of soldiers and some citizens present. a very nice church with an organ in it The mail came I rec'd the Salem Advocate.~

MONDAY SEPTEMBER 21" 1863
Little-Rock Arkansas

There was Brig drill again to day. I went with Frank J. Burrows to See Capt. Joe Thorp of Co."K,, 136" Ills. Infty. they are camped on the north side of the Arkansas river about three miles below us. The main part of the Infantry are camped there at present. The 50" Ind. of our Brig are building winter quarters as though they expected to remain. the weather is more pleasant.

TUESDAY SEPTEMBER 22" 1863
Little Rock Arkansas

I got a pass and went over to town in the afternoon, and bought a pr boots $.12.00 returned and was taken Sick at tatoo with vomiting & purging, and a cramp in my stomach. Serg't Fred A. Niles & A. Whits stayed with me.

WEDNESDAY SEPTEMBER 23" 1863
Little Rock Arkansas

I was sick all day with Intermittant Fever and not able to stir about any to day Dr. Medcalf attended sick call for me this morning. There is thought to be some probability of our staying here this winter 50" Ind are building winter quarters

THURSDAY SEPTEMBER 24" 1863
Little Rock Arkansas

I was better this morning. rested well during last night Dr Medcalf attended sick call again to day. Col. Pease is division "Officer of the day." I took Six large doses of Quinine during the day to break the chills. I paid Stephen Frump $.20.00 to day

FRIDAY SEPTEMBER 25" 1863
Little Rock Arkansas

I had no fever to day, think I will be well enough for duty tomorrow. The Brigade was called out and searched for some stolen property belonging to citizens. nothing found in our Reg't. the 50" Ind Infty found guilty. The boys go foraging, and some times they bring in things they should leave in the country F.J.B. complaining again~

SATURDAY SEPTEMBER 26" 1863
Little-Rock Arkansas

I was on duty to day, and feel very much better. Capt. Cheney returned from home to day and brought me a Henry Rifle. he paid $.45.00 for it, at St. Louis, He is very glad to get back again. there was a mail came, we will get it to morrow trains run to Duvalls Bluff every day now.~

SUNDAY SEPTEMBER 27" 1863
Little Rock Arkansas
I got a pass and Capt Cheney & I went to town to church. there are several churches in town, and our men attend pretty regularly now. Capt Lockwood had preaching in camp this evening. we got a mail to day I rec'd letters from J.F.B. and Lyde~

MONDAY SEPTEMBER 28" 1863
Little Rock Arkansas
Lt. Lemmon and detail returned from Duvalls Bluff. Officer of the guard caught some of the men gambling. among them H. Burt & McKinney Capt Cheney Brigade Officer of the day. usually a field officer is required for Brigade Officer of the day. I wrote to J.F.B. & Lyde~

TUESDAY SEPTEMBER 29" 1863
Little Rock Arkansas
I went with Capt Cheney to Little Rock. saw the Penitentiary, & Arsenal. then went down to the battle ground but it dont compare with the battlegrounds of Fort Donaldson or Shiloh, nor of some of the skirmishes during the Seige of Corinth. we went to the 10" Ills Cav. to see some of Capts. friends, then to camp at Sundown. we had a fish for supper.~

WEDNESDAY SEPTEMBER 30" 1863
Little Rock Arkansas
I paid H. Burt $.20.00 to day, and went down to Dr. York's Surg. 54" Ills. he is Surgeon in chief of Division. I took my personal Report. I saw Brig Gen'l. Kimball. Dr Flack Surg 50" Ind. was down there also. Report say Rosecrans has been repulsed. During the past month we have had some hard service. Marching during very hot Weather, over very dusty roads, finding water very scarce and also very bad, and yet making very long and hard marches, without any necessity Existing for it. And it has told seriously on the health of the Command. When we reached Clarendan on White River, the health of our regiment was Excellent, and by the time we reached Brownsville, we had very many sick men

in camp and several deaths in consequence of the <u>unnecessary</u> <u>hard</u> campaigning under circumstances. We reached Brownsville before Gen'l Steele Expected us, and before he was ready to proceed to Little Rock. during this Month we having Experienced the other side of the drama of a soldiers life, from what we have Experienced during the last year.=

THURSDAY OCTOBER 1" 1863
Little Rock Arkansas

I paid Capt Cheney $.20.00 on my gun, paid the Mess $.10.00 for board and Paddy $.2.00 for cooking I went to see Lt. John L. Stanley he is sick again Ad. Ward & John Lemon with the Ambulances have been transfered to the Ambulance Corps.~ I went to the Hosp't and got my horse and Saddle and brought to camp. Our Hosp't, Ambulances & Reg't are badly scattered~

FRIDAY OCTOBER 2" 1863
Little Rock Arkansas

Col Pease & Lt. Spiro marked off the ground for building barracks. Lts Lemmon & Whaling went out foraging for our mess to day. Lt. Dobbleman is Act. Brig. Commissary he issued for the first time to day. Dr Bridges relieved from Hosp't. and gate [given the gate--dismissed] to 27" Iowa for duty to day.

SATURDAY OCTOBER 3" 1863
Little Rock Arkansas

I went up a mile above camp on a high elevation known as Big Rock. The name Little Rock is antithetical to this. I killed pidgeon to day with my Henry Rifle. I was over to town this evening and bought two news papers for fifty-cents.

SUNDAY OCTOBER 4" 1863
Little Rock Arkansas

We had three baked turkeys for dinner to day, in our mess. I went to the woods and dug out a trough to feed my horse in. Companies are building houses for winter I have made up my mind to resign when Dr Mercer returns. I have all the work to do.

MONDAY OCTOBER 5" 1863
Little Rock Arkansas

I helped Co. "D,, put up their barracks. the Knapsacks which were stored at Memphis came to day Capt Laur went for them. some are missing. Burggraf made me a stand table to day. Mail came. we got the Invoices of our three months supply of Medicines I got nothing except papers our medicines were shiped at Memphis Sept. 26. by the Med. Purveyor. Weather cool especially at night. I wrote to K.R. & Em.M.

TUESDAY OCTOBER 6" 1863
Little Rock Arkansas

In camp all day, nothing of importance in camp. Meal time comes and we eat, night comes and we sleep, it is a perfect monotany even a fight would be of interest to break the calm. The right wing of the Reg't is building quarters.   I wrote to S.F.F.M.~

WEDNESDAY OCTOBER 7" 1863
Little Rock Arkansas

I helped Co. "D,, put on the ribs and cover their houses. they miss Tom Hoss now. he always made a good boss or overseer on such occasions.~ A fuss between Lieuts Whaling & Spiro. W. called S. a d--d Jew. S. of a B. about men of Co. "G,, on dress parade wearing straw hats. both like quarrelling.

THURSDAY OCTOBER 8" 1863
Little Rock Arkansas

Some excitement in camp in reference to men joining the regular cavalry 40. of Co. "E,, say they'll go. oppertunity for some men to get a commission in that enterprize. Co "D,, dabed and moved into their houses to-day. two houses are large enough for the entire company now.

FRIDAY OCTOBER 9" 1863
Little Rock Arkansas

I went to the depot for our medicines, but have been sent across the river to the Post. Q.M.'s I went there. he knows nothing of them, sends me to Lieut Seymour, from there I went to Dr. Whitehill's (Med. Director) I found them in Lt. Seymours warehouse. every thing is in a mess here, and mixed up. Pontoon tore up I didn't get back until night.

SATURDAY OCTOBER 10" 1863
Little Rock Arkansas

I went over to town and got our three months supply of medicines. brought them over on the commissary wagons. Capt. Wm Cogan started home to day sick. Capt Kurghoff returned I made 100 opii Pills to night. the health of the Reg't is improving now, some.~

SUNDAY OCTOBER 11" 1863
Little Rock Arkansas

In camp all day. officers making out pay rolls as though we were going to be paid off soon. I went over to town to church at night with Lt. Stanley and Q.M. Serg't Ed. Nixon. Lt. A.S. Chalfin went and took about forty of the men, to church. the house was crowded~

MONDAY OCTOBER 12" 1863
Little Rock Arkansas

Col. Jas. M. True started for home. Col. Jas. I. Gilbert 27" Iowa in command of the Brigade now. I made a cover for my gun. to day a deer crossed the river from the other side and was killed by some of the officers of our Brig. Provision train returned from Duvalls Bluff.~

TUESDAY OCTOBER 13" 1863
Little Rock Arkansas

I went with Capts Cheney & Lockwood, and the Chaplains of the 27" Iowa & 62" Ills and Lt. Hemmenway, to Big Rock and tried our pistols & my gun, and rolled stones down the precipis[precipice] to see them fall and crush trees and stones below. Then we went back north and saw some of the Rebels fortifications, where they expected to meet, and repulse us We didn't come that way

WEDNESDAY OCTOBER 14" 1863
Little Rock Arkansas

I went with Capt Cheney to the woods and cut timbers to build winter quarters for ourselves, now that the men are done. The pay master is paying off part of our Brig. I went to the Hosp't to get my long shot gun but Ad. Ward had it at Division Hd Qrs.~

THURSDAY OCTOBER 15" 1863
Little Rock Arkansas

The pay master, Major Burns came and paid off the Reg't for July & August. he paid me $.224.80cts. I paid Capt. Cheney $.30.00, and H. Burt $.24.60 Col. Pease, F.J. Burrows, Lt. Kerr, Sergts Voris & Breese received orders to go to Illinois on recruiting service for the Regiment.~

(handwritten margin notes: 112.ϟ   224.ϟ   I'ly &   Aug)

FRIDAY OCTOBER 16" 1863
Little Rock Arkansas

Col. Pease, F.J. Burrows, Sergts Voris & Breese, started home to day. John Jenkins was promoted to Commissary Serg't since A. Hesse resigned. Cheney & I put up the walls for our shebangs to day. Pidgeons are flying thick but no shot to shoot them with to be had.~

SATURDAY OCTOBER 17" 1863
Little Rock Arkansas

Lieut. H.W. Kerr started for home to day. I went down to where the Div. was camped and got some brick to build chimneys. then put our tents up on our walls, and have some prospect of comfortable quarter soon I got my long shot gun from Ad. Ward to day. now for the birds, but ammunition is scarce, especially Shot.~

SUNDAY OCTOBER 18" 1863
Little Rock Arkansas

I went with Capt. W.P. Moore Lt. A.S. Rowley and Robbert King (citizens) pidgeon hunting we shot away most of our ammunition and got but few birds. We went to preaching to the 50" Ind. they leave to morrow for some point up the Arkansas River.~

MONDAY OCTOBER 19" 1863
Little Rock Arkansas

The 50" Ind Infty. left for some point up the river. Capt Cheney went and got some lumber to build our houses with. Major T.W. Morgan returned to night. I went over to town with Capt Cheney and got papers of the 9" inst. ten days old. no mail came.~

TUESDAY OCTOBER 20" 1863
Little Rock Arkansas

I tore down my house and built it with White Pine flooring, tongue & grooved to gether. I hired a hand to help build a house for the Mess. "Sutler Bill" came last night and is selling goods fast to day. Capt Laur returned to day went to Memphis for stored property~

WEDNESDAY OCTOBER 21" 1863
Little Rock Arkansas

I settled up with Stephen Frump to day and paid him $.35.85cts in full. There is talk of our leaving here soon. we are getting too comfortably situated to remain here long. Our Hosp't goods came to day, also the blankets and clothing of the Regiment, in bad order. they were left in store at Memphis Tenn. Capt Laur went for them.

THURSDAY OCTOBER 22" 1863
Little Rock Arkansas

It rained most all day, and was very disagreeable. I loafed most of the day with Co."D,, as I have no chimney built to my shebang yet. Masons & trowels are very scarce Mail came to the Reg't after taps to night. I rec'd a letter from Lyde~~

FRIDAY OCTOBER 23" 1863
Little Rock Arkansas

F.J. Burrows Commission came to the Reg't. last night as Adjutant of the Reg't. I was in camp all day. Lt. Rowley is sick. I exchanged Photograps with Capt. Cheney sent his and Capt Kurghoff's home. Cheney's finished his chimney. rec'd letter from J.F.B. and wrote J.F.B. & Lyde~

SATURDAY OCTOBER 24" 1863
Little Rock Arkansas

I went and got a load of brick. in camp most of the day. Went with Capt Cheney to town and bought us each a cavalry overcoat, $.11.50. of the Q.M. Dept. I wrote to F.J. Burrows to bring us some Shot, to shoot, pidgeons and ducks. there is none to be had here.~

SUNDAY OCTOBER 25" 1863
Little Rock Arkansas

The Quartermaster is issueing clothing to the Regiment to day. The Artillery Serg't came down and had some sword exercises. Went over to town to church at night. the Chaplain of the 61st Ills preached the churches were all crowded, with citizens and soldiers promiscuously [intermingled]. went up into the gallery. the night clear cool and beautiful.

MONDAY OCTOBER 26" 1863
Little Rock Arkansas

I went to town and bought a pr. of blankets $.7.20, and 2. pr. of drawers $.1.90. finished my chimney. Went up to Dr Cameron's Surg. 62" Ills to consult the M.D.s in regard to the probabilities of going before a Medical board for a re-examination, by a "special board."

TUESDAY OCTOBER 27" 1863
Little Rock Arkansas

I done nothing but loafed all day. rumor of our returning to Memphis Tenn. Two Hundred Arkansians came in to day and quartered with our Brigade. they are said to be in the State Service. They are recruiting and organizing for the U.S. Service~

WEDNESDAY OCTOBER 28" 1863
Little Rock Arkansas

In camp all day transcribing my diary of 1862. Dr Cameron called upon me to day. O.W. Brokaw & N Lever on a drunk to night. Capt. Cheney and Lt. Mitchell went out hunting and did'nt get back until after dark. but they got no ducks. but very tired.~

THURSDAY OCTOBER 29" 1863
Little Rock Arkansas

In camp writing most all day. company officers settling up clothing accounts for the year. most of the boys behind. clothing is high this year. and the men have had the misfortune to lose considerable in moving. Its been raining most all day and very disagreeable nothing of interest in camp bad weather, makes everything seem dull.

FRIDAY OCTOBER 30" 1863
Little Rock Arkansas
I wrote most all-day. it rained last night, and to day we have cool and disagreeable weather. Capt Cheney Brigade officer of the day. field officers have about played out going on duty as officer of the day. I rec'd letters from Lyde & K.R.~

SATURDAY OCTOBER 31" 1863
Little Rock Arkansas
The Regiment mustered for pay Capt Lockwood building quarters. Capt. Cheney and I went to the timber and cut and hauled a load of wood. he promoted Sam'l. C. Goshorn to Orderly Serg't. and corp'l Pate, to Sergeant, and he suspended Corp'l N. Lever for one month, for drunkenness, and conduct unbecoming a non-commissioned Officer. During the last month the Reg't has built good comfortable quarters and if permitted to remain I think will be satisfied in them. The general health is good. but few sick, either in quarters or Hospital. The citizens are coming in and forming companies and drilling, will be able to defend themselves soon.~

SUNDAY NOVEMBER 1" 1863
Little Rock Arkansas
In camp most all day writing. I paid the Mess $.10.00 boa[r]d money for the month of November. our board cost us $.12.00 per month $.10.00 to Mess, and $.2.00 to Paddy for cooking it.~ I went to church to town at night, heard the Chaplain of the 36" Iowa preach. I exchanged Photographs with Major T.W. Morgan, sent his home.~ Wrote to Lyde & K.R.

MONDAY NOVEMBER 2" 1863
Little Rock Arkansas
I went up to Hospital in the forenoon and got some medicines. Lt. A.K. Dement playing off sick. Lt. S. Sondag refused to go on duty and reported sick also in consequence of Dements playing off. The Sutler moved down to the left again. Weather very warm.

TUESDAY NOVEMBER 3" 1863
Little Rock Arkansas

I got a pass and went with Jim Gray, Gustave Helm & Dillingham seven miles up the river hunting all on foot. We saw four deer. Stoped at a house and got some Sour milk and corn bread to eat. we returned at Sundown very tired, without any game.~

WEDNESDAY NOVEMBER 4" 1863
Little Rock Arkansas

I finished transcribing my diary of 1862. it was badly written, so I got a new diary and transcribed with pen & Ink. Co. "F,, Killed a deer. Capt. Logan been out two days foraging went to Bear-skin-lake and got Sixty wagon loads of corn. The weather is disagreeably warm to day.~

THURSDAY NOVEMBER 5" 1863
Little Rock Arkansas

We cleaned up camp to day, and went to town to a Union Meeting of citizens. heard speeches by Gantt, Rodgers, Fishback & E. Baxter the house was crowded, and the speeches well timed and appropriate to the occation There is realy more Union Sentiment manifested about Little Rock, than at any other point I have visited in the South.~

FRIDAY NOVEMBER 6" 1863
Little Rock Arkansas

Weather pleasant Capt. L.W. Moore returned yesterday from home. I read Gleason's Litterary Companion, "Izana" the mail came though small I rec'd letter from and wrote to Lyde to day. if mails never came soldiering would be, beyond endurance,~

SATURDAY NOVEMBER 7" 1863
Little Rock Arkansas

I made a mistake and got the events of the 7" inst under date of the 5" inst. (above) and will record the 5" here. It rained this A.M. I reported Peyton Smith Co. "I,, for duty to day, for feighning [feigning] to be sick, and peddling whisky in camp. Chaplain got his chimney built to day. he has learned that it is best if you want any thing done, to take hold and do it yourself.

SUNDAY NOVEMBER 8" 1863
Little Rock Arkansas

I went over to town to the Presbyterian church at 10.A.M., to preaching. No papers in town. After church I returned to camp and remained there the rest of the day we got a small mail. I got a letter from Ephraim Glathent he is at Caledonia Ohio & a copperhead

MONDAY NOVEMBER 9" 1863
Little Rock Arkansas

I went to town and bought papers of the 28" ult. and 1st inst. Dr's Allen, Whitehill, & York came and inspected quarters, rations, cooking etc. to day. Dr. Allen is an acquaintance of Capt L.W. Moore's he lives at Alton Ills. I went with Capts Cheney & Logan up on Big Rock and had some target practice while there.~

TUESDAY NOVEMBER 10" 1863
Little Rock Arkansas

In camp all-day reading Atlantic Monthly and the daily papers. We had a big fish for dinner to-day caught by Wm Flake of Co. "D,, with a gig. We might have fish here in abundance if we had some[one] to try who understands something about it.

WEDNESDAY NOVEMBER 11" 1863
Little Rock Arkansas

Capt Cheney got new company Books and is transcribing the old ones. I was in camp all day reading. at night I went with Major Morgan, and Capt Cheney to the theatre. the house was full, and the performance tolerable good. I rec'd letter from E.M.

THURSDAY NOVEMBER 12" 1863
Little Rock Arkansas

Major Morgan takes command of the Regiment to-day. I was in camp all day Weather warm and smoky. Capt Cheney brought a can of Oysters to my tent and we eat them as a matter of cours[e]. "Eating was our fort[e]." I wrote to E.M.

FRIDAY NOVEMBER 13" 1863
Little Rock Arkansas

Capt. W.P. Moore reported to be captured by guerrillas to day. he started to a little town south of Little Rock with a train. I was in camp until evening then went over to town Harrison Burt and [others] saw Capt. W.P. Moore, he was not captured as reported. Train came in from Duvalls Bluff and brought papers from the north of the 3" & 6" instant.

SATURDAY NOVEMBER 14" 1863
Little Rock Arkansas

In camp almost sick with a cold. at 3.P.M. we received Orders to be ready to Move at an early hour to-morrow morning, with C. & G. Equipage to Duvall's Bluff. Our Regiment and the 27" Iowa Infty are to go. the Reg'ts are getting ready. rec'd a letter from R.M.L.~

SUNDAY NOVEMBER 15" 1863
Little Rock Arkansas

We got our plunder packed up and loaded and left camp at 7.A.M., and reshiped to the train and left the depot at 8.30.A.M. The Q.M. left behind to turn over his wagons & teams. we arrived at Duvall's Bluff at 2.P.M. found several boats in the river in waiting for us~

MONDAY NOVEMBER 16" 1863
Duvall's Bluff Arkansas

Took breakfast with Capt. Joe. Thorp Co."K,, 126" Ills went aboard the Sallie List, and started at 7.A.M. down the river. we found it a very crooked stream. guerrillas reported to be along the river below Clarendon but we saw none and tied up to the bank at dark for the night.

TUESDAY NOVEMBER 17" 1863
On board Str. Sallie List

We started at Sun-up Lt. A.S. Rowley very sick we met a convoy of boats in the afternoon they reported guerrillas along the left bank companies were immediately ordered under arms on the hericane deck, but no enemy seen. we tied up at dark on the right bank and put out pickets and lay by all night, and the boys cooked.

171

WEDNESDAY NOVEMBER 18" 1863
On board Str. Sallie List

We started at day-light, and rounded-to, at the mouth of the river and wooded. run slow all day up stream. beside[s] government pays to well for Steamboat men to get in a hurry. They are employed by the day, and try to make it last as long as posible~ tied up at 9.P.M.

THURSDAY NOVEMBER 19" 1863
On board Str. Sallie List

Started at an early hour. we past dry wood and took on green Cotton wood for fuel. we arrived at Helena in the P.M. we anchored out in the stream several miles above Helena, and the cable broke and we drifted down several miles. Rained from 10.P.M. & wind high.

FRIDAY NOVEMBER 20" 1863
On board Str. Sallie List

Weather cool and disagreeable. drizzling rain all day and we run slow. arrived at Memphis Tenn. after dark. we will remain on board until morning. we got the papers and perused them with interest, but found nothing of importance.

SATURDAY NOVEMBER 21" 1863
Memphis Tennessee

The Regiment moved off the boat and went two miles out on the Hernando road and went into camp, near where we were encamped last June in the Suburbs of the City. I went to town with Lt. Jim Mitchell and we eat Oysters, Eggs & Chickens. we filled up a little.

I wrote to R.M.L. & Lyde.

SUNDAY NOVEMBER 22" 1863
Memphis Tennessee

The weather clear and cool to day. Most of the Companies drew tents and put up. Tricillion came out to day to see the Reg't and gass a little. Paddy had chickens for dinner characteristic of Tennessee and Tennesseans. I wrote to F.J.B. & E.M.

MONDAY NOVEMBER 23" 1863
Memphis Tennessee

I went down town and bought a pr pants for $.15.00 a pr boots $.9.00, Druitt's Surgery for $.6.00, and stationary $.2.00. have orders to make out pay rolls immediately prospect of our getting pay soon Brig. Gen'l Veatch is conscripting citizens for the defense of the City.~

TUESDAY NOVEMBER 24" 1863
Memphis Tennessee

I went to the 119" Ills and bought a sheet Iron stove for $.2.50, and put up in my tent. the pay rolls sent off to day. the Quarter Master drew two wagons and teams, to day to hauld wood etc with for the Reg't. I rec'd letters from A.K.A. F.J.B. J.F.B. & Lyde

WEDNESDAY NOVEMBER 25" 1863
Memphis Tennessee

The U.S. Pay Master, Major Mayborn came and paid off the Regiment. he paid me $.223.35cts. The clothing accounts were settled. hence some of the men drew but little pay in consequence of large clothing bills, and loss of clothing in frequent campaigns. The weather is cool and pleasant now.~

THURSDAY NOVEMBER 26" 1863
Memphis Tennessee

I went down town to day and bought photographs of Grant, Rosecrans, Meade, Thomas, Gilmore & Mrs. S.A. Douglas and of Pemberton & Morgan for $.2.00, and sent home. Thirteen recruits came to day for Co. "I,,~ I wrote to Lyde.~

FRIDAY NOVEMBER 27" 1863
Memphis Tennessee

Dr. Medcalf left for home to day. N. Washburn came to see us. We have Orders for five roll call per day now to keep the men in camp. Dr. Medcalf's "Invalids" left for the Invalid Corps to-day some of them in perfect health. I rec'd letter from Lyde

Chatanooga

SATURDAY NOVEMBER 28" 1863

Memphis Tennessee

I sent my Reports to Dr. Boomer of the 27" Iowa I went down town and bought a hat $.8.00. loaned O.W. Brokaw $.10.00 til pay day. favorable news from Chatanooga. rebels repulsed by Gen'ls Grant, Sherman & Hooker. Weather cool and rainy.~

SUNDAY NOVEMBER 29" 1863

Memphis Tennessee

I was in camp all day. weather quite cool. Lt. A.K. Dement took the Stripes off of Corpl John S. Schneider. "S. cursed him for everything that was mean that he could think of. Several of the boys drunk to day in camp. women bring whiskey concealed under their clothing and sell to the boys. it is imposible to keep it out of camp, and admit citizens.

MONDAY NOVEMBER 30" 1863

Memphis Tennessee

I made Monthly, and Personal Reports, and sent in to-day. I went to the Med. Director's Dr. A.B. Cambell's to see about getting a Stove for the Hosp't. says we will have to make requisition on the Quartermaster I went to the Theatre at night with Capt. Kurghoff. play "Arora Floyd." I rec'd letter from Lyde. I paid Paddy $.4.00 for cooking.~

Thus the End of this Month finds us back at Memphis. we have been in West Tennessee until it seems next to getting home to be permitted to return and go into Camp here. Where we can get Mail and papers with some regularity, and have the advantage of the general markets it affords us.

TUESDAY DECEMBER 1" 1863

Memphis Tennessee

I put up the Hospital tent to day, and paid the Mess $.10.00 for board for this month, making $.114.00, I have paid to the Mess and Paddy since I first went into the Mess, on the 17" of last March. I called upon the Misses Lenox to day with Capt Kurghoff. they reside near our present camp~   Rec'd letters from J.F.B. & E.M. wrote Lyde

WEDNESDAY DECEMBER 2" 1863
Memphis Tennessee

We had a man in camp very sick from a Spider bite to day I received a letter from Aunt Martha M. Higgason to day, and answered with $.6.00~ I went with Capts Kurghoff & Laur to Capt. Lenor's to see a game of dominoes played. Rec'd letter from & wrote to M.M.H.

THURSDAY DECEMBER 3" 1863
Memphis Tennessee

Mrs. Col. Bishop came last evening on a visit from home, to see the Col. she spends considerable of her time in camp Camp full of peddlers & hucksters of every description. money is getting scarce with the boys again.~

FRIDAY DECEMBER 4" 1863
Memphis Tennessee

In the afternoon I went with Capt. Cheney to Elm-Wood Semitery east of camp, half a mile. during our absence Mr. Patten & family, were in camp and enquired for us. boys building quarters again. Rebels said to be threatning this place. weather warm & pleasant.

SATURDAY DECEMBER 5" 1863
Memphis Tennessee

I made a Weekly Report for the first time since I have been making reports. The rebels and our men have been fighting up at Colierville. Col Hatch of the cavalry said to be killed, though we have conflicting reports in regard to the results. I cleaned up my Rifle & Pistol to day we may be called out yet if the fighting continues.

SUNDAY DECEMBER 6" 1863
Memphis Tennessee

Lieuts Spiro & Whaling left for home on recruiting service. neither of them are worth much in camp, and are sent off in consequence I think. I had a Sore-Eye and remained in camp all-day. no papers nor mail camp dull~ I wrote to E.M.~

175

MONDAY DECEMBER 7" 1863
Memphis Tennessee

Two young ladies in camp to day soliciting money for Loyal League Society for benifit of sick & wounded Soldiers. I gave $.5.00 Capts Cheney, Houston, & Kurghoff gave $.10.00 after a little bantering~ I went with Capts Cheney & Kurghoff to a show got a wetting. Rec'd letter from K.R. & Lyde

TUESDAY DECEMBER 8" 1863
Memphis Tennessee

I drew a fly for Hospt tent. then went to town and bought a set of chess men & board $3.50, and paid a Tailor $3.00 to take my measure for a Suit of clothing. Capt. Cheney sent for a suit & for a coat for me, to Woods & Henkle Springfield Ills. I wrote to K.R.~

WEDNESDAY DECEMBER 9" 1863
Memphis Tennessee

I Sent Lyde $20.00, to day, and paid Capt. Cheney $.25.00, on my coat. it is to be paid for by his father, at Springfield, and I am to pay him here. I was in camp all day. saw Lt. Rowley beat Capt Cheney at chess. Rowley is a good chess & checker player also plays well at billiards. I rec'd letters from J.F.B. & E.G. wrote Lyde

THURSDAY DECEMBER 10" 1863
Memphis Tennessee

Co. "G,, Started to Alton Ills with prisoners to day. Lt. Dement detailed and went with them. I sent to Maj. Robb for some Sanitaries to day, a good supply on hand there. Capt Cheney building a floor and putting his tent upon it. I rec'd letter from J.F.B.

FRIDAY DECEMBER 11" 1863
Memphis Tennessee

Raining most all day. The "long roll beat" and the bugle sounded "to Arms." we fell in, formed line and took position on the left of the battery. Orders to get one day's rations ready. farther the deponent [one who gives evidence, especially in writing] sayeth not. we returned to camp. I wrote to E.G.

SATURDAY DECEMBER 12" 1863
Memphis Tennessee

I went to town and took a bath. bought some papers to read tomorrow to help while away the time. I saw Lt. Rowley and Houston play at billiards. they rathey [rather] play than eat. still raining~ we got no mail to day~~

SUNDAY DECEMBER 13" 1863
Memphis Tennessee

The "long Roll beat," again at Sun up, and Reg't out in line, until noon. one of the 27" Iowa left his post last night, is said to be the occasion of the scare. but it is a question in my mind whether that was the real cause, or whether Col. Gilbert wanted to see if he could hurry Col. Bishop out with the Reg't.   I rec'd a letter from K.R.

MONDAY DECEMBER 14" 1863
Memphis Tennessee

I was in camp all day. nights cool and disagreeable. I went with Capt Kurghoff to Capt Lenor's to spend the evening, and see them play dominoes, and Euchre. Mr. Lenor flatters himself that he is an excellent domino player. I didn't play at either.

TUESDAY DECEMBER 15" 1863
Memphis Tennessee

Dull and disagreeable to day. I had a case of Smallpox at Sick call this morning from Co."B,, and sent him to the Pest [an epidemic disease associated with high mortality] Hospital. I went with Kurghoff & Lt Lemmon to the theatre at night. play, "Hidden hand" the house was crowded. I wrote to K.R. ["Smallpox" written in margin]

WEDNESDAY DECEMBER 16" 1863
Memphis Tennessee

Rained all day. F.J. Burrows returned to day from Ills. A mule-team & wagon run over Lt. Rowley's tent, breaking & Squelching things generally to wit [namely], cots, desks, chairs, stove, and other things to numerous to mention. And is it to be wondered at, that he Swore a little?~

THURSDAY DECEMBER 17" 1863
Memphis Tennessee

I went to town and bought a pair of Cavalry pants, and two pr socks $.5.25.~ I saw Lt. Reed A.C.S. formerly of Germantown. Sergts Foster of Co."K,, and Corpl. F.B. Ervin of Co."D,, are ordered to Ills. on recruiting Service. I saw Lt. Rowley beat Capt Cheney playing Chess. Capt is not much of a chess player.~

FRIDAY DECEMBER 18" 1863
Memphis Tennessee

I went to town with Frank J. Burrows and he was Mustered into service as Adjutant of our Reg't. I bought a Haversack for $.3.75. then went with Cheney & Lt Lemmon to the Photograph Gallery, and got negatives taken and ordered pictures~

SATURDAY DECEMBER 19" 1863
Memphis Tennessee

I went with Major T.W. Morgan to the City to help him get his leave of absence we eat dinner at the Gayoso house, then went and called upon Miss. Kate Rhoads at Pettit's. Nick Burns found a box of pipes burried. Burggraf made me a bunk. I rec'd letter from J.F.B.

SUNDAY DECEMBER 20" 1863
Memphis Tennessee

Very fine weather to day. I went to the depot to see some of Co. "E,, sick. I eat dinner of Oysters with Lt. Mitchell. Read "The Man of the Golden Mask" most of the day~ 3 of Co."D,, in the commissary for missdeeds Rec'd letters from E.M. & Lyde. wrote to J.F.B.

MONDAY DECEMBER 21" 1863
Memphis Tennessee

I was in camp all day. Paddy Burns returned from home to-day. now we will have something to eat again. Uncle Milt Hensley stoped over with me to night. he is on his way from home, to his Regiment The 1st Tenn. A.D. at Corinth Mississippi. he is looking well and is well satisfied with his branch of the service.~   I wrote to Lyde.~

TUESDAY DECEMBER 22" 1863
Memphis Tennessee

Some guerrillas fired from the Arkansas shore opposite the city into a boat and killed one man, and wounded another. heavy firing at the fort, or gun boats, since dark, and heavy firing during the night above the City. I wrote to E.M.~

WEDNESDAY DECEMBER 23" 1863
Memphis Tennessee

Co. "C,, detailed and sent to the Navy Yard for duty. Lt. Hemmenway of the 27" Iowa came into our mess to board to day. Lt. Dobbleman is A.D.C. to Col. Gilbert comdg our Brigade. Weather cloudy and prospect of rain. I spliced my tent so as to keep the wind out.~

THURSDAY DECEMBER 24" 1863
Memphis Tennessee

Co. "A,, went to the Navy Yard for duty to-day. I went with Major Morgan to the Surgeon in Chief of Division and got his papers through. Eat dinner at Gayoso house went and got my Photographs. (2. Dozen) $.8,00~ Went to the theatre at night performed the "Duke's Mottos"~ I am here.~

FRIDAY DECEMBER 25" 1863
Memphis Tennessee

We have very pleasant weather. to day we had a Christmas Oyster dinner Col. J.I. Gilbert eat with us, and we had a feast indeed. A much more agreeable ordeal than I past, on last Christmas at Bethel Tennessee. We have our mess in a house and can have thing[s] in good order. too much "bust head" in camp. I rec'd letter from & wrote to J.K.Jr.

SATURDAY DECEMBER 26" 1863
Memphis Tennessee

Wet and disagreeable all-day. Capt Cheney got a baked turkey from home to day by Express, so we had another good dinner in camp for Christmas. When we are at Memphis we generaly live well can get almost any thing we want to eat.~ I rec'd letter from M.M.H.

SUNDAY DECEMBER 27" 1863
Memphis Tennessee

We had another Oyster dinner to day some that was left over from Christmas dinner It rained again to day. to bad a day to go to church so I stayed at home and read the papers. We are on the look out for Forrest and his command.

MONDAY DECEMBER 28" 1863
Memphis Tennessee

In camp all-day. no passes given to go to town to-day. prospect of an attack I suppose, or rather an imaginary one which answers the same purpose as well, to Keep men & officers in and about their respective quarters. The boys are getting old.

TUESDAY DECEMBER 29" 1863
Memphis Tennessee

Dr. Medcalf returned to the city from home, last night, and to camp to day, I was taken sick with a chill, head ache, and a very high fever, and past a very disagreeable day. Dr. Medcalf called around to see me in the afternoon. I am doubtful I am going to have Varioloid [mild form of smallpox, in persons who have been vaccinated or have had smallpox] or Smallpox. I was exposed to it fourteen days ago.~ ["Varioloid" written in the margin]

WEDNESDAY DECEMBER 30" 1863
Memphis Tennessee

I past a very hard night, and am feeling very bad to day. My head, Eyes, and back are very painful. am taking Dr. Medcalf prescription of medicines, but without any effect so far. not been able to set up any to day, nor to ly, in bed with ease. Rec'd letter from Lyde

THURSDAY DECEMBER 31" 1863
Memphis Tennessee

I am not much better to day. intimations extant that I have Varioloid. I am satisfied that I have but I have no disposition to go to the Pest Hospital. and I would be sent if Dr. Medcalf should observe close enough to see that I have it. I sold my revolver to day to Marion Richardson for $.15.00. Another year of our service performed and endured, and one more to come yet the last was not attended with as many hardships and privations as the first., and all hope that the next, (if we should be kept another year) may be even more agreeable than this has been. yet we have had no very long continued hardships or privations during 1863.~

FRIDAY JANUARY 1" 1864
Memphis Tennessee

1863. left me sick with Varioloid. I got up to day for the first, after four days confinement and went to Paddy's mess for dinner. The ground is covered with snow. and wood scarce and the weather for this section of the country is very cold. To me the holidays have been very dull indeed. I paid the mess $.10.00 to day to square up the accounts of last year. I rec'd a letter from E.A.B.

SATURDAY JANUARY 2" 1864
Memphis Tennessee

This was a very cold morning. some of the boys on the picket lines got their ears and fingers frosted. Not much stir in camp. I loafed from Frank's to Capt Cheney's Where they kept best fires I stoped longest. I loaned Cheney $.5.00 sent Phot. to L. wrote to E.A.B. i.e. A.E.B.

SUNDAY JANUARY 3" 1864
Memphis Tennessee

Camp very dull and quiet. raining and sleeting most of the time. I regain my strength very slowly though I attend regularly to the mess at meal time, and have good enough appetite. ought to improve faster.   I rec'd letter from R.M.L.

MONDAY JANUARY 4" 1864
Memphis Tennessee

The ground frozen and icy. disagreeable getting about. Capt. Wm P. Moore detailed as A.A.I. Gen'l on Col. J.I. Gilbert's (brigade) staff. Lieut James Lemmon detailed, mustering officer for veteran organization. Men drunk on the picket lines 'Liquor & other articles found there. I wrote R.M.L.~

TUESDAY JANUARY 5" 1864
Memphis Tennessee

Very cold. Mr. James Lyle Co. "I,, fell on the ice to day and hurt himself. I fear seriously. Capt. John G. Berry returned from home to day. I remained in camp all day. I had a game of Whist with Rowley, Cheney & Houston. Rowley & I beat them. Whist Peakmaker checkers chess and such games help to while away many a leisure hour in camp~

WEDNESDAY JANUARY 6" 1864
Memphis Tennessee

I went to town and bought a diary, for this year, and some reading matter to wit, East Lynne and Oakenshow to help "drive dull cares away" I loaned Lt. A.S. Rowley $.25.00 until pay day. We have orders to have our transportation in trim prospect of our having some Campaigning to endure.

THURSDAY JANUARY 7" 1864
Memphis Tennessee

Capt Lockwood cold to day. he called for a detail to cut and haul him some wood. four commissioned officers went and cut & hauled it for him. Weather cold. ground icy. I was in camp all day reading East Lynne and find it one of the most interesting books of the Kind I ever met with.

FRIDAY JANUARY 8" 1864
Memphis Tennessee

A great want of events to break the monotony of camp life. I read all day. some of the boys who went home with Co. "G,, returned but no Co "G,, yet. they went to Alton Ills with prisoners I loaned Capt Cheney $.5.00 to day making $.35.00 in all I have let him have~

SATURDAY JANUARY 9" 1864
Memphis Tennessee

I hired Harrison Austin to chop a load of wood for me (for the mess.) I went and helped haul it. some of Co. "D,, taken to Brig. Hd Qrs to day on suspicion of taking private property from citizens. Co. "D,, have some hardened cases in it. among them Noah Byrum, Tom Farro, & O.

W. Brokaw they are reporting to Hd Qrs to frequently, to be exemplary soldiers~

SUNDAY JANUARY 10" 1864
Memphis Tennessee

I went to church at 11 A.M. to day, with Cheney Logan & Burrows, to the Union church heard a good sermon preached. Geo. E. Dillingham sick to night. I loaned John Hook Co. "D,, $.5.00 Camp very quiet. weather pleasant. the ice is most all gone much pleasenter getting about.

MONDAY JANUARY 11" 1864
Memphis Tennessee

I read Oakenshow most all day. I went to the theatre at night. play "Romeo & Juliet" I saw Major Gen'l Wm T. Sherman there. a fine looking officer. I loaned Frank J. Burrows $.20.00 til pay day. weather pleasant. prospect of our leaving here soon~

Sherman

TUESDAY JANUARY 12" 1864
Memphis Tennessee

Our Reg't drew new Springfield Rifles to day, turning over the Enfield Rifles per order, requiring the 16 A.C. to be armed with the former guns they are the best arm in the service I think. Though many of our men make the exchange with considerable dissatisfaction~

WEDNESDAY JANUARY 13" 1864
Memphis Tennessee

I went to the Navy Yard to day, to see the boys on duty there. Co. "G,, returned from Alton Ills to night. I went to the theatre. Rob't McWade's benifit play "Camilla," afterpiece "Soldiers on a bender" house full. half dozen generals were present Sherman, Hurlbut Grierson and others. The theatre is a success now, every thing went off well. a good house every night.~

Sherman

THURSDAY JANUARY 14" 1864
Memphis Tennessee

Exchanged Photographs with Col. Bishop. I sent Lieut Fischer & one man with Varioloid to Pest Hosp'tl. The prospect still indicates that we will leave here soon. other troops coming in to do duty on the lines at this place.

Rec'd letter from E.M.

FRIDAY JANUARY 15" 1864
Memphis Tennessee

I went to town and bought an album $.6.00 and to the express office but no goods. several boats coming down, ice breaking up roads muddy. weather warmer. The officers of the Reg't are getting picture taken with a view to exchanging all around, and filling albums

SATURDAY JANUARY 16" 1864
Memphis Tennessee

I went to Richmond's and ordered another dozen Photographs. went to the theatre at night play "Hunters of the Mississippi" and "Don Juan" good house. came back with Lt. McGregor & Nixon Co. "A,, came up to re-enlist as veterans. They have the fever now. Rec'd letter from J.F.B.

SUNDAY JANUARY 17" 1864
Memphis Tennessee

Rained most of the day, and is very muddy hence I stayed in camp. sent a Co. "H,, man to Pest Hospt. orders came for pay rolls to be signed and sent into Hd Qrs. prospect of our getting some pay soon. many of the men and officers short of money now. some keep to little, and others spend to much. I have plenty yet and to spare.   I wrote to E.M.~

MONDAY JANUARY 18" 1864
Memphis Tennessee

In camp all day. Wm Brokaw and some recruits came for the Reg't to-day several boats collecting at the Wharf probably to transport our (16) Army Corps. to some other field for duty We have been here about long enough. our men are learning the ropes to well. snow on the ground. Wrote J.F.B.

16th Corps

TUESDAY JANUARY 19" 1864
Memphis Tennessee

Another day without events of interest in our camp, save the enlistment of veterans. very fine weather, except it is muddy under foot.

We heard from our clothing to yesterday it will be here soon it is to be hoped as the present suit has veteraned.

WEDNESDAY JANUARY 20" 1864
Memphis Tennessee

We were reviewed by Major Gen'l David Hunter to day. I went to town and Exchanged Knapsacks, Teeth Extracting Inst's and other unserviceable articles. The officers of Reg't held a meeting in regard to re-enlisting the Reg't as veterans. a little interest manifested by them will do it~

THURSDAY JANUARY 21" 1864
Memphis Tennessee

I went to the Photo. gallery and got another dozen pictures. We received orders to be ready to move by Sunday morning. all astir and likely to be so in the mean time. a great deal to be done. I want to buy a horse, and we need another ambulance and team for it. we have but one and it is an indifferent affair.   I wrote to Lyde.~

FRIDAY JANUARY 22" 1864
Memphis Tennessee

I went to town and got our clothing, my coat and Cheney's suit. I bought a pr of straps $.5.00 Loaned F.J. Burrows $.10.00. Major T.W. Morgan returned I went to the threatre at night. play "Hamlet". I packed up my medicines chest, to be ready to move. Rec'd letter from A.K.A.

SATURDAY JANUARY 23" 1864
Memphis Tennessee

I took my books to the Express office to send home drew an ambulance and pair of mules. packed up our medicine. The 27" Iowa being paid off to day sewed my straps on my coat to day. wrote a letter to father in refrence to my books, Expressed.

SUNDAY JANUARY 24" 1864
Memphis Tennessee

I dressed to go church, but sent the ambulance for the Pay master, and didn't go, and he didn't come. I went to Mr Richmond's during the evening. we are still awaiting orders rumors says we are not going, but not a reliable rumor. Weather very fine.

MONDAY JANUARY 25" 1864
Memphis Tennessee

I went to town and got a permit to send our sick men to the Gen'l Hospital. went to the theatre at night. play "Cricket." house full. The troops are coming in from Corinth. they are evacuating the Memphis & Charleston R.R. There is no particular worth attached to that line now We are probably going to open a new one some where else. perhaps farther south.~

TUESDAY JANUARY 26" 1864
Memphis Tennessee

We packed our baggage and stored it, tents and all. Reg't paid off by Maj. Reynolds (2 months) he paid me $.224.35 Rowley paid me $.25.00, Burrows $.30.00, Hook $.5.00 & O.W. Brokaw $.5.00 I went to the theatre at night. play "Fanchon" & conscription. we are now about ready to leave here.~

WEDNESDAY JANUARY 27" 1864
Memphis Tennessee

I went to town to buy a horse, but didn't find one to suit. all the good horses has been drawn for cavalry & artillery. I will try at Vicksburg. The Reg't moved in the P.M. to the Wharf and went on board the Str Polar Star, and crossed to the opposite side of the river.~

THURSDAY JANUARY 28" 1864
Memphis Tennessee
On board 'Str Polar Star'

We started down the river at noon with Seven other boats in company. The weather very fine. run all day, and most all night we past Helena at 11.P.M. I didn't see the place I was in the cabbin at the time of passing~

FRIDAY JANUARY 29" 1864
On board Str. Polar Star

Tied up awhile in the forenoon in consequence of a dense fog. Some of the boys went ashore and killed some hogs and set some buildings on fire near the river, just for the love some of them have for doing mischief. They deserve severe punishment for it. but Col. Bishop commands and that is sufficient evidence that they will not be.

SATURDAY JANUARY 30" 1864
On board Str Polar Star

Very foggy. rained awhile to day. we arrived at Vickburg at 1.P.M. Like ancient Rome it is situated on a number of hills. We went ashore and lay on the ground with-out shelter in the rain. I saw John Green he is a Lieut. in the 58" Ills Infty.

SUNDAY JANUARY 31" 1864
Vicksburg Mississippi

We lay around on the ground all day awaiting orders. troops moving out to the rear of town. I took a stroll over the place to see the fortifications some of them very strong. the town is a filthy, dirty place, streets narrow and crooked, houses small and smoky. filled with a lot of land-sharks & sutlers selling goods at anormous prices, and have but poor assortments, at that. our mess bought a wagon and pair of mules to carry our provisions, as our transportation has been cut down to three wagons to the Reg't. Lieut Rowley was left behind with our wagons and teams for want of river transportation. I am going to leave my sword with Lieut Bliss til I return

MONDAY FEBRUARY 1" 1864
Vicksburg Mississippi

I tried to buy a horse to day, but could'nt find one to suit. my prospect is pretty good for a long walk. The horses have been issued to the 17" A.C. I went to the theatre at night the play "A grist to Mill" some of the command moved to the rear of the city this evening preparatory to starting on the campaign. we are down below the town near the river at present.~

TUESDAY FEBRUARY 2" 1864
Vicksburg Mississippi

Our brigade moved out three miles to the rear of the city at 4.P.M. We got a mail I received a letter from Ella Moody containing the sad inteligence of the death of father, at the hands of some deserters. It was addressed to Adj't Burrows for me~ He was Murdered near Salem Ills. Jany 22" 1864.

[margin handwritten: Father Willis Killed at Salem Il]

WEDNESDAY FEBRUARY 3" 1864
Vicksburg Mississippi

Capt. J.W. Cheney went with me to see General S.A. Hurlbut, to see if I could get a leave of absence. he would not let me go, but said I should have a leave as soon as this expedition was over. We marched early in the morning in an easterly direction over a rough and broken country.

THURSDAY FEBRUARY 4" 1864
Camp 12. Miles out Miss.

We moved out early. I walked all day. my feet getting very sore. Col. Bishop and Doctor Medcalf monopolize the ambulance. there horses were left with the Q.M. and are still behind. skirmishing at the front this evening. three or four men wounded. one of the 58" Ills Infty.

FRIDAY FEBRUARY 5" 1864
Camp in the field Miss.

Our brigade (3rd brig; 3rd Div; 16th A.C.) in the front to-day. 52nd Ind. done the skirmishing and had two or three men killed. a regiment of the 17" A.C. crossed over from a paralel road on which they were marching, and captured a rebel gun, and some Johnies in front of us. We camped five miles west of Jackson Miss. We were shelled this evening a little while.

[margin handwritten: 3rd brig. 3rd div. 16th A C]

SATURDAY FEBRUARY 6" 1864
Camp near Jackson Miss.

The weather quite comfortable. we lay by all day and the men rested their feet which are getting quite sore, and killed a few hogs for the sake of having a little fresh meat. so far the country is poor the soil is thin, and the fields yellow.

SUNDAY FEBRUARY 7" 1864
Camp near Jackson Miss.

Moved early this morning. reached Jackson near noon and stoped awhile. the central portion of the town has been destroyed by fire our advance captured the rebel pontoon in Pearl river. we crossed on it and then it was destroyed. We camped at 8.30 P.M.

MONDAY FEBRUARY 8" 1864
Camp near Brandon Miss.

We moved early to town, and stoped until noon. I bought some corn bread at a house. The boys got a lot of tobaco. most of this town has been destroyed. we went on fourteen miles and camped at sundown. we got some commissaries to-day.

TUESDAY FEBRUARY 9" 1864
Hickham's Bridge Miss. (Lin Creek)

started early this morning, but were delayed by the trains. we past the 17.A.C. at Morton at sundown and it was "seven miles to camp" which place we reached, half past one oclock in the morning every body tired, and the men swearing incessantly. we marched (23) twenty three miles to day. the two A.C.s have considerable train which frequently delays the march for hours.   Orpas

WEDNESDAY FEBRUARY 10" 1864
Camp in the field Miss.

Moved out early again this morning and were again delayed by the trains and bad roads. We marched but (12) twelve miles to day and it took us til mid night to do that. Men very tired many sore feet, and Diarrhoeas, some chills. Col Bishop in the ambulance considerable~

THURSDAY FEBRUARY 11" 1864
Camp in field Miss.   Hillsboro

Marched early, past Hillsboro at noon. the most of it was burned by our army. sad hour to the citizens. Our cavalry skirmished with the rebels and killed and left on the field five which were burried by the infantry in the evening. We have but very few cavalry with us.

FRIDAY FEBRUARY 12" 1864
Camp in field Miss.

Our Reg't detailed to guard the wagon train. moved early; past Decatur at 10.A.M. burned most of the place. Lieut James Reed and part of our brigade train mist the road and didn't get in on time, and are said to be captured but came in subsequently.~

SATURDAY FEBRUARY 13" 1864
Camp in Field Miss.~

We lay in camp all day and were to move at night. one of Co. "I,, shot his fingers off while on picket just after dark I think he did it intentionally. Marched after night awhile, the Reg't divided among the train. I rode some body's horse. houses burned along the road I made a pot of mush for the mess.

SUNDAY FEBRUARY 14" 1864
Camp in Field Miss. Tallahatchie River

We moved .1/4 of a mile and camped the ballance of the day. The train was corralled to day and the invalids of the army left with us, the main army went on east. Pickets fired on to day by a guerrilla and the rebels skedaddled. foraging parties sent out.

MONDAY FEBRUARY 15" 1864
Camp in Field Miss. Tallahatchie River

In camp all day. Capt. L. Kurghoff bussted my Henry Rifle to day trying to shoot a beef but made no reparation for it. We moved 200 yards and camped. rain fell upon us to day a[s] hard as it ever falls we had no shelter. clear at night again.

TUESDAY FEBRUARY 16" 1864
Camp in Field Miss. Tallahatchie River

Our Reg't went out foraging. skirmished all the way out eight miles, captured several prisoners got a fine lot of corn and fodder, and some meat. returned at sundown, tired and with sore feet. We found the country poor, and the inhabitants destitute.

WEDNESDAY FEBRUARY 17" 1864
Camp in Field Miss.~ Tallahatchie River
We changed our camp, by moving 100 yards on to a ridge, and lay in camp all day. we gathered up leaves and pine tops and made us comfortable beds, but at 8.P.M. were ordered on picket by Gen'l Chambers. relieved the 20" Ohio Infty. Lt. Dobbleman remained in camp and slept on our beds. the night was cool. we have seasoned pine logs to burn which makes excellent fires~

THURSDAY FEBRUARY 18" 1864
Camp in Field Miss. Tallahatchie River
On picket all day. had a nice time, eating corn-bread, and molasses which Lt. John Stanley and I made of Sugar. Paddy moved out and cooked for us. at night I slept in a house with Major T.W. Morgan and F.J. Burrows. the first night in a house since we started.

FRIDAY FEBRUARY 19" 1864
Camp in Field Miss. Tallahatchie River
Relieved off picket by the 20th Ohio Infty. returned to camp and received orders preparatory to returning to Vicksburg. the object of the Expedition having been accomplished and "the problem of the war having been solved." the rebels skedadled and Meredian destroyed~ *Moredian*

SATURDAY FEBRUARY 20" 1864
Camp in Field Miss.~ Tallahatchie River
We marched at 10.A.M. in the train, many refugees accompanying us. Dr. Davis (a prominent rebel of this section of the country) a prisoner. I was sick all day. we reached Decatur at sundown. Killed a hog and calf and had a splendid supper of them.~

SUNDAY FEBRUARY 21" 1864
Decatur Mississippi
Marched at 5.A.M. in front of the train Went 17. Miles and camped at 2.P.M. in an old field. we went to the branch near by and striped off and washed ourselves Cheney, Burrows, & I and changed our clothing. the rear of the army did'nt get into camp until after dark. so it takes the army about 5. hours to pass any given point

MONDAY FEBRUARY 22" 1864
Camp in Field Miss.

We marched at the rear to day. our Reg't at the rear of the brigade at 10.A.M. Camped at sundown after marching 17. Miles, at Hillsboro Miss. I had a lot of sick men on my hands to day Capt. Wm Cogan officer of the day. he has a horse to ride, and will have a good time.

TUESDAY FEBRUARY 23" 1864
Hillsboro Miss.

We lay in camp all day. part of the army was still behind until to day they came up. I saw three Major generals viz Sherman McPherson & Hurlbut. The 17" A.C. past us, and the 16. A.C. came up. I saw Hanly King he is a member of the 124" Ills Infty. 1st brigade; 3. Div. 17" A.C.

WEDNESDAY FEBRUARY 24" 1864
Hillsboro Miss.

Marched at 7.A.M. on the Canton road 16 Miles and camped early; Paddy foraged to day and came into camp with some chickens, Potatoes, & geese. I was on duty at the rear of the brigade to day; Gen'l Sherman was fired at by a guerrilla from the brush.

THURSDAY FEBRUARY 25" 1864
Camp in Field Miss.~

We moved at 6.A.M. Part of the 17. A.C. came in a head of us, and we past them again and cam[p]ed in the road at Pearl River after marching 6. miles had to make a pontoon to cross on. a battery and a few Infantry crossed and the pontoon failed so it had to be repaired and no more crossing done to night. Weather fine, and roads good.

FRIDAY FEBRUARY 26" 1864
Pearl River Miss.

We crossed the river at day-light, then cooked breakfast, and marched at 11.A.M. a great many negroes & refugees accompany in the army We went 12 miles and camped near Canton the prettiest place, and finest country I have seen in the State. Command on 1/4 & 1/2 rations.

SATURDAY FEBRUARY 27" 1864
Canton Mississippi

Lay in camp all day. Gen'l Hurlbut came to the 52nd Ind Infty and made them a speech told them if they would re-enlist, they should go home to-morrow. Col. Bishop tried our Reg't but they would'nt re enlist. I made an application for a leave of absence, and took it to brig Hd Qrs.

SUNDAY FEBRUARY 28" 1864
Canton Mississippi

The 49" & 117" Ills went out to tear up track on the R.R. - guerrillas fired into a wagon train near by, and Col Bishop took Co "I,, to the rear of the 117" Ills disgracefully leaving the rest of the Regt without orders. We sent off our sick to Vicksburg under charge of Dr. Martin 52" Ind.

MONDAY FEBRUARY 29" 1864
Canton Mississippi

In camp all day. a petition being circulated requesting Lt. Col. Wm. M. Bishop to resign immediately in consequence of his disgraceful conduct yesterday, and during this campaign generaly. Lt. A.S. Rowley rejoined us bringing 12. days rations of hard bread & salt. we have orders to move to morrow. Co. "G,, dug up some china ware.

TUESDAY MARCH 1" 1864
Canton Mississippi

Raining hard this morning. We marched at 8.A.M. Col Bishop waited until the Division train got in between him and his position in the column. then the regiment in trying to regain it position in the line became shamefully scattered, of which Gen'l Hurlbut took notice. Marched 18 miles through the mud, and camped near Livingston. I bot pr shoes of Q.M.

WEDNESDAY MARCH 2" 1864
Livingston Mississippi

Marched at Sunup, went 7. miles and stoped to repair a bridge. artillery firing at the rear. three pieces of artillery and a detachment of rebels captured by a brig of the 17." A.C. We marched on 10 miles further and camped in a very broken old field.

Brownsville

THURSDAY MARCH 3" 1864
Camp in Field Miss.~
Moved at 9.A.M. We past Brownsville a small villiage, and crossed Big Black River at dark on a pontoon and camped after marching 18 miles to day. it seems as though we are on our own territory now that we have crossed this river and are home

FRIDAY MARCH 4" 1864
Big Black River Miss.
We moved at 7.A.M. at the rear of the brig I was on duty at the rear had three wagons to pick up invalid straglers. We reached the rear of Vicksburg at 5.P.M. and camped. all tired and many with sore feet. received a large mail. I rec'd one from J.F.B. E.A.B. & Rev Cliff

SATURDAY MARCH 5" 1864
Vicksburg Mississippi
I paid the Mess $.10.00. I washed and changed clothes, and went to town and bought some provisions for the mess. I bought a gold pen $4.25. and a pocket Knife for $.3.00. I saw the 30" Ills going home as a veteran organization on furlough. Our boys are re-enlisting and will probably make it yet. Co "H,, have not made a start at reenlisting yet.~

SUNDAY MARCH 6" 1864
Vicksburg Miss.~
Capt. James W. Davis our orriginal quartermaster came out, and made a speech, and got up a little excitement, and the boys went to work re-enlisting and made t[h]e 49" Ills Infty. a veteran organization. a little interest manifested by the officers was all that was needed. I wrote to J.F.B.

MONDAY MARCH 7" 1864
Vicksburg Miss.
Major T.W. Morgan reported the Reg't to Gen'l Hurlbut as a veteran Reg't. and asked a furlough for them but was to late. we were already assigned to the Red River Expedition, and orders to move to-morrow. I went to town and bought an oil-cloth and other necessaries for field service

TUESDAY MARCH 8" 1864
Vicksburg Miss.~

Our orders to move at 6.A.M. changed to the P.M. When we marched down through town and stoped on the river bank below town, I lost my Henry Rifle out of the ambulance. Col Bishop is going to leave us his resignation being accepted by Gen'l S.A. Hurlbut.

WEDNESDAY MARCH 9" 1864
Vicksburg Mississippi

Rained all day. We were assigned to the Steamer Liberty a small stern wheel boat, with capacity of 500 men. We went aboard and took our rooms. then Cheney, Burrows & I went to town and bought one Doz cans Peaches, 2 cans green corn, Pineapples, Peas, Honey & etc. to carry with us on the expedition as we will not likely get much after we leave here

THURSDAY MARCH 10" 1864
Vicksburg Mississippi

Lay at the shore and wrote letter. received a mail we received an order from Gen'l Sherman promising furlough to all Veteran Regiments as soon as this expedition is completed. not very cheerfully received. I rec'd letters from J.F.B. & R.M.L. & wrote J.F.B. & Lyde.

FRIDAY MARCH 11" 1864
Natches Louisana [Mississippi]

Past the above place at sun up. Saw some fine Sugar plantations. arrived at the mouth of Red River at 3.P.M. found quite a number of gun boats there. The boys burned a house while guards were all around it alledging that it was rebel property. a poor justification.

SATURDAY MARCH 12" 1864
Red River Landing Louisiana Sims poat

Moved at noon past the mouth of Red River and went down the Atchafalaya river about 30. miles and tied up at Simsport the boys went a shore and cooked rations Threatened to burn a building here but was prevented by a strong guard.~

SUNDAY MARCH 13' 1864
Simsport Louisiana

Brig. Gen'l A.J. Smith Sent out a brigade to reconoiter they found no enemy; the ballance of the command disembarked and drilled most of the day in an old field on the river bank. after dark we moved out in a Westerly direction six miles, past a little fort built by the rebels but not occupied at present. We camped at 2. oclock in the morning, with orders to be up at 4.A.M.~

MONDAY MARCH 14" 1864
Camp in Field Louisiana

Marched at 6.A.M.; the rebels destroyed the bridge over bayou De-glaze at Mooresville, fired a few shots at them past a little town Cocoville. The rebels were in front of us until we came to Monsura they turned to the left We past Marksville 2 hours by sun commenced fighting immediately. works were charged at dark by 58. & 119. Ills & 24 Mo. & 89 Ind

TUESDAY MARCH 15" 1864
Fort De Russy Louisiana

I went to Fort De Russy and saw the prisoners (175) also the guns captured on the Indianola by the rebels below Vicksburg, and yesterday recaptured and will be taken aboard to day. The charging party were under command of Brig General Joseph A. Mower. the works were destroyed to day we re embarked and started up to Alexandria La

WEDNESDAY MARCH 16" 1864
On board Str Liberty

Moved early. saw some fine sugar plantations. we arrived at Alexandria at 2.P.M. found no enemy they left yesterday. We disembarked with wagons and provisions. our ammunition was left on board the boat, except what is in cartriage boxes. this is very pretty little town.~

THURSDAY MARCH 17" 1864
Alexandria Louisiana

The Surgeons confiscated a drug store. I appropriated a can of honey and a few articles of medicine. We lay around camp all day Many rumors and speculations extant as to our future movements. Three pieces of

Artillery found and brought in to day which the rebels had left in their haste to save themselves yesterday. There was not a gunboat around with us yet.~

FRIDAY MARCH 18" 1864
Alexandria Louisiana

The gun boats are taking on cotton, sending to the country for it. Naval officers taking pictures and other private property from citizens they are acting in rather a disgracefull maner Their facilities for carrying such articles has a demoralizing effect. there is no restraint.

SATURDAY MARCH 19" 1864
Alexandria Louisiana

The Steamer Lauruel Hill came up and said to be going down soon with a mail. all hands at the tables writing letters to send by her. Many conjectures as to what will be our future movements and when they will take place. I wrote to E.M., J.F.B. & Lyde.

SUNDAY MARCH 20" 1864
Alexandria Louisiana

Aboard the boat all day. some of Major Gen'l N.P. Banks' cavalry in town, most of them Eastern troops, Mass. Maine, Penn etc. they look rather hard as though they had seen some active service. saw one Louisana cavalry Regiment among them

MONDAY MARCH 21" 1864
Alexandria Louisiana

A stir got up in camp in the evening and regiments called out in line and stood in the rain until they were wet then ordered to camp when everything was wet, at dark. There was probably no enemy within a dozen miles of here, some imaginary danger I think. our men are in camp just below the town on the bank of the river

TUESDAY MARCH 22" 1864
Alexandria Louisiana

Genl. J.A. Mower captured 200 prisoner and four pieces of artillery, 30 miles up the river at Catile Landing without firing a gun. The Str

Luminary came up bringing St. Louis papers of the 12th inst. We are still laying here apparently awaiting orders or for the river to rise.

WEDNESDAY MARCH 23" 1864
Alexandria Louisiana

I saw a lot of prisoners and four pieces of Artillery in camp captured by Gen'l Mower also saw a lot of refugees to night who have been driven from their homes on account of their Union proclivities. many of them are in destitute circumstances at present.

THURSDAY MARCH 24" 1864
Alexandria Louisiana

I was on the boat all day reading "Cepherine or the secret Cable" we have been here eight days now and no more prospect of our moving now than when we first landed. steamers coming up from New Orleans occasionally, and others going down camp very quiet though full of vague rumors.

FRIDAY MARCH 25" 1864
Alexandria Louisiana

The Reg't went aboard the boat and it went down the river 20. miles for wood. We landed at a Sugar plantation and got our wood, and rolled on Six Hhd. [abbreviation for hogshead, a large cask or barrel] of Sugar and several Bbls. of molases, and the boys got lots of chickens. the planter and family had gone to Texas. We returned at 3.P.M. and found Gen'l N.P. Bank's Infantry in town.

SATURDAY MARCH 26" 1864
Alexandria Louisiana

We marched out at 9.A.M. along bayou Rapides. we past several squads of Cavalry we traveled through a fine section of country. Marched 17. miles and camped at sundown near a small stream of water. men very tired. a hard, dusty, march.~

SUNDAY MARCH 27" 1864
Bayou Rapides Louisiana

Started at 7.A.M. marched in a circuitous Rout and camped at Catile Landing at 1.P.M. after traveling a distance of 10. miles The country is not so rich as that we past through yesterday. our camp is in an old field full of weeds and briars.

MONDAY MARCH 28" 1864
Catile Landing Louisiana

Lay in camp all day. Major Morgan went out with a detail foraging and got some fine beeves for the brigade. The commissary, and some gun boats came up in the P.M. transports came up after night I had gone to bed and didn't get up~

TUESDAY MARCH 29" 1864
Catile Landing Louisiana

I went to the boat to get breakfast and found a lot of invalids aboard belonging to Banks' army and other Reg'ts of our army. A detail of five companies sent with the boat up the river for fuel. we got a lot of rails and returned. the wagons and ambulances put aboard after night. Indications of a move soon somewhere think we are going to re-embark this time~

WEDNESDAY MARCH 30" 1864
Catile Landing Louisiana

Cos. "D,, & "C,, on picket I went out and took Capt Cheney his dinner, and stayed there an hour or two then went to Col. Blanchard's house (a rebel citizen who vacated the premises, on our approach) and found everything destroyed, feather beds riped open, and all a perfect wreck of destruction.

THURSDAY MARCH 31" 1864
Catile Landing Louisiana

We are still waiting for the word, "forward" A portion of Bank's or all of them having gone up by land. it seems very uncertain about our going higher up, except Bank's army is to small to accomplish the objects of the Expedition which is not very probable as there seems to be but few rebels in the country. Two transports came up this morning empty from below. Officers of our Reg't making out roll for the veterans in order that they may get pay, when we get back to a Pay-Dept. I borrowed $.20.00 of Capt. Cheney to day rather than break a $.100.00 bill. We have quite a number of cases of Diarrhoea in the Reg't. from bad water, and eating sweet potatoes and fresh meat.

199

FRIDAY APRIL 1" 1864
Catile Landing Louisiana

I paid the Mess $.3.75 the amount required this month. Major Morgan drilled the Reg't. this evening. the boys says its a sure of our receiving marching orders. The Str. Lumminary came up from New Orleans with papers of the 27th ult. though not much news in them of importance to far from the seat of war.~

SATURDAY APRIL 2" 1864
Catile Landing Louisiana

We re-embarked on the Str. Liberty and started at 2.P.M. up the river. we ran until after dark. we passed two gunboats in the evening travel'd through a rich country and tied up for the night. the river is to narrow and crooked to run after night with safty.

SUNDAY APRIL 3" 1864
On board Str Liberty

We started early, and found the river narrow and extremely crooked. it required hours to pass some places in consequence. there are some tolerably large boats in the expedition especialy some of the Rams, and gunboats we tied up again at 8.P.M. at Grand Ecore.

MONDAY APRIL 4" 1864
Grand-Ecore Louisiana

L. Dow. Williams of Co. "B,, fell overboard and was drowned. we moved up a little and disembarked and encamped in a very pretty woods. I went on board the Str Adriatic with Lt. Col. Taylor of the 119th Ills. Infty. We are now in a rich and level scope of country.

TUESDAY APRIL 5" 1864
Grand-Ecore Louisiana

We went up the river foraging for fuel and provisions We got a lot of rails, and some hogs, and beeves. We went out to a house and got some cistern water to drink, and had an interesting time, talking to the women. We returned and I devoted the ballance of my time letter writing. I loaned John Hook $5.00 until pay day which is an uncertain period. I wrote to J.F.B. J.K. & Lyde.~

WEDNESDAY APRIL 6" 1864
Grand-Ecore Louisiana

I went ashore to march at day light across the country, got ready, then ordered to remain. I went back and stayed aboard the boat all day some of the ballance of the army not ready to march yet I suppose. Col. Moore 117th Ills Infty is commanding the brigade on this expedition.

THURSDAY APRIL 7" 1864
Grand-Ecore Louisiana

We marched at 9.A.M. on the Natchatoches road. it commenced raining at 11.A.M. and continued all day. at night we were 14. miles out. passed through a poor pine country, but sparcely settled by a class of poor people. rained at night. some of the officers slept in the Negro quarters.~

FRIDAY APRIL 8" 1864
Camp in Field Louisiana

Marched at 7.A.M. Weather delightful. the country continues poor. in the afternoon we heard heavy canonading at the front. We camped near Pleasant Hill, after dark. learn that the rebels captured a considerable portion of Bank's train and artillery and got the best of the fight.~

SATURDAY APRIL 9" 1864
Pleasant Hill Louisiana

We learned this morning that the 13th A.C. of Bank's army was over powered, and demoralized yesterday, for want of support. We moved up and took position in the town. Bank's troops fell back in the rear of Smith's guerrillas, and at 4.P.M. the rebels horde came upon us with deafning yells, were received cooly and repulsed after a desperate encounter of about four hours. and we held the field.~

SUNDAY APRIL 10" 1864
Pleasant Hill Louisiana

At sunup I found my self in a field hospital and the army five miles off, on a retreat, having drawn off at 2.A.M. under cover of night. I was on foot and in company with John Jenkins we pushed forward and overtook the army after traveling ten miles. camped at 2.P.M. and dressed the wounded

MONDAY APRIL 11" 1864
Camp in Field Louisiana

We started at 7.A.M. and got back to Grand Ecore before night. found the boats had gone up the river and rations scarce. We went into camp near where we were before. found Gen'l Bank's army in camp. also found some of our missing, who we had supposed lost on the field of action.

TUESDAY APRIL 12" 1864
Grand-Ecore Louisiana

We lay in camp all day. I went to the general Hospital and helped to dress the wounded. there seems to be a good many of them for the time the fight lasted, and the number engaged. Lt. Kerr returned from home. also a large mail was received; I rec'd letters from J.F.B. & Lyde

WEDNESDAY APRIL 13" 1864
Grand-Ecore Louisiana

Major T.W. Morgan's resignation came back to day approved; which was sent off last winter while at Memphis Tenn, and was supposed to be lost, and he had abandoned the idea of quitting the service at present. He made the boys a little speech and bade them fare well. and thus we lost the best officer the Regt ever had. he left for home. Capt Wm P. Moore went down the river wounded. Our brig. & Col Shaw's went up the river by land after night.

THURSDAY APRIL 14" 1864
Campti Louisiana

We moved up to the town, and found the rebels had left. found the transports considerably riddled. by rebel shots. I found Wm Davis of Co. "E,, wounded in the arm. lay by until afternoon when we returned We left the 117th Ills to guard some boats that were a-ground and disabled. I rec'd letters J.F.B. & Lyde.~

FRIDAY APRIL 15" 1864
Grand-Ecore Louisiana

In camp all day. I slept three hours to make up lost time, while up to Campti to rescue the boats the rebels had. had a battery below them, and wouldn't let them pass. they had started to Shreevesport all quiet at the front. the 117th still up at Campti.   I wrote to J.F.B. & Lyde.~

SATURDAY APRIL 16" 1864
GrandEcore Louisiana

I settled up with Capt. J.W. Cheney to day, and loaned Lt. John L. Stanley $.15.00. The Governor of Mo. was here to day and the Mo. troops were out on review Gen'l Smith; Mower; Totten and others made speeches to them. J.A. Smith of Co."I, died at 8.P.M. considerable Diarrhaeas in camp now~

SUNDAY APRIL 17" 1864
Grand-Ecore Louisiana

I sent off nine of the sickest men of the Reg't to Alexandria, which indicates that there is a move in comtemplation at no distant day~ I loaned S.T. Gray $.2.00. The river is falling one of the gun boats sank below here This has been a dull day every-body is tired of the place, and anxious to move one way or the other. any thing is preferable to remaining here.

MONDAY APRIL 18" 1864
Grand Ecore Louisiana

Moved out to camp except the sick the boats are going down the river. I left my Valise on the boat in room "C,, it is to heavy to carry along in an ambulance Gen Banks is fortifying this place as though he thought he had "gave the rebels time to con centrate."

TUESDAY APRIL 19" 1864
Grand Ecore Louisiana

We were up and in line of battle at day light but no enemy made his appearance. Banks is fortifying. the boats are ordered to Alexandria, to tie up there, and await Gen'l Smith's orders The indications are that we will go down the river soon. and all are anxious.

WEDNESDAY APRIL 20" 1864
Grand-Ecore Louisiana

Lt. Wm Whaling reported dismissed the service, in the Army & Navy Journal. we got up a petition to have him reinstated. At 3.P.M.

~Smith's army moved out to Natchitoches skirmished with the rebels and took position on the western border of the town and camped for the night.~

THURSDAY APRIL 21" 1864
Natchitoches Louisiana

We lay in camp and skirmished with the rebels all day after night we moved back across Cane river and started down the country. our move out here had been to cover Bank's retreat. he hadn't got into the road in advance as intended, so we had to wait for him all night without orders, even to camp. we stood in line of march til day. every body tired and out of patience. the rebels discovered our move in the night.

FRIDAY APRIL 22" 1864
Natchitoches Louisiana

Moved at an early hour. the rebels attacked the rear at noon, while Banks' had found obstructions at the front. F.J.Burrows & I went forward to the wagon train and got some dinner. We marched until a late hour at night, and found the advance stoped by an enemy at the front, at Cloutierville

SATURDAY APRIL 23" 1864
Cloutierville Louisiana

Corralled the teams and fighting commenced at the front at an early hour, and at about 11.A.M. we were attacked at the rear. the "guerrillas" were about faced and drove them off. the 49" made a gallant charge. The command moved forward a few miles and camped for the night on a very pretty place for a fight.

SUNDAY APRIL 24" 1864
Camp in Field Louisiana

Our pickets were attacked at 2.A.M. Gen'l Mower opened on the rebels with artillery. at 7.A.M. we went into position, and into the fight in cool earnest. Smith Masked [Massed] a brigade of inft. and a battery and punished the rebels severely. We lost 8. Killed, and 30. Wounded. We crossed Cane river, and reached Catile Landing after night.

MONDAY APRIL 25" 1864
Catile Landing Louisiana

Marched at 8.A.M. the rebels fired at us without effect, from Pine Hills. drove them back and skirmished all day. Banks' army came down the river road, a shorter way. we camped after marching about 12. miles, rations scarce and feet sore. This is soldiering under difficulties It is buying glory at an advanced rate. Not getting much credit for our services either~

TUESDAY APRIL 26" 1864
Bayou Rapides Louisiana

Started at 7.A.M. for Alexandria with high hopes of getting out of the Dept soon. We arrived at Alexandria at 4.P.M. amid the hayahs [harrahs] & cheer of the men of the 13. A.C. Gen'l John A. McClernand's and some of his A.C. just from New Orleans. Banks' men came in the near way. I loaned S.C. Goshorn $.5.00, to day~

WEDNESDAY APRIL 27" 1864
Alexandria Louisiana

We rested from our labors to-day. lay in camp not even an interesting rumor afloat. I tried to buy a pair of shoes but the sutlers are all closed "by order" The river has fallen so that the boats cannot pass over the falls just above the town. I wrote to J.F.B. & Lyde~

THURSDAY APRIL 28" 1864
Alexandria Louisiana

We were out in line of battle in the P.M. fighting on the right. We lay in line of battle all night, not heard the result, several fires in the country not far off. Our boat ordered to take on 200 bushels of coal, which we think indicates a move soon, and we can not [determine] how soon

FRIDAY APRIL 29" 1864
Alexandria Louisiana

We were ordered to camp without a fight, no rebels of any consequence near. some of Banks' men burned a lot of government property, in the way of forager yesterday on the strength of their scare~ The river full of boats, they pass and repass below here. those of our fleet ordered to draw five days rations. the gun boats are above the falls and unable to pass. weather warm and pleasant.

SATURDAY APRIL 30" 1864
Alexandria Louisiana

We received orders to be ready to move at 6.A.M. with one days rations. we waited all day and didn't move, troops being thrown across the river, for fatigue duty. the river has to be damed up befor the boats can pass, the falls. the current is rapid and it will take considerable time and work. The weather is pleasant and the season about as far advanced as June 30" in Ills. I bought a pair of boots yesterday for $.12.00. Soldiers have to pay exorbitant prices for every thing bought of sutlers here~ a month ago we were at Catile Landing on our way up the river, thinking there was sufficient rebel force west of the Mississippi river to seriously impede our progress. but it seems we failed to accomplish the objects of the Expedition. but it is generally conceeded to be more from the stupidity and incompetency of our General (N.P. Banks) than from the Numerical strength of the rebel force, or the Extraordinary generalship of the opposing Commanders. The Campaign has Cost heavily in Men & Means. in Men by casualities of battle but, worse, in the impaired health of the troops= to say nothing of the vast expence, to the Government= in supplying the fleet= and Army for so long a time=

SUNDAY MAY 1" 1864
Alexandria Louisiana

I paid the Mess half a month's board $.5.00. Sent ten sick men to Hospital to day. there are numerous rumors in camp in regard to what we are going to do. It is currently reported that there is a battery (rebel) below us. Cavalry had a skirmish with rebels a cross the river to day; Men are at work daming the river from the opposite bank.

MONDAY MAY 2" 1864
Alexandria Louisiana

We were ordered out at 1.P.M. up the Bayou Rapides road. found the enemy in considerable force three miles from town, skirmished until dark, and then our brigade drew off and were replaced by an other. We lay on our arms for the night. no serious damage done on either side

TUESDAY MAY 3" 1864
Bayou Rapides Louisiana

We marched at 6.A.M. on the Appalosous road, 8. miles and found the rebels in force, near Gov Moore's (rebel) plantation skirmished with them pretty lively. drove them back and burned some cane, and then fell back to Moore's plantation and camped

WEDNESDAY MAY 4" 1864
Gov. T.O. Moore's Plantation La.

We were in the second line to day; skirmishing went on all day. I was sent to the front and found a rebel wounded by the name of Wm. Tulley formerly of Salem Ills. and cousin to John Tulley Wagons foraging for horse feed and sugar at the skirmish line to day.

THURSDAY MAY 5" 1864
Gov. T.O. Moore's Plantation La

Still at the same place Lieut. A.S. Rowley R.Q.M. came out with some rations. I sent to town for medicines, heavy canonading heard in different directions to day. Cavalry at the front doing the skirmishing to day; Weather dry and roads very dusty Medicines very scarce, as we did not contemplate this expedition at our last drawing, and have had no opportunity of drawing since.

FRIDAY MAY 6" 1864
Gov. T. O. Moore's Plantation La.

Ordered to be ready to move at 6.A.M. but moved to the rear at _P.M. to guard a crossing there. some fighting at the front but not many casualties there We are about one and a half miles from the front guarding a crossing to the rear of the right flank on Roberts Bayou.

SATURDAY MAY 7" 1864
Robert's Bayou Louisiana

Lay around all day no excitement in the field very little fighting done. the rebels were driven six miles and we hold the field. I bought some chickens, and had some dinner to day. Eating is the Exception, and doing without the rule since we have been out here~

SUNDAY MAY 8" 1864
Robbert's Bayou Louisiana

Our forces drawn off to their former position Not quite ready to advance yet. the dam is doing fine and will be ready for the boats to pass soon. then we will show the rebels that we can go where we please, asking them no addos but driving them out of our way.~

MONDAY MAY 9" 1864
Gov. T.O. Moore's Plantation La

I sent to the river for my boots by Dr Jennings of the 117" Ills Infty quite a number of men and officers went back to town to-day Orders received preparatory to a move down the country. I think we will not be here many days longer. The men are suffering for some new clothing. many of them have not a change, nor even one, decent suit of clothes.

TUESDAY MAY 10" 1864
Gov. T.O. Moore's Plantation La.

Skirmishing this morning at the front, our Brigade went out to meet the enemy, but he retired. Gen'l Mower sent for a section of Artilery and shelled them, a little. I got some Opium and Quinine from Dr. Jennings Ass't Surg. 117" Ills. one man wounded in the arm to day.

opium

WEDNESDAY MAY 11" 1864
Gov. T.O. Moore's Plantation La

I went to Alexandria to day. was up at the falls Work of daming progressing finely. Gun boats will get over soon. I saw Lieuts Stanley & Mitchell in town, returned to camp with them. I bought some black berries in town to-day. Lt. James Reed in arrest by one of Mowers aids.

THURSDAY MAY 12" 1864
Gov. T.O. Moore's Plantation La

In camp all day. a flag of truce sent out to day to the enemy, with regard to the exchange of prisoners. no fighting to-day. there was one man wounded last night on the picket line. arrangements are being made for a move, to take place soon.

FRIDAY MAY 13" 1864
Gov. T.O. Moore's Plantation La.

Gun boats all over the falls, pioneer parties sent out to day to repair the roads. Troops moving out from Alexandria on the river road. All quiet at the front lines to-day. Gen'l A.J. Smith came out from town this evening. Every thing now indicates a move immediately. Orders rec'd from Bank forbidding the destruction of private property. Orders rec'd to move.

SATURDAY MAY 14" 1864
Gov. T.O. Moore's Plantation La.

Marched at Sun-up on the road along the river bank. found the boats going down the river. We protected them on the right, but several of them were fired into from the opposite bank of the river Eli Porter, Co. "F,, was wounded in the foot on a boat. skirmished with the rebels on the right bank in P.M.

SUNDAY MAY 15" 1864
Red River Louisiana

We moved down the river again. we took a near cut, and left the river several miles, and arrived at Fort De-Russy after dark. had another skirmish with the rebels near there. found the boats had gone on down the river without us. we expected to re-embark here. the men are out of patience

MONDAY MAY 16" 1864
Fort De-Russy Louisiana

Marched at 3.A.M. to Marksville firing at the front. Moved out on an open prairie and opened with artillery some fine manouvering. we drove the enemy off the field and took up the line of march, after the finest display of troops I ever witnessed; We crossed Bayou De-Glaze and camped for the night.

TUESDAY MAY 17" 1864
Bayou De-Glaze Louisiana

Heavy skrimishing at the rear; The Cavalry suffered considerably; We moved at noon and fought most of the day at the rear. Gen'l Mower opened on the enemy with a ten gun battery, and drove them off Col.

Pease rejoined the regiment this evening after an absence of Seven Months Oct. 16" 63. Months, on recruiting service in Illinois.

WEDNESDAY MAY 18" 1864
Yellow Bayou Louisiana

We moved across yellow Bayou, but fighting commenced on the other side in which the 1st & 2nd Brigades suffered severely, though they captured 150. prisoners. We relieved them before dark, and, we removed to our former position near the Bayou. By order of Gen'l Smith

THURSDAY MAY 19" 1864
Yellow Bayou Louisiana

Moved but little to day; had no fighting of any consequence; A flag of truce came in to day from the enemy. rumor says with a mail from prisoners they hold; but more probably with a view to the Exchange of prisoners, and perhaps to take observations.

FRIDAY MAY 20" 1864
Yellow Bayou Louisiana

Moved across the bayou and took position behind it. the rebels came in sight, and exchanged a few shots at long range, without effect on either side. we drew off and crossed the Atchafalaya at Simsport, and now have to march to the mouth of old river.

SATURDAY MAY 21" 1864
Simsport Louisiana

Marched at Sunup, and arrived at the Mississippi river at 10.A.M. I found my Henry Rifle which was lost at Vicksburg. I paid the man $.5.00 for finding, or stealing it, I dont know which. I paid the Mess $5.00 for board. The 52nd Ind. Infty. rejoined our Brigade this evening, have been absensent, since we left Canton Miss, on veteran furlough, and have mist the hardest campaign of the season perhaps by it.

SUNDAY MAY 22" 1864
Mouth of Red River Louisiana

Re-embarked and started up the river at 10.A.M. tugging the Str. Sioux City. We are about the 15th boat in the fleet and are running very slow. Lieut. S. Sondag Co. "H,, in arrest for drunkenness. The river in fine stage for boating, being most bank full. weather warm~

MONDAY MAY 23" 1864
On board Str Liberty La.

I spent most of the day in the cabbin as it is very warm and nothing of interest in sight any where. the river is high and the country level, and fertile, and in times of peace has been quite wealthy. We arrived at Vicksburg at midnight. Very glad to get back even here.

TUESDAY MAY 24" 1864
Vicksburg Mississippi

We dis-embarked on the level land below town among the carcasses of the dead mules and horses that have been hauled here during the War. I paid the for pair pants $.2.50 Loaned Col Pease $.10.00 to day. The R.Q.M. drawing clothing for the Reg't. I went to town and eat ice cream, it is a luxury with us.~

Ice Cream

WEDNESDAY MAY 25" 1864
Vicksburg Mississippi

In camp all day Most of the boats went across the river to take on some coal, and ours didn't return until after midnight I lay on a log at the river bank until it came. All hands making payrolls, some prospect of our getting some money soon, it is a scarce article with most of the men. I wrote to J.F.B.

THURSDAY MAY 26" 1864
Vicksburg Mississippi

I made a special requisition and drew some medicines to day. A boat fired into near the mouth of the Arkansas river, on the Mississippi. Col. Shaw's Brig. said to be going up there to morrow. Hanley King came to see me. I wrote to R.M.L.

FRIDAY MAY 27" 1864
Vicksburg Mississippi

The Q.M. drew a new Ambulance and team for us, and turned over the old one to-day. this time he got a tolerable good pair of Horses The weather is warm, dry and dusty. we are using the river water and it is'nt good. I wrote to A.K.A.~

SATURDAY MAY 28" 1864
Vicksburg Mississippi

Nothing in camp of interest only a general desire to go up the river. Many rumors in regard to our being paid off, and leaving here but it seems to end in rumors. good news from Gen'ls Grant and Sherman.

SUNDAY MAY 29" 1864
Vicksburg Mississippi

I got up sick this morning with Diarrhaea. I attended sick call though it required quite an effort to get out to camp. I couldn't eat any thing all day. The health of the Reg't is fast failing Many of the men got Diarrhaeas owing to bad water and the warm weather, and ther having no good shelter from the hot sun; and cool nights.

MONDAY MAY 30" 1864
Vicksburg Mississippi

Still sick. I feel tolerably well while lying down, but dizzy and weak when walking about. I have my usual duties to perform whether sick or well. Dr. Medcalf is on duty with the Division Commander, a Sinecure Col. P. Pease paid me $.10.00 borrowed money to day.

TUESDAY MAY 31" 1864
Vicksburg Mississippi

I made out monthly reports to day; also Personal Reports. I sent J.S. White Co. "F,, & John Smithschneider Co. "A,, to Gen'l Hospital here to day. I had a difficulty with Capt Laur Co. "K,, in refrence to sending Wiggins of his company to Hosp't. Medcalf interfered in his behalf and prevented me sending him; I sent for ice; to the Medical Director for the use of the sick remaning in my charge, but it was refused, after being fully assured by the Div. Surg. that any thing essencial to treating the sick would be furnished upon application; S.T. Gray Co. "D,, very ill with Pneumonia his recovery very doubtfull.~ No news from the north except rumor.

WEDNESDAY JUNE 1" 1864
Vicksburg Mississippi

I eat some peaches and Blackberries as usually the case with sick persons those things least suited to their case are the ones most desired, and will generally be indulged regardless of ulterior consequences; I had a little settlement with Dr. Medcalf before Col Pease in refrence to sending men to Gen'l Hospital yesterday.

THURSDAY JUNE 2" 1864
Vicksburg Mississippi

There was not much stir in camp until evening, when we got orders to load our transportation on to the boat, preparatory to starting up the river, and an order to be ready to start at an hours notice. The weather very warm.

FRIDAY JUNE 3" 1864
Vicksburg Mississippi

It rained this morning the Reg't re-embarked and waited all day impatiently for the signal to start. (one long whistle.) but no signal heard. Went up town and bought one dozen cans of fruit, to eat on the way. Rec'd a letter from Lyde.

SATURDAY JUNE 4" 1864
Vicksburg Mississippi

Our boat, (with the rest of the fleet) lay at the shore until noon, when the long whistle announced the glad tidings that all was ready. We shoved out, and bid a final farewell to the Maiden City as we rounded the point at the mouth of Yazoo River

SUNDAY JUNE 5" 1864
On board Str. Liberty No. 2

We run along fine all day, until about 4.P.M. when we rounded-to at the point where the rebel battery was said to be located. We disembarked and got ready to move out, but were ordered to camp for the night, so we camped and fought mosquitoes. The Cavalry went out on a reconnaisance artilery and ambulances being unloaded.

MONDAY JUNE 6" 1864
(Chicot Co. Arkansas)

The command moved out through the rain and mud, and found the enemy in considerable force, on the opposite side of a bayou, in a strong position Gen'l Mower charged and drove them out, loosing forty men Killed, and one hundred wounded. Henry Risley Co. "K,, accidently wounded. We camped at Lake Villiage.

TUESDAY JUNE 7" 1864
(Lake Villiage Arkansas)

I went to the Hosp'tl and helped to load the wounded into ambulances. we started at 7.A.M. and drove over a very rough road a distance of eight miles and arrived at Columbia Ark. where the boats were in waiting. We reembarked the rebels came up and captured a man, and skirmished all the evening.

WEDNESDAY JUNE 8" 1864
(Columbia Arkansas)

We started early, and run all day and night we past the mouth of White river at dark, stoped for wood but did'nt get any, as the wood was not very convinient and the bank was very muddy. it rained at night and was quite dark, but we kept running nevertheless. all hands are in a hurry.

THURSDAY JUNE 9" 1864
(On board Str Liberty)

We stoped this morning and took on wood. arrived at Helena at 11.A.M. stoped and Frank & I went up town and got paper of the 6th inst. I got a $.100.00 bill changed and loaned F.J. Burrows $.10.00. We started at noon again. most of the companies got some fresh bread; some of the men whisky and were a little boisterous in consequence of it.

FRIDAY JUNE 10" 1864
(Memphis Tennessee)

Arrived here this morning at day light and re-mained on the boats til afternoon Dr. Mercer returned to the Reg't after an absence of Ten Months found Lt. Spiro and others of the Reg't here, in waiting I sent fourteen sick men to Gen'l Hospital to day sick. We moved out two miles on the Hernando road & camped.

SATURDAY JUNE 11" 1864
Memphis Tennessee

I went to town to day and bought a linnen coat, and left my dress coat at Isaac Isaacs to be repaired and cleaned. I loaned Capt. J.W. Cheney $.20.00 to day and S. Bacon $.1.00. I went to see Col. David Moore Div. Commander in regard to drawing an ambulance and medicines~

SUNDAY JUNE 12" 1864
Memphis Tennessee

In camp all day. disastrous news from Gen'l Sturgis' command, said to be falling back in disorder. has lost 180. wagons and about 16 pieces of artillery. Another Banks affair only on a smaller scale. he has most of the colored troops from this place

MONDAY JUNE 13" 1864
Memphis Tennessee

In camp until afternoon then went to town; Saw a lot of Gen'l Sturgis' men coming in, stragling. It seems his defeat has been disgracefully disastrous, inferior to Bank's only in point of numbers   I went to the theatre at night play, "Satan in Paris" Gen'l A.J. Smith was present   not a very large house to night.

TUESDAY JUNE 14" 1864
Memphis Tennessee

Our (3rd) Brig. returned from White's Station to night where they have been to protect Sturgis' stragling column. We had company drill to day in our Reg't. The Q.M. drew some drums for our Musicians and we had dressparade this evening. In camp all day.

WEDNESDAY JUNE 15" 1864
Memphis Tennessee

Prospect of our going out east to morrow, to do Gen'l Sturgis' work for him. Our officers are making every effort to get our veteran furlough, which it seems is being strongly combated by some of our commanding officers either division or A.C. Corps

THURSDAY JUNE 16" 1864
Memphis Tennessee
We had orders yesterday to be ready to move at 2.P.M. to day; but didn't get the order to march. It rained in the afternoon. The Q.M. drew another ambulance to day. Dr. Mercer went on duty to day. I went down town and got my coat, and bought a hat.

FRIDAY JUNE 17" 1864
Memphis Tennessee
Some of the colored troops went out towards Moscow on the train to-day. Some one-hundred-day men in camp here now. Capt. Wm. P. Moore returned from home to day been absent since we were at Grand-Ecore his arm is not well yet, where he was wounded at Pleasant Hill La. April 9" 1864. Gen'l. A.J. Smith is a Major General, now.

SATURDAY JUNE 18" 1864
Memphis Tennessee
Some talk of our getting pay now; but it is hard telling when we will get it, though. Dr. S.F.F. Mercer put on duty with the 32nd Iowa Infty for the time being. Surgeons are very scarce in this part of the army now, owing to sickness and detached service.

SUNDAY JUNE 19" 1864
Memphis Tennessee

In camp all day; preaching in the 49" & 117" Ills. and in the 52" Ind Infty. to day. I sent a Co. "H,, man to Gen'l Hospital. I heard to day that Frank Black [J.F.B., James' brother] was wounded in the leg in one of the recent fights in Georgia. I wrote to J.F.B. & Lyde.

MONDAY JUNE 20" 1864
Memphis Tennessee
Rained this morning, the 1st Brigade being paid off to day; peddlers & husksters are all attracted there now; Money has great attractions for them, as well as for most other classes of individuals. There is another move in contemplation.

TUESDAY JUNE 21 1864
Memphis Tennessee

The 117" Ills is being paid off to day. our regiment will be left until after the Reg'ts are paid off that are going to accompany Gen'l. Smith in his expedition over the teritory where Gen'l Sturgis made such disastrous failure; It is not positively decided yet so far as we know whether we will get home or not now.

WEDNESDAY JUNE 22" 1864
Memphis Tennessee

The 52" Ind. 117" Ills & 178" N.Y. Reg'ts started for the depot of the M.C. R.R. I let Dr. Garrison have my ambulance to take some sick men to Gen'l Hospital; A lot of men of the Brigade behind on a big drunk, to day There are always some straglers.~

THURSDAY JUNE 23 1864
Memphis Tennessee

After considerable trouble we received the order to go to Illinois on veteran furlough. Leaving behind six line officrs and one Surg. I went down town with the ambulance and took Capt. Cogan & Lieut Lemmon to see Genl Smith in regard to the details.~

FRIDAY JUNE 24" 1864
Memphis Tennessee

The Reg't was paid off to day by four paymasters; I was paid $.445.20 by Maj. Jamison. Then the Reg't, except the non veterans, packed up and marched down to the wharf and went on board the Str. Hanibal, and started up the river for Cairo during the night.

SATURDAY JUNE 25" 1864
On board Str Hanibal

We only run part of last night it being very dark. Started early this morning and run all day, though not very fast. weather very warm and dry. all are anxious to get along as fast as posible; some of the boys have not been home since their first enlistment the furlough was the principle stimulant to re-enlist.

SUNDAY JUNE 26" 1864
On board Str Hanibal

We past Island No. 10. at day light. We stoped at Columbus Ky. and drew some rations Then came on to Cairo. Saw Calvin Scott, & B.F. Marshall. We embarked on train, and lay there all night; to be ready to start in the morning for Centralia Ills.

MONDAY JUNE 27" 1864
Cairo Illinois

Started at 6.A.M. and arrived at Centralia at 4.P.M. making very poor time. I sent the sick to Soldiers home, and then got permission and left for Salem. I found all well and expecting me home. I only got leave for the night, return to morrow.

TUESDAY JUNE 28" 1864
Salem Illinois

I returned to Centralia at 9.A.M. Capt. Wm P. Moore returned from Springfield with furloughs for the men, and all hands are busy preparing their rolls & papers. I called upon E.M. and at night I wrote to R.M.L.~

WEDNESDAY JUNE 29" 1864
Centralia Illinois

Wm P. Moore returned to day instead of yesterday, and is commissioned Major of the Reg't. The men were furloughed and most of them left for their homes this evening. I called upon the Misses Jackson this evening with F.J. Burrows and found them very agreeable young ladies and spent a very pleasant evening. I got my furlough and came to Salem to night.

THURSDAY JUNE 30" 1864
Salem Illinois

I went out to George Williams with Mother to day, to see Magrett. I went to see the meadow but the grass on it is not worth cutting. The corn looks very small to me after seeing corn much larger two months ago in Louisiana. the weather is very dry~

One month ago we were at Vicksburg anxiously awaiting orders to come up the river to Memphis and two months ago we were at

Alexandria La. with but little knowledge of when we would get out of that disastrous Campaign.= it requires a good share of equanimity to patiently endure all the vicissitudes of war, and by the way the active campaigning and fighting even, is not always the hardest part of the service, but laying at some out of the way, place, where mails, and news, are not obtainable, and no known object for remaining at the place, with its attendant inconviniences and embarrassments, sometime puts a Soldiers powers of Endurance to a severe test.= but in the coming Month we hope circumstances will make some reparation for the hardships, and privations of the past few Months.

FRIDAY JULY 1" 1864
Salem Illinois

Frank J. Burrows Started for his home in Pennsylvania; called upon Capt Lydick to-day. We had a fine shower of rain; not many citizens in from the country all busy harvesting; hands scarce and high wages from $.2.00 to $.2.50 per day~ though I am not desirous enough of company of the male persuasion to follow them to the harvest field.

SATURDAY JULY 2" 1864
Salem Illinois

I went to the depot and telegraped to Nashvile Tenn; to find if Frank Black was in Hospital there; I took dinner at D.P. Myers, and spent the evening at Uncle T.J. Black's. quite a number of ladies in during the evening. I went with Lyde to Moody's.

SUNDAY JULY 3" 1864
Salem Illinois

I went to church this A.M. Zue came home with us. Uncle Mark Lovell came to town this evening. Lt. E.B. Harlan came home to day; he is going to be married to morrow to Miss Mary Crundwell at Uncle Tom's I am going to be at the wedding.

MONDAY JULY 4" 1864
Salem Illinois

I went up town and saw Lt. Harlan. Then to Moody's and took dinner, and at 4.P.M. to Uncle Tom's and saw Harlan Married by the

Rev. T.F. Houts. they left on evening train Picnic at the fair ground. S.L. Bryan Schaffre & T.E. Merritt made speeches.

TUESDAY JULY 5" 1864
Salem Illinois

Col. P. Pease and a delegation of the Union-League from Centralia came up and held a meeting at the Court House; C.R. O'Neill was in town He & the Col. took supper with me; then I got aboard the train and went to St Louis Mo. with the Col. to make a little draw on the Pay Master; we stoped at the Everett House at 1. Oclock at night.~

WEDNESDAY JULY 6" 1864
St. Louis Missouri

I saw Capt. Cogan Lt. McGregor & Jim Pickett there. We called upon Major O.W. Ballard and I was paid $.223.35 to include June 30" 1864. Then I bought a Saddle and rigging for $.64.00. bought a velvet vest $.15.00 or rather left my measure for one. I returned to Salem Ills at night.

THURSDAY JULY 7" 1864
Salem Illimois

I went out to New Middleton to buy a horse I eat dinner at H.W. Eagan's, and supper at Granville Cheeley's but didn't find a horse to suit. I saw Matt Arnold. I visited at Sol. Smith's Most of the land near the station is in cultivation since I left here~

FRIDAY JULY 8" 1864
Salem Illinois

I sent to Memphis Tenn. for some Photografs spent the day in town. not many in. business dull, weather warm, with occasional showers. I went down to Moody's in the evening. and to day I wrote to R.M.L., J.F.B., & S.F.F.M.~

SATURDAY JULY 9" 1864
Salem Illinois

In town all day. all quiet. Mother went to Georges. Tom. brought the filley home. I went to Uncle Tom's to see him in regard to his be-comimg a candidate for Circuit Clerk this fall on the Union Ticket. he consented and I wrote to Col. P. Pease in refrence to it, as he wants to announce his name at Centralia.

SUNDAY JULY 10" 1864
Salem Illinois

I went to Preaching in the A.M. in the M.E. Church. Matt Cunningham, John White & Bart Barnes returned from the army to-day. This has been a dull day. I made no calls, and received none. home seems very dull, not stir enough.

MONDAY JULY 11" 1864
Salem Illinois

Mrs Pruden; & Miss. Torrence were at our house to-day. I was in town all day. not many people in from the country; harvest is still on hand. The weather is warm and pleasant In the evening I wrote to Lt. J.L. Stanley

TUESDAY JULY 12" 1864
Salem Illinois

I went to Centralia to day with Zue. spent a pleasant evening at Mrs Baker's. I stoped at the Merritt House; I saw Capt. L. Kurghoff and the boys that were left there in charge of the arms and Regimental property.~

WEDNESDAY JULY 13" 1864
Centralia Illinois

I went down to Richview to see Lt Rowley and Capt. Houston; Lieut. James Reed Co. "F,, died there July 1st 1864.= he was very ill when he arrived. I returned to Salem and Judge S.L. Bryan & Lady called to see me; also the Misses Moore. Commissions came to day for Wm. P. Moore & J.E. Gauen for Moore as Lt. Col. and for Gauen as Major of the Reg't. The germans are enraged.

THURSDAY JULY 14" 1864
Salem Illinois

I left town at 10.A.M. and went to Omega with Lyde & Lute, by way of Red Lake prairie arrived at Uncle Mark Lovell's at noon; and stoped there for the night; I saw Mr. Hammond for the first time, he is keeping a little store at Omega, and doing some business at it.~

FRIDAY JULY 15" 1864
Omega Illinois

I went with Dr. Smith to see some patients. then went to Uncle Will Hensley's and to Aunt Martha's then went to C.R. O'Neill's to stay over night. found all in tolerable health and enjoying the comforts of home and its associations a blessing only appreciated fully by us soldiers.

SATURDAY JULY 16" 1864
Omega Illinois

Started home, and called at Uncle Will's then drove to Stringtown and stoped at Mr. H. Pruden's for dinner. then came to town P.M. and went to D.P. Myers to a party given by him for the soldiers of Salem that are at home. We had a pleasant evening of it.

SUNDAY JULY 17" 1864
Salem Illinois

I was at home all day, and spent seemingly the warmest; and the dullest day of the season; There was preaching at the M.E. Church, but I thought it to warm to be confined in the house so long hence I stayed at home, and enjoyed myself as best I could under the circumstances. I wrote to John Keen Jr.

MONDAY JULY 18" 1864
Salem Illinois

I went out to George Williams' to spend the day but T.M. Smith (formerly of Co. "D,,[)] came out to see me in refrence to a certificate for pension. I returned to town with him; I settled with Uncle Tom. J. Black and paid him $.63.40 in full. I set up with D.P. Myers. (sick)

TUESDAY JULY 19" 1864
Salem Illinois

I went with Lyde & Lute to Uncle Wm. Black's to spend the day Zue Moody went with us. Uncle Wm was stacking wheat, found him a Union Man. We spent a very pleasant day. Lizzy Black returned to Salem with us, on a visit. The weather is warm and dry.

222

WEDNESDAY JULY 20" 1864
Salem Illinois

We went out to Uncle Wilk. Allmon's to day by way of Geo Williams'. Zue, accompanied us again to day. We spent the day there, and came to Wm. Marshall's for supper, we returned to Salem after dark the evening quite cool. we spent a pleasant day.

THURSDAY JULY 21" 1864
Salem Illinois

In town all day. Not many people in, harvest is on hand, and hands are scarce and hard to get. I paid B.B. Smith $.18.67, on account of Smith & Castellow; an error in the amount I think. it should be but $.5.30 he agrees to correct it, if it exists. The acct was made with Castellow and he is in the army now.~

FRIDAY JULY 22" 1864
Salem Illinois

I was in town all day; Not much doing. Uncle Robt. Black was in to see me, and staid for dinner; he is a copperhead. Uncle Wilk was in town; also Julia Allmon I loafed most of the day, and found it quite stale amusement.

SATURDAY JULY 23" 1864
Salem Illinois

I went to the train for papers, and met Ella Moody there, went home with her. Mother & Lyde came down and we all took dinner at Moody's Then went to Mason's gallery, and had some Photograps taken for all present. I got my H. Rifle from Freeman's shop.~

SUNDAY JULY 24" 1864
Salem Illinois

I was to church in A.M.; I went to Moody's with Lyde & Lute; Mr. Geo. Holton was there; he took Ella to Centralia in a buggy Misses Story & Lackey were at Moody's Went to church at night. Rev. Mr. Clifford preached. I took Zue and went home with her after church and we were engaged to night.~

MONDAY JULY 25" 1864
Salem Illinois

We had Moody's; Myres; Lt. Walker's and Albert Allmon to our house for supper this evening. I redeemed my land from P.P. Hamilton's tax title to day. I paid him $.30.00 on the N.W. qr; of the S.E. qr; of Sec. one; of Town two North; of Range three East. W.W. Willard took the acknowledgement of the deed Paying taxes is a profitable business~

TUESDAY JULY 26" 1864
Salem Illinois

I went to Centralia; and Ella Moody went with me to Richview. We called upon Miss Ella Barnes at a Mr. Walker's then I bought a horse of a Mr. Howard for $.160.00 left him there and returned to Odin and stoped with Uncle Benj. Woodard for the night. Em Turner was there.

WEDNESDAY JULY 27" 1864
Odin Illinois

I returned to Salem, and hitched up and took the girls, and went out to Mr. Pruden's on a visit. We went down to Mr. S.B. Arnold's a little while in the evening, then returned to Pruden's to stay over night. We find this much pleasanter than soldiering~

THURSDAY JULY 28" 1864
Stringtown Illinois

We went down to Mr Arnold's and took dinner then we called at Mr. Torrence's a little while then at Pruden's; then home. Misses. Matt. Arnold & Ann Pruden accompanied us. F.J. Burrows came down in the evening and we had a good time generally then.~

FRIDAY JULY 29" 1864
Salem Illinois

In town all day. I sent Sol. Smith $.15.00 by mail. due to Smith & Rollings Lyde & I went over to Mr. Blessing's and took supper. In the evening Zue & Hellen Moody came up Margrett Williams came to town in the P.M. to see me. this is the last day of my furlough, and it seems to me to have been the shortest month of the year.

SATURDAY JULY 30" 1864
Salem Illinois

I went down to Centralia on the 9.A.M. train Lyde Lute & Tom, and Zue Moody went with me Lyde & Zue & I called at Col. P. Pease in the evening. Lute went home with Lizzy Johnson; then we went to the ice cream saloon. A Det. of the Reg't sent up to Vandalia to quiet a disturbance. I went to Richview for my horse.

SUNDAY JULY 31" 1864
Richview Illinois

I got my horse from Mr. Howard paid him $.4.00 for keeping him for me, and rode him to Centralia. The roads were very dusty until I got most to town. The officers and men of the regiment are coming in very slow. I washed and dressed to go to church but was to late. I went home with Lyde & Lute. took Capt. Cheney with me. Frank J. Burrows went up the road to Kimmundy to take another lesson in millinery. Capt. J.H. Lockwood came in from home. he has bought a young horse. a difficulty up the road at Ramsey Ills. between the copperheads & Union men. There is a regular organization of men in that vicinity committing murders, arson & robbery in defiance of the laws.

MONDAY AUGUST 1" 1864
Salem Illinois

As there was to be no train on the O.&M. R.R. we hitched to the hack; and Tom started with us at 8.A.M. for Tonti; but when we arrived the train had gone; so we went to Odin and then to Centralia in the hack. twenty five of the men of our Reg't are gone up to Ramsey to quell a disturbance there. The men are coming in very slow.

TUESDAY AUGUST 2" 1864
Centralia Illinois

Our detachment returned from the north at 12. O'clock last night. Noah Byrum was arrested and taken up the road for shooting a man last night. I went with Col. Wm P. Moore to Central City and called upon the Misses Stubblefield I went with Zue to a concert at the Presbyterian church

WEDNESDAY AUGUST 3" 1864
Centralia Illinois

The officers of the Reg't held a meeting and passed resolutions in regard to the decease of Lt. Jas. Reed. I bought some watermelons and went to the Milliner's shop with Capt. J.L. Stanley to eat them. Ella, Zue, & Miss Thompson were there. Most of the Regt is here.

THURSDAY AUGUST 4" 1864
Centralia Illinois

We received orders in the A.M. to be ready to move at 2.P.M. We started at 3.P.M. stoped at Jonesboro for supper. Arrived at Cairo at Midnight Met the 50" Ind Infty there going home on vet furlough. they are from Arkansas. We put up at the St. Charles Hotel.

FRIDAY AUGUST 5" 1864
Cairo Illinois

I left the St. Charles and went to the Louisiana House. I saw Joe. Williams, (the tinner) and Mr. Boswell. We took our horses to a livery stable and put them up there. Dock Castle returned, from Salem. We went to the theatre at night. An actress on the stage here that was at Vicksburg last February. Night very warm and play not very good.~

SATURDAY AUGUST 6" 1864
Cairo Illinois

I saw Calvin Scott of Salem here. I loafed all day around town from one place to an other. No boat to take us down the river yet. the place is getting to be very dull with me. Co. "K,, are at a ball to night with a lot of Irish at a drinking saloon.

SUNDAY AUGUST 7" 1864
Cairo Illinois

We embarked on the Str Mollie Able and started down the river for Memphis at 9.A.M. run about half way down and tied up for the night. Lt. Col. Moore had a fuss with a gunboat-man about the table set for the officers of our regiment~

MONDAY AUGUST 8" 1864
On board Str Mollie-Able

We started at day light, and passed Fort. Pillow at 11.A.M. stoped at noon on account of a bar, unloaded the stock & freight and tied up for the night. The Str Belle Memphis passed on over the bar and down the river. the weather is exceeding warm~

TUESDAY AUGUST 9" 1864
On board Str. Mollie-Able

Run down to Randolph and disembarked and the boat returned for the stock and freight left at the bar. We gathered some green corn and roasted. It rained while we were here, and the chaplain went into a church here and preached. We called on an old citizen and got some water, reembarked and started at dark~

WEDNESDAY AUGUST 10" 1864
On board Str. Mollie Able

We landed at Memphis at 8.A.M. disembarked and moved out to the M.&C. R.R. depot. rained this A.M. I rode up town with Col Pease in the rain; Went to the city at night with most of the officers of the Reg't. saw Col. Bishop to day. I wrote to Lyde & Zue.

THURSDAY AUGUST 11" 1864
Memphis Tennessee

Started at 8.A.M., the Reg't. on two trains. I went on the first as far as La-Grange. was left there while trying to get something to eat. We arrived at Holly Springs at 5.P.M. I paid the Mess $.10.00. We met the 119" Ills & 89" Ind. going back to La-grange. We went into camp.

FRIDAY AUGUST 12" 1864
Holly Springs Mississippi

I rode around the town with Col. Moore We embarked on a train during a hard rain and went down to the Tallahatchie River and disembarked to guard some supplies. I saw Uncle Milt Hensley, he has heard of Jennings, one of the murderers~ in the 122" Ills.

SATURDAY AUGUST 13" 1864
Tallahatchie River Mississippi

I was going to Holly Springs to day; but there was no train went up. We are camped in the river bottom on the north side of the stream; and on the east side of the railroad; the bridge has been destroyed by the rebels; hence this is the termination of the road at present, to all practicable purposes. the ballance of the army are three miles across the river.

SUNDAY AUGUST 14" 1864
Tallahatchie River Mississippi

I rode over to Brig Head Qrs. with Col Moore Capt. Cogan & F.J. Burrows; returned by noon and went with Lt. Kerr & Capt. Cheney to Holly Springs to see if I could find, and catch Jennings one of the men that murdered father, Jennings is dead; and John Wm. Thomas is not in the 122" Ills.

(Attached on a separate note with this date)
John Wm Thomas, alias John Wm Conley, 14" Ills Infty Now a battalion of the 14" & 15" Ills. His mother & step father, Robt Ross live 1 mile south of Palmyra Macoupin Co. Ills. His grand father Ienae Conley lives 4 miles south of Waverly Morgan Co. Ills. John Wm Thomas' wife's people live 10. miles South East of Jacksonville.

J.W. Thomas is 24 years old, 5. feet 8. inches high; Blue eyes, Black hair, and spare built.

Refrences
Capt. A.C. Hulse Palmyra he is son-in-law of Ross.
Lt. T.G. Capps Co. E. 122" Ills
Col. John I. Rinaker 122 Ills.

MONDAY AUGUST 15" 1864
Holly Springs Mississippi

We got breakfast at an Irish Shebang, dinner and supper at Lt. Hemenway's of the 29" Iowa Infty. There was no train went down the road to day Lt. Rowley came to Holly Springs to-day. part of Smith's command is in camp here yet. I wrote to Uncle T.J. Black my information

TUESDAY AUGUST 16" 1864
Holly Springs Mississippi

Capt. Cheney left at 5.A.M. for Memphis Tenn. Lts. Kerr, Rowley, & I started at 7.A.M. for the front a car got off the track at Waterford and detained us two hours. We called on T.O. Hoss while there. Most of the colored troops are there We reached camp at noon all quiet.

WEDNESDAY AUGUST 17" 1864
Tallahatchie River Mississippi

Dr. Mercer; Capt. Logan; Lts. Sondag; Kerr; Whaling; Dohrman & Mitchell started home on leave of absence (30. days.) I sent some sick men to Memphis; trains came at last, and left during the night. The weather is wet It rains most of the time, every thing we have is wet including our blankets, & clothes. all quiet. Rec'd letter from & wrote to Lyde.

THURSDAY AUGUST 18" 1864
Tallahatchie River Mississippi

The troops from above are moving to the front to day through the rain; preparations making for a forward movement soon Would be glad to move most any time or place to get away from this camp in the bottom Rec'd letters from J.F.B., E.B.H., & Lyde.

FRIDAY AUGUST 19" 1864
Tallahatchie River Mississippi

We pulled up stakes and moved this morning passed the entire command except our Brigade which is still four miles in advance of us We put up with a Mr Jacob Fudge and took part of his house for quarters. It rained all day & night.~

SATURDAY AUGUST 20" 1864
Abbeville Mississippi

We stayed at Mr Fudge's, and eat watermelons until 4.P.M. We moved four miles to the Brig. on Hurricain creek. I went to see some sick children to a neighbors of Fudges by the name of Walton's. Col. Shaw, (Div. Commander) came over to see us to day. We camped after dark.

229

SUNDAY AUGUST 21" 1864
Hurricane Creek Mississippi

We moved at 7.A.M. to day one mile, had a slight skirmish and camped in an open field about four miles north of Oxford. The clouds cleared away and we dried our blankets & clothing etc. and had a very pleasant day. We gathered some green corn and fed our horses, and cooked, some for our selves. The train and troops generally came this far and camped.

MONDAY AUGUST 22" 1864
Four Miles from Oxford Mississippi

We were up and ready to march at 8.A.M. but remained until after noon, when news came that the Rebels had attacked Memphis and we turned back and camped at the Hurricane for the night. My horse has had too much green corn and is foundered. *g" 5ṣod?*

TUESDAY AUGUST 23" 1864
Hurricane Creek Mississippi

We moved at 5.A.M. Went back to the south side of the Tallahatchie and camped. Col. Moore went out with a detail foragin for the brigade some of the foragers were attacked and ours reported captured; one of Co. "B,, wounded in elbow. they came in without loss, with forage O.K.

WEDNESDAY AUGUST 24" 1864
Tallahatchie River Mississippi

Lay in camp all day. the advance are building a bridge over the Tallahatchie river. Parties sent out foraging again to day and preparations making to move soon This expedition has been a fruitless one so far as we can see at present.

THURSDAY AUGUST 25" 1864
Tallahatchie River Mississippi

We marched at 7.A.M.; across the river and halted for the cavalry to pass. The day was hot and many of the men gave out. Water was scarce along the road. Arrived at Waterford at 3.P.M.; and camped sent out foraging details and got forage I got my saddle bags full of fine peaches to day while the command was resting

FRIDAY AUGUST 26" 1864
Waterford Mississippi

Marched in the rear of the command at 9.A.M. Col Shaw has ordered straglers to be fired upon if found away from the column. I was on duty at the rear to pick up the Sick lame & lazy of the whole army that might be left by the way-side. We camped at 4.P.M. at Holly Springs~

SATURDAY AUGUST 27" 1864
Holly Springs Mississippi

In camp all day; a detail sent out foraging in charge of Major. McWilliams 117" Ills. They were fired into by the rebels, and considerably demoralized Lt. A.S. Rowley R.Q.M. brought in a fine lot of corn. We got some peaches & apples to cook to day

SUNDAY AUGUST 28" 1864
Holly Springs Mississippi

Up at 3.A.M. and moved at 5.A.M. took some invalids to the supply train to be hauled. Two men Killed to day by our own men shooting at hogs, one of them belonged to the 58" Ills. We camped at dark on Cold Water. (creek.)~

MONDAY AUGUST 29" 1864
Cold Water Mississippi

We moved at 5.A.M.; through a muddy bottom and over a hilly country; arrived at Olive Branch at 1.P.M. and after lunch Col. Moore Frank J. Burrows & I went across the country to Germantown distant ten miles and called upon Miss Kate Rhoads & the Misses Rodger's Frank and I took supper at the latter place and returned to camp at 8.P.M.~

TUESDAY AUGUST 30" 1864
Olive Branch Mississippi

Marched at 6.A.M. in the middle of the division, turned an Ambulance over to day. We arrived at Memphis Tenn at 5.P.M. and camped on the State Line Road tired, hungry, and many sore footed. I rec'd letters from R.M.L., Lyde & Zue.

WEDNESDAY AUGUST 31" 1864
Memphis Tennessee

Rained this A.M. I sent Dr. Wm. H. Medcalf to officers Hospital sick. I made out Monthly & Personal Reports. Sent an ambulance to the city for officer's desks & trunks; Capts Cheney & Berry returned to the Reg't also many of the men from Hospts. convalesent camp & Soldier's Home etc. The regiment mustered for pay. I borrowed $.25.00 of Capt. Cheney. he promoted S.T. Gray and John Hook to Sergeants, and W.J. Gray & John Ward to corporals to day. My horse has had to much to eat or drink and is foundered again. The Q.M. drew some oats & hay for our horses to day. everybody is busy to day many letters written to day by the men I wrote to Lyde & Mrs. Bliss for my sword.

THURSDAY SEPTEMBER 1" 1864
Memphis Tennessee

Col. Pease's brother is here on a visit he belongs to the gun boat Service. I got a five days pass and went to the city and got it extended at Post. Hd. Qrs. to ten days. I bought a camp stool. We put up our tents and got our goods that were stored from the city, and made things as comfortable as possible.   I wrote to E.B.H., & Zue.

FRIDAY SEPTEMBER 2" 1864
Memphis Tennessee

In camp all day. This said to have been the warmest day of the season. Captain Cogan making Muster Out rolls for the Non Veterans of Co. "A,,. To day Col Pease was ordered to take command of the brigade.
I rec'd letter from Lyde.

SATURDAY SEPTEMBER 3" 1864
Memphis Tennessee

I went to the city and took dinner at Gayoso. got a dozen Photographs. Went to the city in the P.M. with two men to Gen'l Hospitl, and bought hdkfs socks etc. bought Photos of Gen'ls A.J. Smith & J.A. Mower.

SUNDAY SEPTEMBER 4" 1864
Memphis Tennessee

In camp all day. preaching in the Reg't. had dressparade this evening for the first time in months. Wm. Bronson was relieved from duty as

Com. Serg't at his own request, and Wm Heinzelman promoted to fill the vacancy. I wrote to J.F.B. & Lyde.

MONDAY SEPTEMBER 5" 1864
Memphis Tennessee
I made a requisition and went to the city and drew a small lot of Medicines; then went to see Uncle Milt Hensley. he says the A.C. Elder note has been paid by him to Elder some years ago, and he failed to take it up. Our division moving to the river, we expect to go soon. an other Expedition in contemplation I think.~

TUESDAY SEPTEMBER 6" 1864
Memphis Tennessee
Two Regiments and this battery of our Brig left to day; I turned over a Medicine chest and some books to Hemel Stevens Medical storekeeper, belonging to Dr. Wm. H. Medcalf Surgeon of our Reg't. Col. Pease went with the Brig. he is in command. Col. Moore commands the Reg't

WEDNESDAY SEPTEMBER 7" 1864
Memphis Tennessee
Our Regiment moved at 9.A.M. to the wharf and were assigned to the Str. Stephen Decatur went on board after dark and waited for the rest of the Brig. to embark. I took dinner at the Gayoso Hotel to day, and borrowed $.15.00 of Capt Cheney~

THURSDAY SEPTEMBER 8" 1864
Memphis Tennessee
The boats started after day light but I was not up to bid adieu to the city of Memphis Major. O.T. Turney U.S. Pay master is on board and paid the Reg't four Months. he paid me $.222.20 two months pay to August 31" 1864. Geo. E. Dillingham paid me $.8.40 to day~

FRIDAY SEPTEMBER 9" 1864
On board Str. Stepen Decatur
We run all day without an incident, or stoping until we reached Columbus Ky. at 8.P.M. the weather clear and warm We run on a bar just below Cairo owing to the fog and stoped for the night. We have but

an indefinite idea of our final destination. rumors are rife, but with us facts are scarce~

SATURDAY SEPTEMBER 10" 1864
Cairo Illinois

Landed at 7.A.M. and took breakfast, then re-embarked and moved three miles up the Ohio river and dis-embarked and camped in the weeds on the Illinois bank of the river I bought a blouse for $.23.00 and a hat $.5.50 I saw Col. Haynie; Capt. Scott; & Judge, & Marshal, to day.

SUNDAY SEPTEMBER 11" 1864
Cairo Illinois

I commenced copying the Register for refrence Col. Pease gave me permission to go home and return to morrow night. started at noon, the engine broke at De Soto and detained us 4 hours. I got off at Tonti and walked home arrived at mid night~

MONDAY SEPTEMBER 12" 1864
Salem Illinois

I remained in town until noon then went out to George Williams' in the P.M. & took supper returned and went down to Moody's Maj. Mabry's called on me. I left in the evening for Cairo again. Ella came with me as far as Centralia I saw Miss Thompson there.

TUESDAY SEPTEMBER 13" 1864
Cairo Illinois

Arrived at 7.A.M. and went out to camp We had an oyster dinner in our mess to-day. I rode up to Cairo in the evening with F.J. Burrows; Capt. Lockwood; & Dr. Medcalf got a paper. prospect of our leaving here to morrow Col. J.I. Riniker 122" Ills says we go up the Mississippi river to Sulphur Springs. We have'nt a good camp ground here~

WEDNESDAY SEPTEMBER 14" 1864
Cairo Illinois

We re-embarked and started up the river at noon Frank J.B. got left We stoped at Cape Girardeau and tied up for the night. I went up to see the town with Col Moore a lot of the boys on a drunk at a billiard saloon up in town to night.~

THURSDAY SEPTEMBER 15" 1864
Cape Girardeau Missouri
Started at day light run five miles and snaged the boat and sank at Devil's Island dis-embarked and put the pumps to work, and the carpenters built a bulk head, and she came up at dark; worked the pumps til late the river is very narrow and crooked here~

FRIDAY SEPTEMBER 16" 1864
Devil's Island Mississippi River
Reloaded our stock, and plunder. The regiment marched one mile & a half to the head of the Island, and re-embarked, run pleasantly the ballance of the day. We passed Chester and several other small towns along the river bank. country broken.~

SATURDAY SEPTEMBER 17" 1864
On board Str. Stephen Decatur
We started early and run regularly most of the day; landed a few minutes at Sulphur-Springs, but the troops had gone on up the river. We started up the river again and stoped after dark at Jim Pickett's father's and wooded. I went up to the house with some of the officers. McGregors *Iuleina* lives here.

SUNDAY SEPTEMBER 18" 1864
On board Str. Stephen Decatur
Started at day light, and arrived at Jefferson Barracks at 7.A.M. We dis-embarked and put up tents on the bank of the river. got up a series of resolutions, recomending the officers, & crew, of the Str Stephen Decatur to the public, as worthy of their patronage.

MONDAY SEPTEMBER 19" 1864
Jefferson Barracks Missouri
Col. Pease is in command of the Reg't again and according to his custom we pulled up stakes and moved camp. We moved back from the river two hundred yards into the brush. details were made and cleared up camp and we put up tents again.

TUESDAY SEPTEMBER 20" 1864
Jefferson Barracks Missouri

Capt. J.W. Cheney started home on a twenty days sick leave. We all went over to the Barracks to see a Sword, belt, sash, and pr. Spurs, presented to Major Gen'l. A.J. Smith speeches made by different officers. I saw Maj. Gen'l Rosecrans and Brig. Gen'l. Tom. Ewing, Jr.

WEDNESDAY SEPTEMBER 21" 1864
Jefferson Barracks Missouri

I went to Carondelet and got my horse Shod for $.2.00. took some clothes to wash. several of the officers went to the city yesterday on a tour with Genl. Smith and are returning to day. I paid the Mess $.10.00, and loaned Dave Luttrell $.3.00 to go home on. the weather is dry and dusty, and we have to cary water from the river. many of the men absent.~

THURSDAY SEPTEMBER 22" 1864
Jefferson Barracks Missouri

Frank J. Burrows & I made an application to day for five days leave of absence to go to Salem Illinois Col. Pease went to St. Louis. Capt. Kurghoff in command Lt Dobbleman returned from Veteran furlough. Lt Chalfin left for home. I went to Carondelet.

FRIDAY SEPTEMBER 23" 1864
Jefferson Barracks Missouri

I went to Carondelet to day for my washing~ Our leave of absence came back O.K. and we mounted our horses, and Nick went with us to St. Louis. Frank forgot his leave and inserted his name on mine, and passed the guards. We had a rain & wind storm, arrived at Salem at 8.P.M.~

SATURDAY SEPTEMBER 24" 1864
Salem Illinois

In town all day. Saw Dr. Mercer he talks some of rejoining the regiment. saw Maj. Mabry & others belonging to the Service. Frank J.B. & I went out and had a shooting match on the railroad and called at Moody's on our return, and had some music.~

SUNDAY SEPTEMBER 25" 1864
Salem Illinois

Frank J. Burrows & I went out to Metcalfs camp ground, to Camp Meeting to day in a buggy. saw a great many people. we eat dinner with Sam'l. B. Arnold's. met a great many acquaintances. We returned to Salem in the P.M. had a race on the road with Mrs. Dr. White and passed her and numerous others. paid $.4.00 for buggy hire.

MONDAY SEPTEMBER 26" 1864
Salem Illinois

A circus in town to day many citizens in town F.J.B. & I went to the show. saw Capt Castle to day he has just returned from the 111th Ills. We went down to Moody's in the evening with the girls, had some music and a good time generally.~

TUESDAY SEPTEMBER 27" 1864
Salem Illinois

We saw Capt. Milton H. Lydick Co. "F,, 48" Ills Infty off for the front. to day we took dinner at Uncle Tom. J. Black's. It rained in the P.M. we expected company but the rain prevented. I gave Frank the dodge and went to Moody's to see E & Z at 7.P.M. "returned late."

WEDNESDAY SEPTEMBER 28" 1864
Salem Illinois

We started on the 9.A.M. train and came to St. Louis; took the train there for the front, and was stoped at Carondelet, then at the barracks. the Reg't. was out at De Soto Mo. we stoped at camp, for the night. Dr. Mercer paid me $.20.00 this morning at Salem, borrowed money.~

THURSDAY SEPTEMBER 29" 1864
Jefferson Barracks Missouri

Col. Pease came in this A.M. from the front. the brigade arrived late in the evening, and we received orders to be ready to move at an hours notice. We packed up most of our things including medicines, and Camp & Garrison Equipage but remained all night. the weather is pleasant. Ella Moody is to be married at Salem Ills this P.M. at 7. to George Holton of Centralia Illinois~

FRIDAY SEPTEMBER 30" 1864
Jefferson Barracks Missouri

All quiet, all day, but at dark we received orders to pack up and go to the depot, where we repaired [returned] and after loading our goods on board a train of cars, the Brigade em-barked and started at 9.P.M. to-wards St. Louis Mo. arrived and stoped there several hours waiting for something pertaining to rail road affairs. Perhaps the train crew are Killing time; so as not to venture very far from St. Louis during the night. This past month has brought us to a new field of action. We wound up last month in West Tennessee at Memphis, and we had been so long in that Section, that it seemed almost like home, to get back into that part of the country= New fields open up requiring our services= and new development of the rebels movements. Price, Cabell and others with considerable force are approaching from Arkansas= and have to be met and repelled by the Union forces and, we have to make a part of that force. hence we are here and our Brigade leads the advance of the Union Inft= other forces will probably follow in our wake soon.

SATURDAY OCTOBER 1" 1864
On board train Pacific R.R. Missouri

Cloudy and raining I lay in an ambulance all night on the train. We were fired into this morning at 9. O'clock. We stoped and three Reg'ts disembarked the 52" Ind. Infty, the 49" & 117" Ills Infty and moved up in line of battle. found the rebels in considerable force at Franklin Mo. they had some artillery we attacked them and drove them off at noon. We had seven men wounded.

SUNDAY OCTOBER 2" 1864
Franklin Missouri

The depot & telegraph office and all public property; to gether with a bridge near by were burned here by the rebels yesterday morning, owing to the R.R. men's delaying us at St. Louis friday night. The enemy are said to be approaching with 20,000 men. ordered to lay on our arms, at night. a train came.

MONDAY OCTOBER 3" 1864
Franklin Missouri

A train came in this morning with forage. I paid the Mess $.10.00. Gen'l A.J. Smith and the advance of cavalry came in this evening. I went to see a german citizen sick in town to-day. We have possession of a large brick house for Reg't. Hd. Qrs.

TUESDAY OCTOBER 4" 1864
Franklin Missouri

Dr. Mercer came this morning after an absence of 48. days instead of 30. as was granted him Rec'd orders to be ready to move at an hours notice sent baggage to the R.R. sent one Mess-chest. Dr. Mercer detailed with the 52" Ind. Dr Cooper 178" N.Y. returned; we had a hard rain in the P.M.~

WEDNESDAY OCTOBER 5" 1864
Franklin Missouri

We moved this morning five miles to Gray's Summit. went into camp in an open field. found water scarce and indifferent Officers sent back most of their Valieses we our Mess chest, in order to haul more rations for the men; transportation is out down now until it is most imposible to cary the necessities. I let F.A. Niles have $.1.00 to buy a pad lock~

THURSDAY OCTOBER 6" 1864
Gray's Summit Missouri

In camp, many rumors afloat. We are said to be awaiting rations. News good from the East. I received Mr. & Mrs. Holton's Weding cards to day. I sent four men back to St. Louis to Gen'l Hospital to day. this is a good time to get sick just the eve of an expedition.

FRIDAY OCTOBER 7" 1864
Gray's Summit Missouri

We started out in the morning with the impression that we were going to change came[camp] merely. went into the woods and stoped most of the day then started and marched twelve miles, and camped after night at or near Union Mo. the 178" N.Y. ambulance upset to night.~

SATURDAY OCTOBER 8" 1864
Union Missouri

We marched at 6.1/2.A.M. three miles to Union and passed the Millitia then marched Twenty Eight miles and camped on Beff creek. the left of the Reg't & the 117" Ills got lost this evening, in the woods The Chaplain bought 10. Doz. Eggs this evening. passed over a rough & hilly country to day.~

SUNDAY OCTOBER 9" 1864
Beff Creek Missouri

We lay in camp all day. The Millitia came up in the afternoon and, went into camp. they are very tired, and cant march with old troops. their knapsacks are too large and they are not accustomed to marching. I spent the day in looking around. the country is very poor and broken in this region

MONDAY OCTOBER 10" 1864
Beff Creek Missouri

We marched about 18 miles to day and crossed the Gasconade River at sun down it was about 100. yds. wide, and 3. feet deep The men waded it. I carried quite a number across on Charley. We camped on the west bank. The chaplain bought some eggs.~ *horse*

TUESDAY OCTOBER 11" 1864
Gasconade River Missouri

We started at 6.1/2A.M. and passed Lynn at noon and camped at Marrie's river a small stream of pretty water, after a march of 22. miles, over a poor hilly country, our Reg't. at the front of the Brig. It rained during the night.

WEDNESDAY OCTOBER 12" 1864
Marrie's River Missouri

We started early our Brig in the advance and crossed the Osage river at noon it [was] from 2. to 3 feet deep; and was near 200 yds wide. the men waded it except a few. We arrived at Jefferson City, at dark. Embarked on the cars and left at midnight for California.

THURSDAY OCTOBER 13" 1864
California Missouri

Arrived here at 6.A.M.; disembarked and went into camp near a Mr. Ross; had Hd Qrs in his yard, a fine blue grass, shaded with black walnut trees. We had a good dinner. We are on the edge of a fine prairie, rich and level we are about 25. miles west of Jefferson City. This is the first fine looking country we have seen since we left St. Louis, except it was a small bottom or scope.

FRIDAY OCTOBER 14" 1864
California Missouri

Capt. Cheney returned from home. (off his sick leave) I loaned F.J. Burrows $.40.00 and Lt. A. McGregor $.20.00 he is going to Springfield Ills to copy our Muster-in rolls. The 1st and 2nd Brigs. came in to-day passed Reg't Hd Qrs at "Shoulder Arms" perhaps thinking it was the general's. wrote to M.J.M.

SATURDAY OCTOBER 15" 1864
California Missouri

We were in camp all day Nothing startling to narate This man where we are camped, is very anxious to sell out and leave here. to many of the vicissitudes of war experienced here to suit him business to uncertain, and unsettled even to reside here with any comfort, at present.

SUNDAY OCTOBER 16" 1864
California Missouri

Marched at 7.A.M. the men thought when we started that we were going on the train the ambulances were sent on ahead; we passed Tipton & Syracuse and over a fine country, 25 miles and camped at Otterville Lt. Brewer joined us to night. The country is a little broken right here~

MONDAY OCTOBER 17" 1864
Otterville Missouri

In camp all-day. I went over to town and bought some butter for the mess; then went down and saw the ruins of the bridge destroyed by the rebels as they passed through here. I saw part of the first division in camp here to-day, some of the 11th Mo. We have our engine & train of cars west of this place in running order

TUESDAY OCTOBER 18" 1864
Otterville Missouri

Marched at 9.A.M. We passed Smithton, Farmer's City and Sedalia and camped two miles west of the latter place after traveling fifteen miles to-day. this latter town is situated out in an open prairie, surrounded by a good country.

WEDNESDAY OCTOBER 19" 1864
Sedalia Missouri

Went to town and got dinner and moved at 2.P.M. in the advance to-day. rained in the evening, and at night we camped at 8.P.M. in the woods by the road side after a march of 15. miles pretty well for a wet evening~

THURSDAY OCTOBER 20" 1864
Camp in the Woods Missouri

I paid Mess $.5.00. We marched at 7.A.M. I went off the road with F.J. Burrows and got some chickens & butter. Dr. Medcalf got some butter to day. It snowed this AM and was disagreeably cool. we camped off the road, to night. The Brig. lost in the brush by the Adj't.

FRIDAY OCTOBER 21" 1864
Camp in The Brush Missouri

Marched at 7.A.M. to-day. F.J. Burrows & I went off the road to day for butter, eggs & chickens; stoped at a house for dinner the man tried to scare us off, telling us of the danger of being captured by guerrillas, but we stayed for dinner. Lieut. Baker A.D.C. was captured to day by rebels near the road. We camped at Lexington Mo at dark after a march of 23. Miles~

SATURDAY OCTOBER 22" 1864
Lexington Missouri

Started at 7.A.M. after going three miles the non-veterans of Co. "H" were found missing. Col Shaw stoped the column and sent back for them they had "stacked arms" at the camp this morning their time having expired. Shaw told the Serg't if he refused to do duty he would have him shot in two minutes. 'he done duty.'

SUNDAY OCTOBER 23" 1864
Camp near Wellington Missouri

We started at 7.A.M. marched along the train, to guard it. we passed through a good country but depopulated by millitary order We stoped at little Blue creek after dark for 2. hours for supper having marched 25 miles. then went on to Big Blue 15. miles further, making 40 miles at one run~

MONDAY OCTOBER 24" 1864
Big Blue River Missouri

We got into camp early this morning passed Independence last night. we expected to catch the rebels here this morning but the cavalry couldn't keep them. we saw where Genl Pleasonton charged them. we lay by to-day to rest we lay down and slept five hours after eating a lunch, and rested the ballance of the day~

TUESDAY OCTOBER 25" 1864
Big Blue River Missouri

We marched at 7.A.M. We passed over a part of the battle field saw some dead, rebels, & horses. we passed new Santafee and into Kansas a little ways, and stoped at Big Blue again in the P.M. expecting to march again at night. F.J.B.; J.H.L.; & I went foraging; F. & I got dinner, and we returned to camp, and are not going any farther to night.

WEDNESDAY OCTOBER 26" 1864
Big Blue River Missouri

Marched at day-light in the rear of the Div. We went foraging, and got breakfast, and butter & eggs we traveled 24 miles and camped south of Harrisonville. Moved the Reg't after going into camp to the woods for taking rails off of a fence close by. Weather cool & disagreeable, this evening.

THURSDAY OCTOBER 27" 1864
Harrisonville Missouri

In camp all day. We sent out and bought a hog and divided it among the different messes. one of Anderson's men, (guerrilla) hung in town to day by the Militia. The streets are barricaded by the citizens

243

FRIDAY OCTOBER 28" 1864
Harrisonville Missouri

All quiet. it is rumored that Gen'l Pleasonton has captured Rebel Gen'l's Marmaduke & Cabell and about 2,000 prisoners; 7 pieces of artillery and a large part of their wagon train; it is said to be official to Gen'l Smith and is generally credited by all as being true.~

SATURDAY OCTOBER 29" 1864
Harrisonville Missouri

Col. Wm. Shaw Div. commander, started for home to day to be mustered out the service per expiration of term of service.(with 14th Iowa) rumored we will move this afternoon. The men are out of rations, the train came in after dark with supplies. we received a mail but I got nothing. distributed papers among the men. we will move to morrow morning in an easterly direction, have abandoned the chase.

SUNDAY OCTOBER 30" 1864
Harrisonville Missouri

Marched at 7.A.M. F.J.B. & I went foraging south of the road. got butter, & eggs. We passed Pleasant Hill and waited for the column but it didn't come, so we went back and found it in camp about one mile S.W. of town We marched 12 miles to day, through a very pretty country.

MONDAY OCTOBER 31" 1864
Pleasant Hill Missouri

I paid Wm Whitbread $.5.00 for cooking to day. We moved out in several columns to-day, our Brigade by its self. The 117" Ills turned to the left in the P.M. The supply train & artillery went with Col. Kenney's Brigade. The country through which we passed to day was depopulated two years ago by order of Gen'l Ewing. most of the fencing has been destroyed by the prairie fires. The land is very rich; finely set with blue grass. We camped early, on a farm belonging to a rebel captain. Brig. Hd. Qrs. in his house The Reg't near his fence and we had fine fires made of his rails. Men & officers feasted on his hogs, and we pastured our stock on his grass, and eat his black hams. It rained after night a little Col Pease threatened to tie up old Pat Foley, Co."G,,

TUESDAY NOVEMBER 1" 1864
Camp in the field Missouri

I paid the mess $.10.00 to day. It rained in the after part of the night and part of the day. We marched at 7.A.M. F.J.B. & J.H.L. & I went foraging but got nothing, but got into the brush and I shot at some wild turkeys with my revolver We camped on a little creek near the Lexington road after marching about 20 miles we have many sore footed men~

WEDNESDAY NOVEMBER 2" 1864
Camp in the field Missouri

We started early on the Lexington road, and traveled 20. miles and reached Lexington at night. Three officers of the 1st Brig were killed by guerrillas, and, brought in here by citizens to day. were killed at a house where they had stoped for dinner a Surg. Q.M. & Adjt.

THURSDAY NOVEMBER 3" 1864
Lexington Missouri

Snow fell three inches deep last night, and many of our men are bare footed. some of the officers bought shoes for their men. I bought a pr of gloves of Col. Moore. We passed through Dover to day a little town in the woods and camped after marching about 20. miles. *Dover 20 mi east of Lexington*

FRIDAY NOVEMBER 4" 1864
Waverly Missouri

Started early marched 20 miles over a good country, through one or two small villiagis the roads were good. we camped at night, with Col. Gilbert's Brig. in a little skirt of timber on Crow creek. Most of the country is prairie over which we are passing now.~

SATURDAY NOVEMBER 5" 1864
Crow Creek Missouri

Marched early, passed through a fine country to day; guerrillas were seen off on the prairies to day, this is rebel teritory and is thickly infested by them. We arrived at the Missouri river opposite Glassco and camped after marching 20. miles. We are going to cross the river here and go down on the other side perhaps the roads are better & newer.

SUNDAY NOVEMBER 6" 1864

Glassco Missouri

We crossed over the river and went into camp back of town on a nice walnut ridge. saw many citizens going to & from church to day. I made Weekly & Monthly Reports and sent in, and we rested the ballance of the day this is a nice place

MONDAY NOVEMBER 7" 1864

Glassco Missouri

I sent 25 Men down the river by boat, to St. Charles. Lt Spiro wanted to go said he had tooth ache Dr. Martin "couldn't see it." Marched at 8.A.M. at the front of the command, 12 miles to Fayett and camped at 2.P.M. I went up town and bought some Socks, and eateables. rained at night.

TUESDAY NOVEMBER 8" 1864

Fayett Missouri

Our Reg't marched early, and arrived at Franklin a voting precinct about noon to keep peace at the polls. Hd. Qrs stoped with a Mr Childers, a professed union man (a rebel). rained in the evening and night. Col's Pease & Moore & I stayed in the house took meals & lodgings with Mr. Childers

WEDNESDAY NOVEMBER 9" 1864

New Franklin Missouri

We started in the rain, the roads muddy. we pressed three wagons & teams to help us out with the lame & sore footed I took a guard and went to one man's house to press a team and driver. Three guerrillas were seen just in advance of us to day. We camped at the Fayett & Columbia road at night. had a little house for Hd Qrs.

THURSDAY NOVEMBER 10" 1864

Fayett Road Missouri

We marched at 7.A.M. reached Columbia at noon, and camped on the fair ground, and took dinner at Lieut. Baker's of the Millitia with Col. W.P. Moore; F.J. Burrows, and Dr. Wiley & Maj. McWilliams of the 117" Ills. Columbia is the finest town I have seen in the state and the most thoroughly Union of any.

FRIDAY NOVEMBER 11" 1864
Columbia Missouri

In camp all day. Frank & I bought Shoes & socks for the barefoot, of Co. "D,, Thos. Farro stole a pr of boots was caught at it, and I made him take them back. were invited to Dr. Lathrop's with others to a party in the evening

SATURDAY NOVEMBER 12" 1864
Columbia Missouri

Bernhard Stempel Co. "C,, 49" Ills. was killed by a tree falling on him this morning. We marched at 7.A.M., our Brig. in the advance of the command. We marched 21. miles and camped in the woods. This is a better country than we past through on the opposite side of the river.

SUNDAY NOVEMBER 13" 1864
Camp in the field Missouri

I made weekly reports this morning. we had strict orders in regard to stragling to-day. we traveled 21. miles and camped off the road in a little point of timber. We had fine fires and a pleasant camp, with plenty of water convinient. The country past through on our return is so far generally fair, level, mostly prairie of good quality, and tolerably well improved=

MONDAY NOVEMBER 14" 1864
Camp in the field Missouri

Marched at 8.A.M., passed through Danville We we[re] the front Reg't of the Brig. and got into camp at High Hill in good season; after marching 22. miles. one of Co."D,, cut his fingers off while dividing some beef for the Reg't. his name is Henry Elefritz from Alma Ills cars run from here to St. Charles Mo.

TUESDAY NOVEMBER 15" 1864
High Hill Missouri

I sent off a dozen men by train, and we marched at 8.A.M. I worked Charley to the Ambulance to day: We arrived at Warrenton at 1.P.M. having marched 16 miles to day. by sending men by train saves them having to march=

WEDNESDAY NOVEMBER 16" 1864
Warrenton Missouri

Marched at 9.A.M., in the rear and were in camp at 4.P.M. after marching 21 miles. the most of the men done well to day. best traveling since on this campaign We camped by the roadside (south side) cut trees and had good fires at night.~

THURSDAY NOVEMBER 17" 1864
Camp in the field Missouri

Marched at the usual hour. Col Moore preceeded the command, on his way home. Col. Pease's horse lame the boys say they run him down yesterday. We reached St. Charles at Sun down but didn't get across the river until 9.P.M. Most of the men out of rations. We are bringing another hard campaign to a close=

FRIDAY NOVEMBER 18" 1864
Saint Charles Missouri

Marched at 8.A.M., many of the men without breakfast. We were the advance of the command. arrived at St. Louis at 4.P.M. went into camp at Camp Jackson Most of us went to the city at night. We got an Oyster supper. better fair in the City, than in Camp=

SATURDAY NOVEMBER 19" 1864
Saint Louis Missouri

The Reg't got some wood to day. The weather was very disagreeable, and our camp is out on an open hill exposed to the north winds. The officers are making out their pay rolls. prospect of our getting some money soon.

SUNDAY NOVEMBER 20" 1864
St. Louis Missouri

I paid the mess $.5.00 to day. Well we spent another very disagreeable day. Most of the officers, and men spend their nights and most of their days in the city, at the Hotels. I should like to spend the rest of my term of service here.

MONDAY NOVEMBER 21" 1864
Saint Louis Missouri

It is very cold in camp, but few of the Reg't in camp, the city full to overflowing with soldiers. I had to go to the Western House, and only got in there through the influence of Capt L.W. Moore & Whaling. They put up there it is not so good a house as the Everett or Planter's most of the officers of the Reg't are at the two latter Houses.

TUESDAY NOVEMBER 22" 1864
St Louis Missouri

I went to the city expecting to meet Frank & Lyde Black there but they didn't come I went to the threatre at night and saw Miss Laura Kene & others play "American Cousins." I went with Cheney to his stoping place for the night on Olive street

WEDNESDAY NOVEMBER 23" 1864
St Louis Missouri

I went out to camp the Reg't is being paid off. I returned to the city and found Frank & Lyde had come. I stoped with them at the Everett House. I went with them to the threatre at night. "American Cousins" was the piece for to night again.

THURSDAY NOVEMBER 24" 1864
Saint Louis Missouri

I was paid two months pay, by Major Emmerson to day. ($.220.80.[)] I eat dinner at the Planter's House with Col. Pease & Lady; Frank & Lyde & Lt. Rowley. I bought a Hat $.10.00 Pr boots $.20.00, and the Reg't went onboard the Str Spray to go down the river.

FRIDAY NOVEMBER 25" 1864
Saint Louis Missouri

F.J. Burrows; J.W. Cheney & I bought overcoats for $.35.00 each. We started for Cairo at 1.P.M. Many of the men left behing[d] expecting to meet us at Cairo. several of the officers going through, among them Col. Pease Maj. Gauen; Lt. Rowley & Dr. Mercer and others. Frank Black is going with us to Cairo. Lyde started home yesterday~

SATURDAY NOVEMBER 26" 1864
On board Str. Spray

We had to give up our state room to day to the chamber maid. Went into No. 20. nothing of interest transpired to-day. The wind blew off some hats, and rendered the Hurricane roof untenable. We are not crowded much in the absence of our straglers~

SUNDAY NOVEMBER 27" 1864
On board Str. Spray

Started early from near Cape Girardeau, and arrived at Cairo at 11.A.M. I saw Capt Scott; Dock. Castle, Gen'l. Haynie & C.W. Webster called on the two former J.F.B. left for home stoped at the St. Charles, and left for up the Ohio river at 10.P.M.~ but didn't start.

MONDAY NOVEMBER 28" 1864
On board Str. Spray

Started at day light and run up to Paducah Ky. didn't land however but went on up to Smithland Ky. and landed and took the stock off, and let the men cook rations. one of Co. "E,, fell overboard last night, drunk, and was drowned & lost.

TUESDAY NOVEMBER 29" 1864
Smithland Kentucky

Started at an early hour and run all day. I was quite unwell and kept my room all day, and hence saw nothing of interest saw a few of the setlers along the bank. 2. years ago, early last february, we traveled up this direction, on the Tennessee river instead of the Cumberland however, to be initiated into the realities of a Soldier's life, which most of us remember.

WEDNESDAY NOVEMBER 30" 1864
Fort Donaldson Tennessee

Started at 1.A.M. and didn't get to see the fort where we were innitiated into the realities of War now most three years ago. We saw Clarksville on the left as we went up; The draw bridge there has been partly destroyed. Three years has brought us back almost to where we learned the rudiments of Soldiering= and very likely from indications some of us will get our Muster Out before we get away from this Dep't=

Union Troops are concentrating here from various directions and Gen'l Schofield is being driven back on this place by the rebels, under Hood. and near here will probbaly be fought a general battle, for the Mastery of the field= a month ago we were in Western Missouri in the midst of a Campaign= with as little thought of being here now= as we now have of being at Detroit next month= But such are the uncertainies, and chances of a Soldiers life= This year has been one of great activity with the Forty-Ninth with many privations and incidental Casualties= Many Mound Mark the line of our March= where the loved were lost=

THURSDAY DECEMBER 1" 1864
Nashville Tennessee

I paid the mess $10.00 to day. We landed here during the night, and disembarked this A.M. and moved out by the Capital, to the front. I took some men to the Hosp't, and our Brigade moved to the left, and I joined them after dark, in an old field, little to the right of Col. Acklin's residence: Our troops are all back to camp except, Cavalry.

FRIDAY DECEMBER 2" 1864
Nashville Tennessee

F.J.B. & I went to see Col. Acklin's fine residence, and surroundings. prospect of an attack. We returned: I was ordered to report to Dr. Wiley for duty. took dinner with a Mr. Robberrts We moved to the right, and went to fortifying again and worked all night.~

SATURDAY DECEMBER 3" 1864
Nashville Tennessee

We had to leave our works again and move to the right again, to the Harding Pike on the right of our division, and go to fortifying not much fighting going on; I went out to Lt. Stanley on Picket, and we tried to get a shot at the rebel Pickets but failed.

SUNDAY DECEMBER 4" 1864
Nashville Tennessee

Working on the fortifications the battery built works on our right. We cut the trees in front of us & the battery. artillery firing on the left in the morning, and on Col Gilberts hill at night. the rebels are moving to our right, towards the river below.~

MONDAY DECEMBER 5" 1864
Nashville Tennessee

I went up to Col Kerry's Hill in the A.M. and to a fort west of us, and saw a cavalry skirmish, which was very interesting to look at. Nine of Co. "G,, returned to day who were absent without leave. they were left back at St. Louis Mo. We are still working on the fortifications, no fighting of any consequence going on; only an occasional skirmish.

TUESDAY DECEMBER 6" 1864
Nashville Tennessee

Col. Pease put O. serg't Cy. Daniels and others to work on the fortifications for absence without <u>leave</u>. nothing of interest in camp to day. The batterymen (Bat."G,, 2" Ills) are building their own fortifications with stone and dirt, our men helping some.

WEDNESDAY DECEMBER 7" 1864
Nashville Tennessee

The 117" Ills is building another line of works, inside the former, and on the crest of the Hill. occasional firing on the lines particularly by cavalry pickets. some little artillery firing to at times, but generaly at too long a range to be very effective.

THURSDAY DECEMBER 8" 1864
Nashville Tennessee

I went down to town to day with F.J.B. and got a dish of oysters. returned to camp and Dr. Hawley called to see us. The weather is very windy and disagreeably. The battery firing at the rebels occasionaly nothing of interest in camp to day.

FRIDAY DECEMBER 9" 1864
Nashville Tennessee

Nothing of interest in camp. the weather is very disagreeable it rained snowed and sleated by turns. The officers are making preparations for final muster out at the end of this month, though this is an inconvinient place to make out muster out rolls. We will have to participate in this coming fight. I wrote Aunt Lucy, W.W.B. & J.F.B.

SATURDAY DECEMBER 10" 1864
Nashville Tennessee

We sent our horses to the city this morning and had them shod Lt. A.S. Rowley was relieved from duty as R.Q.M. in order that he might settle up his business, and Lt. J. Foster Co. "K,, detailed in his stead, as he expects to remain in the service.

SUNDAY DECEMBER 11" 1864
Nashville Tennessee

In camp all day; to cold to stir out. Lieut. L.R.H. Dobbleman Co. "F,, sent in his resignation to day, he is going to quit the service and return to Urope as his parrents live there and he has now been over three years in the service.

MONDAY DECEMBER 12" 1864
Nashville Tennessee

I went to the city with Col. Pease and bought two cavalry blankets for $.6.00 The Col. bought a <u>pair</u>; We called upon Mrs Johnson formerly from the vicinity of White's Station Tenn. Dr. Mercer got a tent, and put up after so long a time.

TUESDAY DECEMBER 13" 1864
Nashville Tennessee

We <u>put up</u> Dr Mercer's <u>tent</u> and stove & we had some extra duty men to help us <u>ditch it,</u> and clear the snow out of it. We <u>put some hay</u> in it, to sleep on. it rained during the night. I <u>have been sleeping in our Ambulance</u> since I have been here, in fact for the last twelve months or more as I have not <u>had a tent in the time.</u>

WEDNESDAY DECEMBER 14" 1864
Nashville Tennessee

I made Invoices of the Medicines for which I was responsible to Dr. Mercer and took his Receipts for the same. Was writing most of the day. We received orders at 8.P.M. to be ready to, move on the Enemy at 6.A.M., tomorrow. The entire army to move <u>out</u> in <u>line</u> of <u>battle.</u>

THURSDAY DECEMBER 15" 1864
Nashville Tennessee

We moved out at the appointed hour Gen'l. A. J. Smith's (16") corps, on the right. The 4. A.C. on the left, and the 23" A.C. in reserve. after a feint on the left, Smith attacked on the right vigorously swinging around to wards the left. captured three or four batteries and many prisoners

FRIDAY DECEMBER 16" 1864
Nashville Tennessee

Moved forward early, and attacked the enemy in his works. charged them in the evening, and captured much artillery, and many prisoners among them Major Gen'l Johnson & Brig Gen'l Jackson We lost very few killed and wounded Thos. Burns Co. "A,, was killed yesterday evening~

SATURDAY DECEMBER 17" 1864
Nashville Tennessee

We camped at the foot of the outer line of hills last night, about five miles from the city. We took up the line of march this morning on the Granny White Pike We marched about five miles, crossed over to the Franklin Pike, and camped, after a very disagreeable day through the mud and rain. Saw Major Gen'l Schofield this evening he passed us.

SUNDAY DECEMBER 18" 1864
Franklin Pike 10 Miles out Tennessee

Moved at the usual hour in the rear of the 4" & 23" A.C. Went a few miles and stoped an hour or two. some prisoners past us going to Nashville. Moved on and stoped again thinking we were in camp for the night, but had to go again. We passed the town and camped after night

MONDAY DECEMBER 19" 1864
Franklin Tennessee

Marched about noon in rain passed one of the most disagreeable days I have seen in the service. we camped after night in the mud and rain, found wood scarce We marched but few miles to day but was all behind and, day at it. tongue broke out of one of our wagons.

TUESDAY DECEMBER 20" 1864
Spring Hill Tennessee

Lay in camp until late in the day, then moved about four miles, and camped in a mudhole. another bust day. rained P.M. and at night. left the wagons & Ambulances behing[d], the latter did'nt come up to night. I went into a tent with the field and staff of the Regiment.

WEDNESDAY DECEMBER 21" 1864
Camp in the field Tennessee

We moved over on a ridge east a little ways and found good camping ground and put up tents Dr. Mercer came up after while with the ambulance We have been here all day, and will remain for the night quite comfortable. The other A.C.'s are moving toward the front. It was rumored that we would surround Gen'l Forrest by coming here last night, but its a mistake.

THURSDAY DECEMBER 22" 1864
Camp in the field Tennessee

The men detached from the regiment were returned to their respective companies to day. The Division moved in the P.M.. I was left behind with ambulances for a while, then went forward with the ambulances of the Div. and joined the Regiment at dark on Duck River.

FRIDAY DECEMBER 23" 1864
Duck River Tennessee

We received our orders to return to Nashville and go to Paducah, Ky. to be mustered out, and turn over arms. We turned over transportation including ambulances to night. I was in camp all day. the weather is pleasant again. all are anxious to be mustered out the service

SATURDAY DECEMBER 24" 1864
Duck River Tennessee

The Division moved forward at 3.A.M., and we started back at 9.A.M. had six wagons of the supply train to help us to Spring Hill. I saw Dick Smith of the 21st Ills there. then we got aboard a freight train after considerable delay and started for Nashville, where we arrived during the night.~

SUNDAY DECEMBER 25" 1864
Nashville Tennessee

We dis-embarked and went to a saloon and got breakfast, then moved down to the wharf Then I went to the City Hotel for dinner, with Capt. J.W. Cheney. The Regiment went on board the Str Financier and laid over for the night, as we could not pass the draw bridge after dark. Nashville is not in such commotion, as a week ago~

MONDAY DECEMBER 26" 1864
Nashville Tennessee

All on board, and started down the river at 11.A.M., except Capt. Kurghoff who was left behind. The day was very foggy. We stoped a while at Clarksville then run down to Ft. Donaldson and lay over for the night. officers making muster out rolls~

TUESDAY DECEMBER 27" 1864
Fort Donaldson Tennessee

We started at day light and reported at Paducah Ky. at 4.P.M., and went into camp, on a flat piece of ground west of the fort. The 34" N.J. Infty are on duty here. they are to join our Brig under Col. Wolf. Now, 3rd Brig. 2" Div., 16" A.C.~

WEDNESDAY DECEMBER 28" 1864
Paducah Kentucky

I made out Anual report; Dr. Medcalf is turning over property to Dr Mercer they are a little short on some articles. I think there is not much prospect of my getting out the service at present. Gen'l S. Meredith dont want to let us go.

THURSDAY DECEMBER 29" 1864
Paducah Kentucky

Brig. Gen'l. S. Meredith Commd'g, District West Ky decides that none of us can be mustered out who have not served three years in present grade Except Col. P. Pease and he for want of a proper command, there being two other field officers in the regiment for duty. The Gen'l ignores all orders and circulars from the War Dept. on the subject~

FRIDAY DECEMBER 30" 1864
Paducah Kentucky

I paid the Mess $.5.00 to day and Wm. Whitbread $.4.00   The 34" N.J. ordered up the river, and the 49" Ills to duty here. Major J.E. Gauen, myself and three companies, ("C,, "D,, & "H,,) were ordered to Smithland, Ky. We went up on str. Convoy No. 2. and relieved the Jersies, and went into the Court House

SATURDAY DECEMBER 31" 1864
Smithland Kentucky

I had the boys of the respective companies clean up quarters, then I went to Post Head Quarters and wrote passes for Maj. Gauen. He gave out about eighty passes today. We made requisitions on the Post. Q.M. for fuel, and forage but drew neither. The fuel is across the river and the forage is not due until to-morrow We took our meals at the Elliott House to-day. I received letter from Col. P. Pease stating that Lieuts J.L. Stanley; S. Spiro; A.S. Rowley; and C. Dohrman are among those named by the Gen'l for muster out. The Col starts for home to day. the 34" N.J. Vols stoped here to night on their way to join the Brigade so ends the hardest year of the service to me.

SUNDAY JANUARY 1ST 1865
Smithland Kentucky

New Year's came in quiet and cold, and found me at Smithland Ky. on duty with Co's C. D. & H. of our regiment, (49" Ills. Infty.) quartered comfortably in the Court House. Major Gauen Commanding Post. I went into Mike's mess to day. Snow on the ground. This is the fourth New Year's day I have spent in the service The next I expect to spend at home~

MONDAY JANUARY 2" 1865
Smithland Kentucky

I visited the Post & Pest Hospitals to day, in the one I found six colored soldiers sick, in the other I found twenty three persons with the Small pox. I made requisition for a month's supply of wood. Wrote to Dr. H.W. Davis Med. Director in regard to affairs. Weather pleasant. Wrote to Zue ["Smallpox" written in the margin on January 2 and February 2, 17, 18, 20, and 23.]

TUESDAY JANUARY 3" 1865
Smithland Kentucky

Capt. J.W. Cheney came up this evening from Paducah. most of the Officers gone to be mustered out. Col. Pease, Dr. Medcalf; Capts. L.W. Moore, Berry Kurghoff: Stanley, Lieuts Spiro, Rowley: & Whaling. And Lemmon & Mitchell gone on leave of absence the ballance of the Regt on duty.

WEDNESDAY JANUARY 4" 1865
Smithland Kentucky

I went with Capt Cheney around the lines to try to reduce the No of Non Com's., on the line. visited the Hospitals. I went to the 13" U.S.C. in the evening and vaccinated 25 or 30 of their men. Small pox still spreading. sent two new cases to Hospital. The Hospitals are open and , ill-arranged for the sick.

THURSDAY JANUARY 5" 1865
Smithland Kentucky

Capt Cheney traded his allowance of coal for a cook stove for our Mess. Co. "D,, goes to the fort for duty, and gives us their room for a messroom. I visited the Hospitals and found a Negro dead from Pneumonia in the Post. Wet and disagreeable in the evening. no mail for any of this Detachment yet.~

FRIDAY JANUARY 6" 1865
Smithland Kentucky

We put up our stove, and the ballance of Co. "D,, going to the fort to learn to be artillerymen. We put some bunks into our room so that eight of us can sleep on two bunks and have more room for desks and tables, and office furniture.~

SATURDAY JANUARY 7" 1865
Smithland Kentucky

Weather disagreeable and the wind blowing cold. I have three Lieuts of the 13" U.S.C. sick under treatment, beside many of the men. Dr. John W. Mott, A.A. Surg. has four dead men in the Pest Hospt. to day at one time. He made reports to me, and I to Dr. Davis, by mail

SUNDAY JANUARY 8" 1865
Smithland Kentucky

A pleasant day, most of the snow melted off. I visited my patients and intended going to church but was to late Capt Cheney went. I received vaccinator and crusts from Dr Davis to day. I went to church at night with Cheney had a good Sermon and respectable audience

MONDAY JANUARY 9" 1865
Smithland Kentucky

Doctors Farris & Abbott, Surg. & Asst Surg. of the 13" U.S.C. H. Art. came last night. I prescribed at Hospitals and quarters. I went to Hospts. with Dr. Ferris, and returned and he took dinner with me. I visited the Lieuts McDowell & Crawford both have Varioloid. Capt Cheney issuing clothing to the men. Ab. Whits back and in trouble Capt. prefering charges against him.

TUESDAY JANUARY 10" 1865
Smithland Kentucky

It snowed, and blew most all day, and I spent most of the day in quarters. I went to see the Lieuts. both of them broke out finely with smallpox. I saw the Q.M. of the 52nd Ind. and a Q.M. of the 1st Brig. and a Lieut of our battery (Bat. "G,, 2nd Ills.) on there way to Nashville Tenn.

WEDNESDAY JANUARY 11" 1865
Smithland Kentucky

I got a pass and Marion Richardson & I went out hunting. found a squirrel and opened fire upon him I killed him the fourteenth round. We didn't get much game, but had lots of fun. we called at a Mr Thompson's and got some dinner. returned to camp, found all quiet. thawing some.

THURSDAY JANUARY 12" 1865
Smithland Kentucky

A fine day, though a little windy 6 boats came down the Cumberland with all the hard cases that have been confined in the zollicoffer for a month. they broke into several houses and played thunder generally. Dr. Ferris' medicines came he took Dr. Mott's Sanitaries from him, to day.

FRIDAY JANUARY 13" 1865
Smithland Kentucky

I loaned Capt Cheney $.10.00 to day, until he could send home and get some from his father. Lieut. Col. Moore came up this evening and we went arround to Hd. Qrs. nothing of interest in camp. We spent the time in running back and forwards to Hd. Qrs. Major J.E. Gauen commanding Post. We ought to have Col. Moore here to command Post.~

SATURDAY JANUARY 14" 1865
Smithland Kentucky

We spent the day loafing around town. A citizen here to day from Caditz for a negro brought in by a recruiting party of the 13" U.S.C. and they are trying to bully him out of the darky. John Jenkins up with some sacks & C.C. & G.E. Col Moore returned caught up a citizen for trying to hire a soldier to desert.

SUNDAY JANUARY 15" 1865
Smithland Kentucky

Capt Cheney made application for a ten days leave of absence. I dressed to go to church to day but there was none, in consequence of the smallpox Capt Fischer & Lt. Cogan went riding in the evening. I went to Hd. Qrs. and made charges & specifications against a citizen (Spaulding) arrested yesterday

MONDAY JANUARY 16" 1865
Smithland Kentucky

I made arrangements to go to Paducah to day got the order and transportation. Two boats came at noon, Lt Dohrman & I got aboard the Str. J.S. Hall and waited until dark for them to coal. I concluded not to go and disembarked. Dohrman got no supper.

TUESDAY JANUARY 17" 1865
Smithland Kentucky

I went to Hd. Qrs. and wrote passes for the Major Citizens charging one another with disloyalty and each professing the most devoted union proclivities. hard to tell which is the worst rebel. I played chess with Capt

Cheney. I wrote to the Surg. Gen'l for a statement of my accounts with the Medical Dept. preparatory to being Mustered out the service

WEDNESDAY JANUARY 18" 1865
Smithland Kentucky
Lt. C. Dohrman returned from Paducah, and in getting off the boat fell into the river and got a good ducking. The 23rd Army Corps is passing up the Ohio river going to the Eastern army somewhere, perhaps to Richmond to participate in the last campaign of the war

THURSDAY JANUARY 19" 1865
Smithland Kentucky
Tom Black I got an order and went down to Paducah on the Str. Armada. I met with Uncle Tom Black at the wharf. I went to camp for dinner saw Dr Allen Med. Inspector; I went with F.J. Burrows and called upon Col. Hicks Lt Col Wm. P. Moore has a commission as Colonel~

FRIDAY JANUARY 20" 1865
Paducah Kentucky
Lieut. H.W. Kerr got a leave of absence yesterday. Lieut Jas. Livesay is ordered to Indianapolis with prisoners. Capt Lockwood promised to return with me but got left. I came up on the Str Slice Dear. I went out horseback riding. Capt Cheney got a ten day leave. I bought a pr of blue jeans pants to day for $.8.00.

SATURDAY JANUARY 21ST 1865
Smithland Kentucky
Capt. Cheney turned over all his property to Lieut Latsch of Co."H,, so that if he gets out of the service he will not have to come back here from Paducah. thence home on leave of absence, and if he gits mustered out he will not have to come back to make disposition of his property. he has now been over four years in the service.~

SUNDAY JANUARY 22" 1865
Smithland Kentucky
Cheney waiting for a boat to go to Cairo then home but none came. he payed me forty dollars for F.J. Burrows. It rained this morning, and

was muddy to day. Our Regt have been relieved from Patroll duty, at Paducah by the colored troops.

MONDAY JANUARY 23" 1865
Smithland Kentucky

It snowed during the night, and is quite cold this morning. Capt Cheney left for home. Major Gauen wrote Col Burge, of the Ky recruits a letter in refrence to his men's disobedience. Dr Ferris tried to carry the Maj by storm to day in regard to the Post Hospital, and its management.

TUESDAY JANUARY 24" 1865
Smithland Kentucky

Capt Lockwood came up to day and brought some mail and reading matter for the boys. I wrote a letter to John C. Wilson of Co. "D,, at Baltimore. Lieut Latsch relieved Lt Rodgers of the 13" U.S.C. at the Fort, and of charge of Co. "D,, the boys are well pleased with the change. spent the day at Hd. Qrs.~

WEDNESDAY JANUARY 25" 1865
Smithland Kentucky

A cold day. considerable stir among the "M,, "S,, on account of fuel for Hospitals, and houses for Hospital purposes. No body wants to take the responsibility of saying where the sick shall be taken to. Capt Lockwood & I called upon the Minister of the town Mr. Beardsley at Capt Mill's. lots of ice in the Ohio river now. getting to be bad boating. the river will be closed soon if it dont thaw.~

THURSDAY JANUARY 26" 1865
Smithland Kentucky

Capt Lockwood left for Paducah on the steamer Missouri. I sent $.45.00 by him to F.J. Burrows left in my hands by Capt. Cheney for him. I called on Drs. Ferris & Abbott, and took dinner with them. Dr Abbott is going up the river to morrow with a detachment of his Reg't to Eddyville.

FRIDAY JANUARY 27" 1865
Smithland Kentucky

Very cold. this morning ground frozen hard, river full of ice. boats cant run up the Ohio from here. The Kennett came up to day from Paducah and brought some rations. Serg't. S.T. Gray returned from Paducah. I took the countersign around the lines. Dr Ferris tired of being Post Surg. Abbott in a stew.~

SATURDAY JANUARY 28" 1865
Smithland Kentucky

I went out to Mr. Stinebreaker's with Capt Fischer and got a lunch of milk & bread. got a canteen and bucket full to bring to camp. then went around the picket lines with the countersign. I bought a pr of shoes for $.3.00 goods are cheaper here than elsewhere.~

SUNDAY JANUARY 29" 1865
Smithland Kentucky

A fine day, clear and pleasant. I started to church, but met Dr. Ferris and turned back and heard him "blow hard." We had a good dinner two boats came back that started up the Ohio on account of ice. I went to church at night with Marion Richardson. Sergt Sam'l. C. Goshorn was there drunk. We had a good discourse and attentive audience.

MONDAY JANUARY 30" 1865
Smithland Kentucky

Boat up with papers, Blair's visit to Richmond is the subject of interest in the papers now, at least they are full of it. I went out riding this evening. found a rough, broken and poor country. Mostly timbered, sparsely settled with poor people~

TUESDAY JANUARY 31ST 1865
Smithland Kentucky

I went out to the country on foot with Lieuts Dohrman & Latsch, hunting. I carried a Springfield rifle and revolver the Lts were similarly armed. We went up the Cumberland six miles by land to Green's ferry, got our dinners and started back on the same side of the river (the west.). We found a skift [skiff] full of water at the bank and diped the water out with a gourd and a board. We confiscated it and came down the river in it, <u>nine miles</u>. had our hands blistered pulling at the oars. We had lots of fun, but dont want to go again if we know ourselves. did'nt find any game and got very tired going and coming. "It <u>did'nt pay</u>"

WEDNESDAY FEBRUARY 1ST 1865
Smithland Kentucky

I paid the Mess $.10.00 nothing of interest in camp. two little boats came up but neither of them had any mail or papers. this is a dull place when the river is closed that boats cant run as all that is of interest comes in that way. there is no mail of any importance from any other source, and no papers except those brought by the boats.~

THURSDAY FEBRUARY 2" 1865
Smithland Kentucky

The weather warm cloudy and drizzling rain the ice is fast running out of the river. Several boats came up to day. the long looked for Armada came down bringing a mail. I received three letters. I visited Major Watson to day sick with smallpox. <u>Paper</u> came.

FRIDAY FEBRUARY 3" 1865
Smithland Kentucky

Capt Lockwood went up the Ohio to day in charge of the wounded of the 9" Ind. Batt. who were wounded, by the blowing up of a steamboat at Eastport. John Jenkins came up with some clothing for the Det. Mr Wharton started up the river from Paducah with some rejected darkies, and got them gobbled here

SATURDAY FEBRUARY 4" 1865
Smithland Kentucky

Not much of interest [in] camp to day. I spent the time at Hd. Qrs. writing passes; Maj. Gauen swore into the service twenty of those Negroes in dispute between Citizens, and the officers of the 13" USC Arty (Ky). I loaned John Hook $.5.00 to day until he could make a raise.

SUNDAY FEBRUARY 5" 1865
Smithland Kentucky

Capt Cheney returned this morning in time to catch me in bed. (from Ills.) he and I went to church at 10. A.M. spent the ballance of the day reading. Mr Wharton and some other citizens here after Negroes again. Major's is tired of them. I wrote to Zue in regard to our arrangement of last July Capt Fischer went to church at night~

MONDAY FEBRUARY 6" 1865
Smithland Kentucky

I made application to Lt. McIver A.C.M. Dist. West. Ky. to be mustered out, stating, that I had served over three years in the same organization. The Kentuckian in trouble. Dr. J. Duke Mott absent without leave and they have no place for their sick and no doctor and without medicines even~

TUESDAY FEBRUARY 7" 1865
Smithland Kentucky

I have been in quarters all day. this's the first day that I have not visited Hd. Qrs. since we have been here. Capt Cheney and Lieut Dohrman went down to Paducah to-day. The weather is turning cold again, wind blowing and freezing~

WEDNESDAY FEBRUARY 8" 1865
Smithland Kentucky

Cheney & Dohrman returned. Col Moore has made application for us all to be mustered out, the service some of Gen'l A.J. Smith's command passing Paducah for Mobile. Weather cold, snowed a little last night. I spent the day in quarters too cold to be out much of the time.

THURSDAY FEBRUARY 9" 1865
Smithland Kentucky

I took my horse and went to the country riding. I went about four miles, the roads rough, and the ground not frozen deep enough to bear up a horse. the wind blew cold. I returned and played a game of chess with Capt. Cheney I beat him for once. he generaly gets the better of me at chess~

FRIDAY FEBRUARY 10" 1865
Smithland Kentucky

All quiet. Lt. Latsch went out with a squad of men to help repair telegraph. Capt Cheney & Lt. Dohrman went hunting. I got an order and went down to Paducah on the Str. St. Nicholas, saw the Col & boys, saw Mrs Mercer. I went with them to supper

SATURDAY FEBRUARY 11" 1865
Paducah Kentucky

I got some medicines, called upon Dr. Davis Med. Director. I got an order to relieve Dr. Mott and assign Dr. W. Wist Piper to duty in Pest Hosp't. F.J. Burrows came up with me on Str. Sam'l Orr. I got a reply to my letter from Surg. Gen'l. The 16" A.C. went down the river yesterday.

SUNDAY FEBRUARY 12" 1865
Smithland Kentucky

F.J. Burrows went back to Paducah on the Str. Glendale. Capts Cheney, Fischer & I went to church to day. O'Brien brought the Major a jug of Ale. We wrote a letter (anonymous) to an anonymous coreespondent in town here to day.~

MONDAY FEBRUARY 13" 1865
Smithland Kentucky

I wrote out an order prohibiting persons from selling or giving liquor to Soldiers and got the Major to make it Official. Judge Fowler wants the Court House again. The Major was going to send Capt Cheney down to Paducah to see the General about it but they finally agreed to hold court in another house.

TUESDAY FEBRUARY 14" 1865
Smithland Kentucky

Nothing of interest in camp. all going on after the old fashion, eating, drinking and loafing. We moved back into our room. Court is going to be held in a house down on the levy, so we hold our position, O.K.

WEDNESDAY FEBRUARY 15" 1865
Smithland Kentucky

I paid Mess $.5.00 I was sick with a cold most all day Major Gauen received a letter from Dr. H.W. Davis to make me Post Surgeon in stead of Dr. Ferris. Both the Motts are going to leave here J.W. Mott to see Dr. Davis and J. Duke Mott to Owensboroo with his Regt.

THURSDAY FEBRUARY 16" 1865
Smithland Kentucky

Dr. Ferris was relieved, and I appointed Post Surgeon. I rec'd a lot of papers from Ferris among them the statements of "Hospt Fund" I returned them for correction. I helped make them out after they were done Cogan A.C.S. said they were not right. all to make over~

FRIDAY FEBRUARY 17" 1865
Smithland Kentucky

I put in the day after the old Style at this place running to Hd. Qrs. and back I received a letter from Dr. H.W. Davis in refrence to making Reports. I visited the Pest Hospital. Lt. James Cogans was relieved from duty as A.C.S. to-day. he has not got the statements of Hospt Fund made yet for the month of January hence my reports are not forwarded yet.~

SATURDAY FEBRUARY 18" 1865
Smithland Kentucky

I made and forwarded Weekly Reports. Visited the Pest Hospital. I made requisition and had wood hauled to the Pest Hospital. I returned Monthly Statements of Hospt Fund to Lt. Jas. Cogans for correction. it seems imposible to get them correct.~

SUNDAY FEBRUARY 19" 1865
Smithland Kentucky

I went down to Paducah on the Str Armada called on Dr. Davis to see him about getting statements of Hospt Fund from Surgs at this Post, and to get some blanks. I saw F.J.B. & officers and men generally and returned on Str Clifton to this place~

MONDAY FEBRUARY 20" 1865
Smithland Kentucky

Circuit Court in session again this week. I issued an order to Surgs. Ferris & Mott with refrence to their statements of Hospital Fund for Jany requiring certificates. I returned ten men to duty from Pest Hospt. after thoroughly washing & changing their entire clothing for new.

TUESDAY FEBRUARY 21" 1865
Smithland Kentucky

I made certificates in refrence to the clothing burned yesterday, in accordance with Gen'l Order No. 107. War. Dept. March 16" 1864. I got monthly statements of Hospt Fund. both Hospts in debt, and Dr. Mott in trouble. Surgs will have to pay of[f] the indebtedness. No boats up nor down to day Charleston said to be taken.

WEDNESDAY FEBRUARY 22" 1865
Smithland Kentucky

Dr. W.W. Piper reported for duty. I put him in charge of the Pest Hospital. Capt Fischer went down to Paducah. Lt McGregor came up with some ammunition. A Salute of one hundred guns being fired at Paducah in honor of Washington's birthday, and thirteen for the recapture of Charleston

THURSDAY FEBRUARY 23" 1865
Smithland Kentucky

I was sick all night and quite unwell this morning. I went and installed Dr. Piper in his duties at the Pest Hospt. Lt. McGregor returned to Paducah & Capt Fischer here. The Str Armada came and brought a mail, me a very important one. Scott, Richardson came to day.

FRIDAY FEBRUARY 24" 1865
Smithland Kentucky

All quiet, and dull. weather pleasant, mud drying up. Cheney having coal hauled. Went to the billiard saloon and saw Cheney & Dohrman play. Lt Cogans returned from Cairo got his pay. also Capt Battsman 13" U.S.C. I got leave of Mr Davis to keep my horse in his stable

SATURDAY FEBRUARY 25" 1865
Smithland Kentucky

I recived, and made weekly Reports to day. Dr. W.W. Piper makes the best report of any of those reporting to me. Wash. Boyd came up to day from Paducah on a visit. This is getting to be quite a resort for those at Paducah from the Col. down to the privates. any place to get away from there old camp~

SUNDAY FEBRUARY 26" 1865
Smithland Kentucky

I went to church with Capt Cheney in the forenoon. I had an application to accept a citizen into Pest Hospt. but declined. I saw Col. Picket of the Paducah Federal Union, up here to night. In quarters most all day. Weather pleasant.

MONDAY FEBRUARY 27" 1865
Smithland Kentucky

A report of mine, made out and signed by Dr. Mercer came back to day for correction also Ferris' for January. The Hospt Statements for further investigation. My leave of absence came back all right. Capt Cheney ordered to Paducah. I moved my horse to Mr. Davis' Stable.

TUESDAY FEBRUARY 28" 1865
Smithland Kentucky

I made out my monthly, and Personal Reports and sent them in. Capt Cheney went down to Paducah. I got some lumber and put up a pr of Draw bars. Fischer in a rage about the Darky provosts. Dr. Abbott is ordered from Eddyville to Caseyvill and he dont like to move~

WEDNESDAY MARCH 1 1865
Smithland Kentucky

I made my fuel and forage requisitions took a ride around the picket lines with Capt Fischer. Went over to Dr Ferris after Reports. Saw Dr. Abbott there. Wrote Dr. Davis and asked him whether I should admit citizens to Pest Hospitals and if so upon what terms, to be done, as it is an aggitated question here now.

THURSDAY MARCH 2" 1865
Smithland Kentucky

It rained again last night, and to day the roads are quite muddy. I sent off my Reports except Monthly statements of "Hospital Fund." The Str Armada went down to day though not much mail aboard. the river still rising, full of drift-wood. Two lumber barges broke loose to day

269

FRIDAY MARCH 3" 1865
Smithland Kentucky

I took Drs Ferris' & Mott's statements of Hospt' Fund back to the commissary for farther correction. in quarters most all day Both the Mail packets passed to day, the Armada going up, and the Gen'l Anderson going down I received a letter from home~

SATURDAY MARCH 4" 1865
Smithland Kentucky

Made my Weekly Reports, got the statements of "Hospt Fund" and sent to Dr. Davis with a letter stating that I could not correct the errors though I was satisfied they existed, owing to the commissary's mistake. sent off all my papers preparatory to leaving for home to-morrow morning.

SUNDAY MARCH 5" 1865
Smithland Kentucky

I started for home at 10.A.M. on the Str Robbert Burns. stoped an hour at Paducah. Saw Captains Cheney, Cogan, Houston & Logan, and Lieut F.J. Burrows. Lt. Kerr came aboard and went to Cairo Ills. we put up at the St. Charles. Lt. A.F. Taylor, Gen'l Meredith's A.A.A. Gen'l. at night there was a fire in town burned almost a Square. Lt. White 44" Wis Infty. and a Lt. of the 83" Ills Infty went down with us to Cairo.

MONDAY MARCH 6" 1865
Cairo Illinois

I called upon B.F. Marshall. I saw Dr Hawley and the Lt. Col. of his Reg't. Maj S.B.A. Haynes U.S.A. paid me $.220.80 for Nov. & Dec. '64. I left my measure for coat & pants and order for pr. Straps with Kittridge & Co. paid them $.98.50 for them. I bo'ght a pr boots $.15.00. I took lodging in a sleeping car, and saw no more of Cairo~

TUESDAY MARCH 7" 1865
Cairo Illinois

Started at 1.A.M. I arrived at Salem Ills at 10:A.M. found all well. I called upon a number of friends. I Rec'd $.125.00 of Emit Merritt on John W. Merritt's note. (a sale debt). I went with Lyde Lute & Lizzy,

270

to Moody's to spend the evening. I overstayed and they came home in squads. saw Matt Stubblefield

WEDNESDAY MARCH 8" 1865
Salem Illinois

To day I went out to George Williams' on a visit with Tom & Lyde and Madeline Myres returned in the evening. had a thunder shower in the evening. the day was cold and disagreeable. I saw Mr Corrington to day.~~

THURSDAY MARCH 9" 1865
Salem Illinois

I went to the depot for my clothing but found they had not come, to my disapointment, as I expect to need them in a "few days" I met Dr. E.W. Charles, (formerly of our Regt.) there. he has studdied Medicine attended colledge, and graduated, and came here to see Dr Green to be examined, preparatory to being commissioned as an Ass't Surg.

FRIDAY MARCH 10" 1865
Salem Illinois

I went to the depot again. Uncle Tom came home from Louisville. Ella Holton came up from Centralia. Uncle Ben & Aunt Lucy came up. Uncle Wm Black in town. E.W. Charles & Matt. Stubblefield called. He made me a present of a book I wrote him a letter to Gen'l I.N. Haynie~

SATURDAY MARCH 11" 1865
Salem Illinois

Jerry Williams came in to make some arrangements about Eph's final Statements. I prepared a certificate for R.A. Grunendike to aid him in getting a pention. Zue & Ell came down. Zue remained until after dark. I went home with her Mr Moody came in late from the north. been selling books

SUNDAY MARCH 12" 1865
Salem Illinois

Was at home most of the forenoon reading Lalla Roukh, I went with Tom, Lyde, Lute Lizzy & Zue, out to Geo. Williams to spend the evening. roads good and weather pleasant except the wind blew I stoped at Moody's and stayed until "between the late and early".~~

MONDAY MARCH 13" 1865
Salem Illinois

Uncle Wilk Allmon and Aunt Eliza, came to see me to day. I received my clothing from Cairo the coat, I like very much. I went with Lyde up to Stubblefields to see the girls. had lots of fun with Matt. Then to Moody's, and called at Dave P. Myres to ask them to my wedding, next Wednesday evening 7"P.M. I paid John R. Kell $.74.42 to day, a claim he held againss fathers estate. it was probated~

TUESDAY MARCH 14" 1865
Salem Illinois

I went to the Court-House and paid the Tax, for 1864. $.26.35. on our property. I called at Uncle Tom's but he was not at home. I went in the evening to see the Rev. T.F. Houts. Prospect of rain to day. I called at Moody's this evening to make the final arrangements for tomorrow evening.

WEDNESDAY MARCH 15" 1865
Salem Illinois

Married

Rained this morning. I went over to the court house and got my liscenss, and was married to Zue J Moody at 7.P.M. by the Rev. T.F. Houts. D.P. Myres, Aunt Julia & families, were there all of our folks, except Tom & Margret. Miss Douglass, Lizzy Black, Jenny Black & Marian Black. It rained hard in the evening and again at night.~ ["Married" written in the margin.]

THURSDAY MARCH 16" 1865
Salem Illinois

I went to the depot. the train was behind time We hitched to the hack, and Tom went with us to Odin. the train was two hours behind time Ella accompanied us to Centralia. We took dinner and went to Cairo arrived at 10.P.M. found the Armada waiting we went aboard, the boat started at 11.P.M. I lost my box of books. Cairo is under water.

FRIDAY MARCH 17" 1865
On board Str Armada

We past Paducah at Sun-up, arrived at Smithland at 10.A.M. found
Lt. Col. J.T. Foster of the 13" U.S.C. Art. Ky in command of the Post
Major Gauen had been relieved. We stoped at the Elliott House I tried
to get board at a private house but failed. half the town was under water,
and one half the citizens were boarding the other half. We found all well,
and all quiet in camp.

SATURDAY MARCH 18" 1865
Smithland Kentucky

We spent the day in the tavern. water so high that it is disagreable
getting about. I got my horse and rode up and down town made out my
Weekly, and other Reports. didn't get in until after dinner. Dr Ferris is
gone to Louisville for Vaccine Virus~

SUNDAY MARCH 19" 1865
Smithland Kentucky

Went up to quarters. We thought of going to church but the water
was so high that we didn't get there. We went out riding in a skift with
Mr Whtten & Lady and Mr. McPhearson on the back water. I rec'd a
letter from Dr. Davis asking how Ferris was absent. Dr. Abbott called
upon us~

MONDAY MARCH 20" 1865
Smithland Kentucky

We didn't get away from the tavern to day. as we expected, it is
hard getting a place to board, owing to high water. one half the town is
boarding the other half. It rained again this evening, and the wind blew
hard. I wrote to Dr. Davis, that Ferris was absent on leave from Post Hd.
Qrs.

TUESDAY MARCH 21" 1865
Smithland Kentucky

I went to see Dr. Bush to try to get boarding, but failed to get in
Nothing of interest in camp. The river is still high. We intended going
out skift riding but the wind blew so hard that we abandoned the idea.
The water is still over the principle part of the town.~

WEDNESDAY MARCH 22" 1865
Smithland Kentucky

The wind blowing disagreeably cold. I called to see Dr. Carsons about getting board again, but the prospect is not very flattering. We are destined to stay at the old tavern. John Jenkins came up with clothing to issue to the men of this Detachment, to day.

THURSDAY MARCH 23" 1865
Smithland Kentucky

I paid $.21.00 for one weeks board to include breakfast to morrow morning. Capt Cheney came up, and he and Lt. Dohrman paid us a visit. John Jenkins wrote the names of my photographs in my Album for me Dr. Bush promised to board us soon.

FRIDAY MARCH 24" 1865
Smithland Kentucky

I got some blanks from the Med. Director to day, for current Reports. Capt Cheney went back to Paducah to day he is on duty there. Zue & I went to take a walk this evening. Monthly Statements of Hospt Fund came back for further correction to Dr Ferris~

SATURDAY MARCH 25" 1865
Smithland Kentucky

I made out and forwarded my Reports by the Str Silver Moon to Paducah to-day. Serg'ts Goshorn & Gray got ten days furlough to day to go to Illinois. All quiet in camp, nothing of interest going on. We just go through the regular routine of business every day without chang or modification.~

SUNDAY MARCH 26" 1865
Smithland Kentucky

A fair morning. We went to church to day at 11.A.M. and heard a good sermon. spent the ballance of the day in our room. Nothing of interest occuring, except the trees are getting green and Spring is coming.~

MONDAY MARCH 27" 1865
Smithland Kentucky

I went to the court house this morning and took Zue with me. found Fred Roettger Co. "C,, with Varrioloid and sent him to the Pest Hosptl. I went to the artists he says he will take us to board tomorrow. all right if he does~ [" Smallpox Roettger" written in the margin.]

TUESDAY MARCH 28" 1865
Smithland Kentucky

I settled up my tavern bill $.12.00 and went to the mess to board. borrowed $.20.00 of FJB. We went shoping, bought Zue a calico dress at 30cts. pr yd. & a pr of sheets for $.6.75. took possession of the I.O.O.F.'s room and took possession. The artists backed out. Dr Ferris returned, to day.

WEDNESDAY MARCH 29" 1865
Smithland Kentucky

I paid Capt Fischer cater of our mess $.10.00. Dr Abbott, came over to day to make his Reports for the end of the Month, and took supper with us. I cleaned up our room and piled up the furniture of the I.O.O.F. in one side of the room in one side out of the way as much as possible. Think we are doing fine~

THURSDAY MARCH 30" 1865
Smithland Kentucky

Dr Abbott came over and brought his sword, belt, sash & valise and left with us. he is going up the river with a Det of his Regt. Capt Fischer put six men in jail to day for leaving quarters and staying without leave. The men drew wood & whiskey. Zue called upon Mrs. Snyder.

FRIDAY MARCH 31ST 1865
Smithland Kentucky

In quarters most all day. Col W.P. Moore came up in the evening, to stay till to morrow I made out and forwarded Personal Reports to day. all quiet, and we comfortable, owing the high water = covering a considerable portion of the town. many of the citizens are unable to remain in their own houses, and are being entertained by friends and neighbors= hence most of the tenable houses are full= which renders it almost imposible for strangers to get board except at the old tavern= and there charges are entirely out of proportion to their, fare and accomodations. So we are not going to be dependent upon the citizens=

SATURDAY APRIL 1" 1865
Smithland Kentucky

I went to work to day and made out my Monthly Report to the Med. Director, and sent it off Then I re-vaccinnated the entire detachment I had to send a guard after some of the men, as I had a peremtory order to do it, and some of the men had been vaccinated several times before. The Smallpox is still raging among colored troops, and citizens. ["Smallpox" written in the margin.]

SUNDAY APRIL 2" 1865
Smithland Kentucky

Zue was sick all day with head ache, and I had to remain about quarters most of the day= not much to do here but rotine[routine] duty and I am going to try to get relieved from duty as Post Surgeon of this place, and let the heavy Colored have, it all, to themselves=

MONDAY APRIL 3" 1865
Smithland Kentucky

Col. J.T. Foster promised to relieve me from duty as Post Surgeon at my own request to day. Telegraphic dispatch received that Petersburg & Richmond were in the hand of our troops A Salute was fired at Paducah at noon, and another here in P.M. We attended a party, at Col. Fosters.

TUESDAY APRIL 4" 1865
Smithland Kentucky

The papers confirm the dispatch of yesterday, with some of the particulars of the fighting and capture. The officer of the 13" U.S.C. claim that the Negroes there had the honor of first getting into the rebel works I am not relieved as I expected yesterday.

WEDNESDAY APRIL 5" 1865
Smithland Kentucky

The weather is disagreeable I tried to get in the Monthly statements of Hosp't Fund but after it came, I found it was wrong. I wrote Dr Ferris a note that I would make it out for him my self, in order to get it off without farther delay. It seems he is the most incorageable Medical officer I have ever met with in the Army.

THURSDAY APRIL 6" 1865
Smithland Kentucky

Col. Moore, Lieuts McGregor, & Heinzelman & Sergeant Wash Boyd came up from Paducah. Billy brought some clothing for the detachment. Zue & I went up on the hill near Capt Bush's to see the river. The weather is pleasant again. I went over to see Drs. Ferris & Piper

FRIDAY APRIL 7" 1865
Smithland Kentucky

Col Moore, Lts McGregor & Heinzelman & Boyd returned to Paducah to day. I remained in quarters most of the day. Telegraphic dispatches from E.M. Stanton Sec. of War anouncess farther successes of Gen'l Phil Sheridan in the Shanendaoh Valley~

SATURDAY APRIL 8" 1865
Smithland Kentucky

I made reports and as usual had to carry back those received from the Surgs of the 13" U.S.C. for correction. Zue washed to-day. in the evening Col Foster and Adjt Smith called in, and we had some music on the guitar. Zue & I went to the stores and tried to get some guitar strings but failed~

SUNDAY APRIL 9" 1865
Smithland Kentucky

In quarters all day. the weather was too disagreeable to have church so we spent the day as best we could in reading singing, talking etc. We are not well enough acquainted with anybody to go visiting, and its to wet and muddy to go if we were. so we have a perfect monotony under the circumstances

Lee's Surrender (handwritten margin note)

MONDAY APRIL 10" 1865
Smithland Kentucky

News received of the Surrender of Gen'l Lee's Army; to Gen'l Grant. Salutes fired at different posts; bells rung, boats whistled & guns fired at this post. at night there was an illiumination by citizens & soldiers and apparently unmeasured rejoicings, bonfires huzzahs & patriotic songs~

TUESDAY APRIL 11" 1865
Smithland Kentucky

Colored Officer (handwritten margin note)

Zue had head ache to day and was sick. some trouble between the 49" and Col Foster & his officer of the day. our officers accused of forcing a guard and releasing a man in arrest. one of the colored officers knocked down last night by Some of our men. they dont make much.

WEDNESDAY APRIL 12" 1865
Smithland Kentucky

Major Gauen and Capt Lockwood came up to spend a day or two with us. the Capt was quite unwell. at night he had meeting in the lower story of the court house, but in consequence of his indisposition he made the services quite short. he had good order.

THURSDAY APRIL 13" 1865
Smithland Kentucky

Capture Linchburg Forrest Roddey Selma Montgomery (handwritten margin note)

Capt Lockwood, sick, and in bed all day. Zue went over to Mrs Grujats (the druggist's wife) visiting. News received of the capture of Linchburg, also of the capture of Gen'ls Forrest and Roddey and their commands, together with Selma and Montgomery Alabama I received a letter from Capt. J.W. Cheney containing $.5.40 making he and I square~

FRIDAY APRIL 14" 1865
Smithland Kentucky

Adj't Smith placed Lieut Latsch in arrest because he refused to inspect the negro guards to day at guard mounting. Capt. Lockwood didn't get off, he was quite sick all day with diphtheria. Zue washed to day. I rec'd my box of books, almost a month in coming.

SATURDAY APRIL 15" 1865
Smithland Kentucky
A telegraphic dispatch anounces the assassination of President Lincoln and Secretary Seward in Washington last night. all business is suspended here in consequence. a meeting appointed for to-morrow by the citizens. Capt Lockwood left to day for Paducah in company with Major Gauen.

SUNDAY APRIL 16" 1865
Smithland Kentucky
The citizen's meeting was thronged with officers and soldiers, and quite a number of speeches made some very cutting remarks made by a gun boat officer I was not there, as I understood it to be a citizen's meeting. We went walking in the P.M. I also went horseback riding in the evening.

MONDAY APRIL 17" 1865
Smithland Kentucky
A gun was fired every half-hour, during the day, as a token of respect for the honored dead. I coppied a synopsis of the Rev Mr Thatcher's lectures, recently delivered by him in Paducah Ky. and left with me by Capt Lockwood. I think they must have been quite interesting to those who had the privilige of hearing them delivered.

TUESDAY APRIL 18" 1865
Smithland Kentucky
Lieut Latsch was continued under arrest to day by order of Col. Foster. The river still on the rise. Dr. Abbott called in the morning. while he was here, Mrs. Davis and Mrs Grujat called to pay us a visit. in the evening Dr Abbott called again~

WEDNESDAY APRIL 19" 1865
Smithland Kentucky
The river rose about Six inches last night I made reports, and went through the usual, routine of business to day. A salute of twenty one guns fired here to day. Zue had a very sore finger something like Whitlow or Fellon It rained again this evening.~

THURSDAY APRIL 20" 1865
Smithland Kentucky

Rain, Rain, Rain. It rained most all day. I Rec'd letters from Frank, and wrote Lyde The river still on the rampage. We went to work to day and moved our Colledge to a respectable distance from quarters. Requested Col Foster to move a nuisance from our part of town

FRIDAY APRIL 21ST 1865
Smithland Kentucky

All quiet in camp, nothing of interest going on. I went down town a time or two and waded the back water by the Masonic Hall. skifts and canoes will be in demand again in a day or so if the river continues to rise. some are running now. I wrote letter to Frank and Bob Lovell to day.~

SATURDAY APRIL 22" 1865
Smithland Kentucky

I made the usual Reports to day after the usual trouble of returning them for correction The river is said to be on a stand to day Dr Josiah Abbott received a commission to day as Surgeon of the 119" U.S.C. Infty. he was not expecting it and was very much surprized.~

SUNDAY APRIL 23" 1865
Smithland Kentucky

After making reports Dr. Abbott came over, Capt Fischer went down to Paducah. Zue & I went walking, and borrowed a skift and then went riding on the back water and river in and near town. The Ky 13" went out on dressparade and then on drill~

MONDAY APRIL 24" 1865
Smithland Kentucky

All quiet. the river commencing to fall Nothing of interest going on in camp Zue called upon Mrs Grujat this evening The town authorities filling up the streets in fron[t] of Mr. T.M. Davis' house~ it has been almost impassable.

TUESDAY APRIL 25" 1865
Smithland Kentucky

relieved

Col *Foster ed*

I was relieved from duty to day as Post-Surgeon by order of Col
Foster and Succeeded by Dr Fred. W. Ferris Surg. 13" U.S.C. Art (Ky)
now they have it all in their own hands, and joy be with them for I cant
lay [be covert in action]. The weather is pleasant and the river falling
Zue washed to day. then dried her clothes and ironed them.~

WEDNESDAY APRIL 26" 1865
Smithland Kentucky

Capt Fischer returned from Paducah. Zue and I went out to Mr.
Stinebreakers and walked. took dinner, had Lettus, Radishes Onnions,
Roast chicken fried Ham Milk & butter and Light breadcakes & coffee
etc. We walked back to town in the evening. weather clear and warm

THURSDAY APRIL 27" 1865
Smithland Kentucky

Cloudy to day. We got orders to go to Paducah with the detachment.
Lt & Adjt Smith took supper with us. Miss Littlefield came and called
upon us. Most of the detailed men relieved. We turned over our fuel to
the Q.M. The citizens are loth to see us leave, or to see the darkies come
in.

darkies

FRIDAY APRIL 28" 1865
Smithland Kentucky

Cloudy and raining. we packed up and started. went aboard the Str
Victor No. 2. of the Q.M. Dept. arrived at Paducah at 11.A.M. We
went to camp then to Mrs. Swift's and stoped for the time being. Zue &
Mrs Mercer visited camp. I got lumber to build. I accepted a commission
as 1st Asst. Surg. 49" Ills Infty

SATURDAY APRIL 29" 1865
Paducah Kentucky

I went to camp and saw Dr Mercer attend sick-call then I went to
work, and Wm. E. Farrow helped me. I went to Mr. Harts and bog'ht
five lbs of nails, and at dark we got my quarters done except making the
door. Zue has sick head-ache very bad. I saw Keath and Asa Atteberry

in camp. They are here in the places of Wm. & Jasper Branson, and I suppose to see how they like soldiering~

SUNDAY APRIL 30" 1865
Paducah Kentucky

I made personal Report and handed in for April. Zue was sick with head-ache most all day. We occupied Mrs Swift's room during the day, in the evening we went over to camp, and I made up the bed and fixed up our arrangements as best I could, and concluded that we would spend the night there as we were in the way at Mrs Swifts, not in her way, but in that of Mrs Mercer. Now four months have passed, since we left the front, that we may be said to have "rested from our labors["] = true some of us have not been entirely idle = yet we have been free from campaigning and its consequent hardships = privations = Exposures = and Casualties = No men killed in battle, and but very few deaths from disease = comfortable quarters, good rations, = and moderate duty = is condusive to health, as has been demonstrated every-time the conditions have been enjoyed = while on the contrary when we have endured exposures, in bad weather, poor, or unsuitable diet, and excessive guard and fatigue duties = the contrarin consequences have as surely followed = There may be less glory in this kind of service = but theres a deal more pleasure in it, especially to those who have sought glory on the field =

MONDAY MAY 1" 1865
Paducah Kentucky

I attended Sick call this morning Dr. Mercer made out his Reports. Nick Burns got my horse shod to day, and I turned him into the lot around our quarters to graze. Dr. Davis sent for me this Evening I have to go to Smithland to investigate the Hospital accts of the Surgeon at that place to-morrow. they are not right for April.

TUESDAY MAY 2" 1865
Paducah Kentucky

I attended sick call, then went to Smithland on the Str Fashion, got the Hospt Abstracts from the A.C.S. and went to the Hospt and found a big job and a tedious one. I took supper at the Elliott House. Col. Moore & a Det of men went up the Cumberland river to night. Zue & Laura fell out to day.

WEDNESDAY MAY 3" 1865
Smithland Kentucky

I made the investigation to day found many mistakes in the A.C.S.'s papers. I stayed at the Elliott House last night and took breakfast there this morning. I owe $.1.50 for bill. am broke I left at noon on the Str Baldwin hoping never to see Smithland again while in service

colored

THURSDAY MAY 4" 1865
Paducah Kentucky

I recee'd a letter from Lyde with $.20.00 in it I paid Mrs Swift $.10.00. Rec'd an order to accompany a flag of truce Expedition under Col. Symms started at 10.A.M. traveled 26 miles and camped at Mayfield. I think Dr Mercer was ordered to go but either beged, or lied, out of it, to Dr. Davis.

FRIDAY MAY 5" 1865
Mayfield Kentucky

We started at 7.A.M. after a pleasant night, and splendid supper and breakfast with a Mr. Slaton My horse is lame. We stoped at Boydsville for dinner just at the Tenn & Ky state line. While there a Rebel Major Lewis, a Capt & Lt & private came in on their way to Paducah to surrender, gave their parole [the promise of a prisoner of war to fulfill stated conditions in consideration of his release]. We went 12 miles farther and captured a Capt Dumas stoped with him for the night. Marched 22 miles to day.

Boydsv. Ky

SATURDAY MAY 6" 1865
Mr. Henry's Tennessee

Started at 8.A.M. Met a rebel Col Hewey with a flag of truce. We went into Paris Tenn. and met several rebel officers. took dinner with a Dr. Worthing. Col Hewey went on with us we traveled 24 miles and camped at Macedonia. We found forage scarce, here. My horse has lost a shoe and is quite lame.~

SUNDAY MAY 7" 1865
Macedonia Tennessee

Started at 7.A.M. the weather cloudy and drizzling rain we past Huntington, and stoped at McLemoresville after traveling 13. miles for dinner. We left half the command here with Lt. Murry Col. Hewey stoped with them I went on with the other De't. 11. miles through a swampy country and stoped at dark at Lavinia all night.

MONDAY MAY 8" 1865
Lavinia Tennessee

started at 5.A.M. in the rain, rode Six miles to Spring Creek, and we got breakfast with a Dr Woolfack. then exchanged shots with some rebels. I went in charge of the advance guard. went into Jackson, had a meeting with Col Newsome (rebel) gave his parole. we returned 8 miles and stoped with a Mr. Hays for the night

TUESDAY MAY 9" 1865
Mr. Hay's Tennessee

We started at 5.A.M. went five miles to Spring Creek, and took breakfast with Dr. Woolfack again, then came on to McLemoresville. we took dinner, then went over to Mr Harrolds Fatherinlaw of the Rebel Col Lannins and took supper. Capts Cleybourn & Parkinson came in under flag of truce to cappitulate. We stoped at night with a man near the seminary

WEDNESDAY MAY 10" 1865
McLemoresville Tennessee

started at 6.30. A.M. reached Huntington at 9.A.M. We stoped and paroled some rebels, to meet us at Parris to morrow. eat dinner then went on to within 6 miles of Paris. stoped with a Mr. Carter. found him a very penurious, little, mean, stingy, narrow souled man. he took the crank off his pump to keep the men from drinking water.

THURSDAY MAY 11" 1865
Mr. Carter's Tennessee

Raining this morning, started at 8.A.M. after going about three miles I missed my revolver, and had to go back for it. We stoped at Paris, to dinner again with Dr Worthin. found but few of our rebels here to meet us We went about five miles and stoped with a Mr Young. had some music by the young ladies.

FRIDAY MAY 12" 1865
Mr. Young's Tennessee

Started at 7.A.M. came to Mr Henry's. Met some of our Rebels there. We came on, left two Co's there to receive Pettyjohn's command stoped with a Mr. Adair and got dinner, then to Mayfield and stoped with Mr. Slaton Adjts Taylor & Murry went to Paducah by train. Pettyjohn didn't come to turn.

SATURDAY MAY 13" 1865
Mayfield Kentucky

We started at 7.A.M. and rode briskly. stoped half an hour and rested on the road then pushed on and arrived at Paducah at 2.P.M. and thus terminated the bloodless expedition of the war. We found all quiet and in comfortable circumstances, except Zue was unwell. I borrowed $.40.00 of F.J. Burrows. I paid Mrs. Christman $.20.00 for board. Then went down town and bought two pr of drawers for $.4.00.~

SUNDAY MAY 14" 1865
Paducah Kentucky

All was quiet, and nothing of interest in camp, except our resting after ten days hard riding is rather agreeable. Zue is quite unwell to day. Dr. Mercer has a five days leave of absence to take his wife home and I wish he had a three months leave to stay with her.

MONDAY MAY 15" 1865
Paducah Kenducky

Dr. Mercer started home with his wife on a five days leave. I went to see Dr. Davis and take over Drs. Ferris' & Piper's abstracts I saw Rebel Col Hewey. he is staying about town now, goes and comes as he pleases. I attended sick call and wrote to Lyde by Dr Mercer.~

TUESDAY MAY 16" 1865
Paducah Kentucky

Attended sick call. then went to Hd. Qrs. Post and got an order for an ambulance horse turned in to the Q.M. through mistake. I bought 8. yds calico to make a bedspread. bought Zue a Bible $.4.50. A speaking at the Market house to night by Meridith & Hicks. Capt Fischer got one month pay at Cairo.

WEDNESDAY MAY 17" 1865
Paducah Kentucky

Zue was quite unwell all day. Mrs Swift called in the evening to see her. she has kept her bed all day and eat but little I transfered the list of sick, from the memorandum to the Register Proper for the months of April & May. The health of the Regiment is good at present that is, there is but little serious sickness now.~

THURSDAY MAY 18" 1865
Paducah Kentucky

I attended sick call, then went down town with my boots to get them mended. I bought some ice for Zue to day. She has Dysentery and is quite sick. News of the capture of Jeff. Davis in the papers to day. Capt Lockwood called upon us this evening. nothing of interest in camp to day.~

FRIDAY MAY 19" 1865
Paducah Kentucky

Several commissions came to day one for McGregor as Capt., one for Goshorn as Capt., and as Lts for Niles Laur and others. Zue is much better she didn't go to dinner to day we had Strawberries and cream. Rec'd letter from Ella

SATURDAY MAY 20" 1865
Paducah Kentucky

Zue was very sick this morning I sent to the Hospital, and got a stretcher and Billy Farrow & I carried her to Mr Swifts. wrote to Lyde of her illness. attended sick call, & made reports this morning. Dr Mercer came this evening. brought me a letter & a linnen coat from Lyde. got my boots half soled to day, paid $.2.00 for it.~

SUNDAY MAY 21" 1865
Paducah Kentucky

Dr. Mercer attended sick call. I stayed and attended to Zue, she had a very restless night, and is but little better this morning I stayed at the house all day. she was little better at night and eat some supper, the first for several days. Carrie Christman has been sick several days and is but little better. Dr. Mercer came in several times to day.~

MONDAY MAY 22" 1865
Paducah Kentucky

Weather warm and pleasant. I stayed, with Zue all day. she slept and felt much better in the evening. had some apitite to eat. I wrote Lyde that Zue was better this evening.

I received a letter from Frank to day written April 27". camp quiet again to-day nothing of interest going on.~

TUESDAY MAY 23" 1865
Paducah Kentucky

Another dull day with me. - I lost sleep last night. Zue was quite restless though she is improving some. she does not rest at night. she has some fever, and has to have ice to use night and day.~

WEDNESDAY MAY 24" 1865
Paducah Kentucky

I stayed most of the day with Zue. I went to town and bought her some cracke[r]s, and a little cup to cook soup & panada in for her. I was to camp a little while. Nothing of interest there. - A May festival in town to night. F.J.B. & McGregor and others helped deckorate the room~

THURSDAY MAY 25" 1865
Paducah Kentucky

Frank. J. Burrows is ordered to report at Louisville Ky. for duty as a Mustering officer but he dont want to go. he left some accts with me for collection. Zue was quite uneasy this A.M., but was much better this evening. she is generaly worst during the night. I received a letter from, and wrote to Lyde and Frank~

FRIDAY MAY 26" 1865
Paducah Kentucky

F.J. Burrows left for Louisville Ky. for duty. I think Lt. Harlan got him this order so that he might visit him. perhaps Frank had something to do with it, but it is, little more of a "good thing" than he wanted, just now. Zue is improving slowly now. There is a circus in town at this time.~

SATURDAY MAY 27" 1865
Paducah Kentucky

I went down town and bought some coal-oil, and Harper's Monthly. The circus is in town their charriat past by here this morning. Zue is better. Mr Bough came to tell us good bye, he is going to Illinois

SUNDAY MAY 28" 1865
Paducah Kentucky

Zue is much better now. I was with her most all day. Nothing of interest in camp. We had a very hard shower in the afternoon. The day has been warm and will probably be pleasanter from this time on. it has been

MONDAY MAY 29" 1865
Paducah Kentucky

I made out my personal reports to day so that they might be ready when the time comes to hand them in. I was at the house most all day, with Zue she is able to sit up some. I brought her clothes from quarters to night thing[think] she can sit up some to morrow. The Reg't had dressparade this evening for the first time in almost an age. Wrote to Helen Moody.

TUESDAY MAY 30" 1865
Paducah Kentucky

Zue was better to day, able to dress herself and be up most all day. Charley skined his legs, through the carelessness of some of the boys in giving him to much halter. a festival at one of the churches to night. Nothing of importance going on in camp~

WEDNESDAY MAY 31" 1865
Paducah Kentucky

I helped attend sick-call this morning and, handed in my personal Reports to Dr. Mercer to forward. Zue is improving she is able to be up part of the time. I think she will be well soon if she dont eat to much, as she has a ravinous appetite. Paducah is a pleasant place to live, in many respects. There is considerable wealth, a city on a hill that cant be hid, rolling, Sandy= or rather gravel, streets which dont get very muddy= nor remain wet long after a Shower= but politically there is a large rebel element here, and commercially it [is] a poor place to buy as prices are exorbitant= yet when peace is fully come, Competition will in a great measure remedy things of this character=

THURSDAY JUNE 1" 1865
Paducah Kentucky

I attended sick-call this morning. Then made out Dr. Mercer's Monthly Reports for him, as I have almost always done when with the Regiment at the end of the month. Then went down town and bought papers, and came back and read them. Not much news in them all quiet in camp to day. No excitement

FRIDAY JUNE 2" 1865
Paducah Kentucky

I commenced to make my final Return of Medicines & Hospital stores to day, after attending sick-call. Zue was sick again this morning, had Sick head-ache and was not able to be up until in the P.M. I rec'd letters from Frank & Lyde to-day.

SATURDAY JUNE 3" 1865
Paducah Kentucky

I attended sick call this morning, and made out Weekly Reports. Then called upon Dr. Davis in the afternoon. Worked the rest of the day on my final returns, have everything off my hands except a vaccinator. I got Zue's breast pin repaired.~

SUNDAY JUNE 4" 1865
Paducah Kentucky

Zue had Sarspuin[Sarsaparilla] to day. I attended sick call to day, then spent the rest of the day at the house all quiet, and nothing of interest in camp, so we go through the regular routine of business prescribing [,] making reports etc.

MONDAY JUNE 5" 1865
Paducah Kentucky

I attended sick call, as usual this A.M. In the evening Zue went over to camp and we stayed there for the night for the first time since she has been sick. She has been at Mrs Swift's for Sixteen days, and is barely able to get about now but she had rather be here by ourselves than at the house with all the company and noise.

TUESDAY JUNE 6" 1865
Paducah Kentucky

After sick call, Dr. Allen & Dr. Ball came around inspecting quarters, rations, Men, books etc. found the quarters, in good condition and I think Dr. Allen will report favorably. In the evening Zue & I walked down to the wharf, got some soda water to drink. I went to the river swiming at night.~~

WEDNESDAY JUNE 7" 1865
Paducah Kentucky

I attended sickcall, then Dr. Allen sent for me to help Invoice some Medical &. Q.M. stores he was inspecting for Dr. Mercer. in the evening I went to work making triplicate copies, of the inventory for Dr. Mercer. in the evening Zue & I went walking again. she is regaining her strength slowly~

THURSDAY JUNE 8" 1865
Paducah Kentucky

It rained this morning we had to go to breakfast between showers. I attended sick call then went to the Christian Commission Rooms to see Walker of Co "B,, sick attended a prayer Meeting while there. we had a pair of Exquisites [one who is overly fastidious in dress or ornament] to board with us to day, a Dr. Willard and Lady. I think they are in the wrong pew.~

FRIDAY JUNE 9" 1865
Paducah Kentucky

After sick call, the Pay-Master, Maj J. Fenno came and paid off the regiment at our tent. I received $.217.95 two months pay. I paid Mrs. Swift $.25.00 for board, F.J. Burrows $.60.00 borrowed money. I collected $.6.00 from Co. "D,, boys, for shoes & sock I bought them last fall. After night I went to the uper end of town to see a sick Cavalry man.~

SATURDAY JUNE 10" 1865
Paducah Kentucky

I attended sick call & made Weekly Reports. I paid Capt Fischer $.30.00 for board in the Mess while at Smithland. Went down town with Zue and bought her a lawn dress $.8.00, parasol $.6.00, pr shoes $.4.50 domestic thread, buttons, etc $.3.30, two linnen shirts for my self $.7.00

SUNDAY JUNE 11" 1865
Paducah Kentucky

I attended sick call, as usual, then visited the U.S. Military Prison, that is assigned to me now. I saw Dr. Davis this morning he spoke of the Post Hospital, but says he will not order any one to receipt for the property there. I let Mr. Christman have my horse to ride to day cow hunting.

MONDAY JUNE 12" 1865
Paducah Kentucky

I attended sick-call then the prison, and then cut another window in my house. I paid up my board to, to day. paid Mrs Swift $.12.00 Capts Lockwood Logan & Houston and Lts Livesay Lovejoy & Pence came into our mess at Mrs Swift's to board.~

TUESDAY JUNE 13" 1865
Paducah Kentucky

We went to breakfast through the rain, attended the usual duties of the day. and then spent the rest of the time with Zue. she is making her dress. Our Exquisites are still boarding with us. he pretends to be practicing Surgery, but the general opinion is, that he is a professional gambler and black leg [a swindler; esp. a dishonest gambler]. he is a native of Louisana, so he says~

WEDNESDAY JUNE 14" 1865
Paducah Kentucky

After the usual duties of the day, I took Charley down town to a smith, and got a pr of shoes put on him for $.1.25. then got Frank's horse and Zue & I went riding to the "Three Mile house," started back and got caught in a shower of rain stoped under a shed by the road side, but got slightly damp.

THURSDAY JUNE 15" 1865
Paducah Kentucky

Nothing of interest in camp to day. in the afternoon Mrs. Willard visited us. after supper Zue & I went to Fort Anderson and saw the contents several heavy guns (32.Pdrs) and some field pieces, and the ammunition it is a very strong fort, as Col. Hicks, demonstrated

FRIDAY JUNE 16" 1865
Paducah Kentucky

I attended sick-call, and visited the prison. not much sickness in prison or camp. I can attend the Regt. Prison & Battery, (I have it now.) in two hours. Dr. Willard and Lady called upon us this evening at quarters. I took a bullet out of Clem. Williamson's back to day received at Pleasant Hill La. in Apl. 1864.

SATURDAY JUNE 17" 1865
Paducah Kentucky

I atte[nde]d the sick of the Regt. Batt. & prison then made my weekly reports. Dr. Mercer doing nothing. he has some government property on his hand to dispose of and gets nothing done but fuss about that. Dr. Davis is getting tired of him. Capt. John L. Stanley is in camp to day he came back to see his friends in the regiment. he looks fine.

SUNDAY JUNE 18" 1865
Paducah Kentucky

I performed the usual duties to day and put in the time in the regular routine system. I visited the prison twice to day= The 4." A.C. is passing here to day on their way to Texas. It rained at noon. I staid at quarters except in going to meals.

MONDAY JUNE 19" 1865
Paducah Kentucky

I performed the usual duties. paid Mrs Christman $.12.00 board to this date, to-day. N.M. Hickman Co. "F,, got his face badly cut up by a citizen to-day. Zue had Head-ache. I rec'd a letter from Lyde and wrote her one in reply.

TUESDAY JUNE 20" 1865
Paducah Kentucky

Nothing of special interest in camp to day. Zue & I went shoping got her a belt and pr. gloves. in the evening Zue & Frank went and called up[on] Mrs. Trainer a lady friend of Franks. she came to see Zue while she was sick, also a Miss. Bolinger~

WEDNESDAY JUNE 21" 1865
Paducah Kentucky

All quiet in camp, a perfect monotony rules the hour. We eat, drink and sleep alternately. by the way there was one unusual feature in the dinner to day. we had 'Ice cream' for desurt. I attend all the sick, except, it's an occasional call by some of the boys and have more leisure than I know what to do with, or how to employ.~

THURSDAY JUNE 22" 1865
Paducah Kentucky

What shall I record for the event of to day that I may remember it in contra-distinction from other days.? Where there are such a similarity of circumstances, or such a total wand [want] of events. To day we performed the usual routine of duties, and had nothing unusual except it was the bass drum at tattoo~

FRIDAY JUNE 23" 1865
Paducah Kentucky

By mistake I have recorded the events of to day for yesterday, and yesterdays for this date. Well I got, (that is yesterday) Franks horse, and Zue & I went out to the country riding, stoped at a house and got some plumbs & Rasberries. returned just before dark, and didn't get wet this Time~

SATURDAY JUNE 24" 1865
Paducah Kentucky

After the duties of the morning, I made application to Lt. Taylor for five days leave of absence but it came back disapproved by Col. Symes

Comndg Post. Nothing of interest in camp. Battery "B,, 2" Ills Artillery is ordered to Springfield Illinois for muster out of service. hope we may follow soon.~

SUNDAY JUNE 25" 1865
Paducah Kentucky

I made another application to day for leave: this time for three days Col. Moore will take it in person to the various Hd Qrs for me Frank is trying for one, to we want to get to Salem by the 1st July to the Soldiers reception. We had a shower about noon to day, and the air was cooler afterwards~

MONDAY JUNE 26" 1865
Paducah Kentucky

Dr. Davis sent me to Smithland with a verbal message to Dr. Piper to remain at the pest house with the sick The 13" U.S.C. Art. Ky was just leaving, he went with it. I visited the Hospts, found two dead men in one of them I went up on the Liberty No. 2. and came down on the Horner. Made a written report. I paid the Elliott house $.1.50

TUESDAY JUNE 27" 1865
Paducah Kentucky

I attended sick-call, then copied my report of yesterday and carried it to Dr. Davis, talked with him an hour. he is getting very much out of patience with Dr. Mercer about some property he has on hand, in one of the churches. I then visited the prison. The health is good.

WEDNESDAY JUNE 28" 1865
Paducah Kentucky

I attended my usual duties to day without any thing to mark this, from other days, except the diference in date. I made out my personal Reports to have them ready on the last day of the month. At dark Zue & I went walking four or five squares up town.~

THURSDAY JUNE 29" 1865
Paducah Kentucky

After performing the duties of the day, I called upon Dr. Davis and told him I was going to Salem, he is going to Paris Ills. Adj't. Taylor sent us word that the convoy was going at 1.P.M. to-day. afterwards to start immediately. We left at 10.A.M. accompanied by Col. Hicks, Adjt. Taylor, Dr. Davis & Dr Graham of the 40" Ills. F.J.B & McGregor came down in the evening We had storm on the way. We arrived at Cairo Ills 4.P.M.

FRIDAY JUNE 30" 1865
Cairo Illinois

We took a sleeping car and started at 1.A.M. after fighting muskquitoes all night. Zue had head ache very bad. We got breakfast at Centralia Ills. We met R.M. Lovell Capt Castle & Dr Kell Rainey at Odin and met Frank, Lyde, & Tom at Salem depot with the hack looking for us~ We found all well at home, and big preparations Making for a big demonstration to morrow in honor of Marion County's Soldier boys= and especially on behalf of those of the One Hundred and Eleventh regiment= which but recently returned for Muster Out,= having been Most three years since they left here for the tented fields with its Casualties privations and hardships, and while its return has brought Joy, and Comfort, and, blessing to Many a hearthstone; on the other hand= it has brought, heartaches, and tears= and Mourning to Many others, that but a few years ago, were looking on the bright side of life's picture, without any forebodings of the dark shadings that were in store for them on the reverse=

SATURDAY JULY 1" 1865
Salem Illinois

We went out to the fair ground, followed by the 111" Ills. Infty. found all ready. The Rev. T.F. Houts made the reception speech followed by Bre'd.[Brevetted], Brig. Gen'l. J.S. Martin with response. had music in the intervals, then dinner, then speeches by Gen'l. I.N. Haynie & Col. Hicks. all went of[f] well. Ed. Black was there. all sitisfied [satisfied] except copperheads, which was a compliment to the rest.

SUNDAY JULY 2" 1865
Salem Illinois

I am thirty years old to day. We went out to New Middleton to day to Mr Moody's for dinner to day Lyde, Lute, Art, Hellen, Zue & I. saw the citizens gipsying [gypsying] around town. We saw Ike Lear & Ann

Pruden. Not much improvement going on. We returned to Salem in the evening.

MONDAY JULY 3" 1865
Salem Illinois

Scott Lydick, Lyde, Zue & I went to the fair ground and took down the mottoes of saturday. Mother Frank, Lyde, Lute, Tom, Julia, Mary, Zue & I went out to Margret's. C.R. O'Neill & Aunt Harriett came out there. Zue & I went to D.P. Myres and took supper Frank came up and took supper also *D. P. Myres*

TUESDAY JULY 4" 1865
Salem Illinois

Frank, Lyde, Lute, Tom, Zue & I went out to Tonti in the hack. Col. Hicks went with us. We went to Centralia, then out to the grove through the dust. found many people there but the celebration a failure we eat dinner with Col. Pease, and went to his house, and took tea. returned to Salem via Tonti.~

WEDNESDAY JULY 5" 1865
Salem Illinois

Frank bought a Mowing Machine and hay rake to day and commenced cutting hay F.J. Burrows was down for dinner; Hank & Frank Farsons came Mrs Moody came. Dave Myres & Sarah & Aunt Julia were here for supper. R.M. Lovell came in the afternoon~ George & Margret came in after dark. The weather was very pleasant.~ I borrowed $.50.00 of Frank Black this evening.~

THURSDAY JULY 6" 1865
Salem Illinois

I gave Zue $.10.00 this morning and Frank Burrows & I started at 7.A.M. JFB & Tom took us to Tonti We met Col Hicks at Odin & Lt Taylor at Centralia. had a very dusty and warm trip. We found the Str. Armada in waiting. We heard the first Katedids at Caledonia this evening, for this year~

FRIDAY JULY 7" 1865
Paducah Kentucky

I paid Mrs Christman $.20.00 for board. I attended sick call, then visited the prison, Dr Mercer has been very neglectful during my absence. Mrs Swift returned from her visit to the country this P.M. Dr Best 44" Wis Infty is at Mrs Swifts sick. I went swiming to night. Bed Bugs have routed Frank, Nick, Billy & Jake Haer.

SATURDAY JULY 8" 1865
Paducah Kentucky

The weather is very warm and dry and dusty. I attended the usual duties to day made weekly reports. health good considering the extreme warm weather. Mr Christman went up into Ills to some springs for his health. Lt McGregor came back last night. camp very dull.

SUNDAY JULY 9" 1865
Paducah Kentucky

I performed my usual duties. We had very flattering prospect of rain all day, but we didn't get any of any consequence. I went to the Millitary prison in the P.M. to see a darkey taking smallpox. I sent him to the Pest House for treatment I have been feeling quite unwell all day, and took some *Pelenla Hydragri~*

MONDAY JULY 10" 1865
Paducah Kentucky

After sick call & visiting the prison I went to bed and didn't get up till supper I was very sick with Fever & Head ache, something like an Intermittent, I think. Nothing of interest in camp. rumor that we are going to be mustered out soon. No more furloughs & Leaves.

TUESDAY JULY 11" 1865
Paducah Kentucky

I felt a little better this morning after a very disagreeable night. Dr Mercer got up so late I attended sick-call, then went to work making out my Returns of Clothing Camp & Garrison Equipage. set with my coat off writing, and had a chill I took 5. grs Quinine, 1/2 gr Morphia and cut off the fever

WEDNESDAY JULY 12" 1865
Paducah Kentucky

I attended the usual duties to-day, and worked out my returns of C.C. & G.E. I received a letter from Ella, for Zue, and one from Geo Killburn clerk of the Western House St Louis Mo stating that my sword was still in his possession subject to my order.

THURSDAY JULY 13" 1865
Paducah Kentucky

After my usual morning duties, I went to work at my returns, and worked most all day, and until late bed time at them, and finished them. I had to revisit the prison and send a man to Hospital from there. I've been trying to get my horse shod for some time but have not succeeded the smiths give him a very bad character.

FRIDAY JULY 14" 1865
Paducah Kentucky

Another day after the usual stile my duties have become so regular that it is a regular routine, following the same order each day. I tried to clean my gun but could not, as I found a puzzle in the britch pin I wrote Ella Holton her letter was received & Zue at home

SATURDAY JULY 15" 1865
Paducah Kentucky

At the prison, Lt. Chalfin gave me a Synopsis of the story of Uncle Tom's Cabbin this morning. I rode Charley down town and had him Shod he stood first rate. I think a dollar to the smith would have made him gentle some time ago. F.J.B. & I rode out to the grave yard at sundown.

SUNDAY JULY 16" 1865
Paducah Kentucky

Rained most all last night, and I slept most all day H.W. Kerr joined us at breakfast he has been to McNairy Co Tenn. rumors in camp of our going to be mustered out immediately of the August Elections in this state. The day has been cool and pleasant. all quiet in camp.

MONDAY JULY 17" 1865
Paducah Kentucky

After the usual duties to day, I borrowed $.40.00 of F.J. Burrows, and paid Mrs Christman $.6.00 Squaring my board to this date with her. after noon I took Charley and went riding up above Jersey. got some berries to eat. I called on Dr. Davis. he wants Dr Mercer out of service says we are not entitled to a Surgeon. I rec'd letter from & wrote to Lute to-day.

TUESDAY JULY 18" 1865
Paducah Kentucky

Well it rained and the sun shone alternately to day. during the forenoon Lt McGregor & I made application to be mustered in on our new commissions Frank J.B. is overhauling his old papers, to-day. It rained very hard at night. I set up with light burning tried to keep things dry. my roof leaks.

WEDNESDAY JULY 19" 1865
Paducah Kentucky

We had to wait until very late for breakfast this morning. I attended sick-call while it rained and Frank had guard mounting while it poured. after it quit I went to the photograph gallery and sat three times for a negative. I went to the country and picked some berries.

THURSDAY JULY 20" 1865
Paducah Kentucky

I went to the Picture rooms, and sat twice to day, at dinner I told Mrs Christman I was going into a mess to board I went with Frank to supper, at the prison after supper, Frank, Col. Moore, & I went riding to the uper end of town. We are having Seven roll calls each day now, pr order of Col. Syms Comndg Post.

FRIDAY JULY 21" 1865
Paducah Kentucky

I received an order to go to Smithland Ky and look after the sick there. I packed up my medicine, got transportation to go. then received a telegraphic dispatch from Frank Black that Zue was dangerously ill, and, for me to come, immediately. I went to Col. Hicks and got my Smithland order recinded. Telegraphed Frank I would come by first boat. I thought of going to Cairo on horseback to night but abandoned the idea. I waited and watched at the Wharf until 10.P.M. but no boat.

SATURDAY JULY 22" 1865
Paducah Kentucky

I was at the wharf at 3.A.M., but no boat until 8.A.M. the Selq Lyon started. I went on it, paid $.3.00. arrived at Cairo at 3.P.M. and a freight train started at 4.P.M. I paid $.5.10 run slow and met several trains coming down. I met with a gentleman by name of Hester formerly of the 110" Ills he had been to Nashville Tenn and married. he resides in Richview Ills.

SUNDAY JULY 23" 1865
Centralia Illinois

I arrived at 3.A.M. got a horse & buggy of Noleman paid $.4.00. arrived at Salem at 7.A.M. and learned Zue was better; found Mother sick. Lyde, Tom & I went to Middleton found Zue better yet very ill. Frank Lute & Margret came out to see her. I sent Tom to Centralia with horse & buggy. Frank & the girls returned to Salem in the evening~

MONDAY JULY 24" 1865
New Middleton Illinois

Zue rested tolerable well last night, also to day. I gave her Oleum in P.M. We had a Mess of Squirrels for dinner I wrote F.J.B. in P.M. that Zue was better. not so much visiting to day as yesterday. I find Middleton remarkable for nothing but gossip & gipsying around no improvement of any consequence.

TUESDAY JULY 25" 1865
New Middleton Illinois

It rained and stormed very hard last night. a very bad time for haying. Mrs Moody is sick also and took Oleum this evening. I got some Ice for Zue this P.M. and bought $.1.00 worth of tea for them. Mr Moody is plowing up his lot and ditching around the house. I got Zue up stairs since I came and she is more comfortable. I staid with her all day.~

WEDNESDAY JULY 26" 1865
New Middleton Illinois

Mrs Moody, and Zue are both better this morning. bought some more squirrels for them to day. they both eat harty. I received a note from Frank stating he had received a dispatch from Holton, and answered Zue was better. I wrote F.J.B. I would return Saturday

THURSDAY JULY 27" 1865
New Middleton Illinois

I left the sick, both better and went to Salem. saw Dr. Green at Middleton and went in with him to town at noon on a freight train. Frank was painting the house. I bought a valise or sachel $.3.50 Em Turner came down this evening and we had some music. I had my hair cut.

FRIDAY JULY 28" 1865
Salem Illinois

Cloudy this morning. train behind time I went on it to Middleton found Zue & Mrs Moody both better. Mr. Moody went to Salem this evening I staid with the sick until 9.P.M. then took the train for Salem. Saw Mrs Hill on the train. Met Mr Moody at the depot. I went home and to bed.

SATURDAY JULY 29" 1865
Salem Illinois

Frank Black & I started at 7.A.M. in a buggy, arrived at Centralia at 10.A.M. the train behind time. I eat dinner at the Merritt House. started at 1.P.M. Jake. O. Chance on the train going to Cairo. the 11" Ills Infty on the train going home We arrived at Cairo, 7.P.M. I paid I.C.R.R. $.5.05 I walked in vain two miles up the river to the Lady-Gay, and back. then found the Str. Tacony at the Wharf and most ready. I paid $3.00 and came up on her, Lieut Berz, Co."C,, on board.~

SUNDAY JULY 30" 1865
Paducah Kentucky

I arrived at five this morning. found Col Moore absent, and Dr. Davis relieved from duty, by Dr. Ball, 44 Wis Infty. I attended sick call,

& called upon Dr. Ball as I went to dinner. Dr Mercer has got a supply of Medicine since I've been gone I wrote to Zue, and took a nap to day.~

MONDAY JULY 31" 1865
Paducah Kentucky

I attended sick call. Made and forwarded my personal Reports. Then made out the Monthly report copied all the Old Monthly Reports, since June 1864, in the Register, as well as the weeklies since April last. I went down and called upon Dr. Davis after dark and staid until late bed time. I met Dr. R.M. Humble there Dr. Davis has been relieved from duty, and will leave for home to morrow. he has been Brevetted Lt. Col. for Meritorious Services as Medical Director in this district, Dist West Ky.

TUESDAY AUGUST 1" 1865
Paducah Kentucky

Dr. Davis left for home (Paris Ills.) this morning I paid Lt. A.S. Chalfin $.4.00 for the Mess, he is our catur. [caterer] Will. Brokaw put in the guard house to day by the 44" Wis Infty on various charges. Jake Chance in town but didn't come around I think he is fishing around Col. Hicks for some political favor. -- I went Swiming this evening with Frank, McGregor, & others.~

WEDNESDAY AUGUST 2" 1865
Paducah Kentucky

Col. Moore returned this morning his brother Erod came with him from home. One of Co. "K,. accidently shot this A.M. through the thigh. sent him to Hosp't. also H.H. Hunter. to day Dr. Mercer attended Sick call this morning for the first time in an age, when I was present.

THURSDAY AUGUST 3" 1865
Paducah Kentucky

Six citizens put in prison to-day for not reporting themselves when notified of their being draften. [drafted] another very warm day, it rained a shower in the evening. I brought Charley up and let him graze. I oiled my bridle Halter and Saddle to-day.

FRIDAY AUGUST 4" 1865
Paducah Kentucky

Attended sick-call, then read Hamilton on Fractures & Dislocations, and slept alternately too warm to do either with any comfort. Three women arrested to day by the 44"s fool out side the lines and sent to the U.S. prison but not admitted. turned over to the civil authorities

SATURDAY AUGUST 5" 1865
Paducah Kentucky

After sick call, I made Weekly Reports, then I read & slept alternately Uphoff, Baggs & Odin returned this evening with Billy Heinzelman's horse & the mules, stolen while I was absent. they brought two of the Thevies. The weather was very warm to-day. I went to the Market at night and heard some of the candidates make speeches or harrangues. Col Husbands made a speech. he claims to be a Union man now; Citizens say he is not.

SUNDAY AUGUST 6" 1865
Paducah Kentucky

Attended Sick call then wrote to Zue. while writing, I rec'd one from her stating she was improving The weather is quite warm to day. I would have attended church but the heat was so intense I didn't want to endure a coat. I had to build a smoke in my Shebang to drive the mosquitoes out.

MONDAY AUGUST 7" 1865
Paducah Kentucky

Weather cooler to day quite pleasant. Election in Kentucky to day Lt. McGregor Officer of the day, and spent most of his time at the poles. Not much interest manifested the rebel candidates ahead. Dr. Davis took his final departure this evening. I read Hamilton on fractures & Dislocations. find him very interesting indeed.

TUESDAY AUGUST 8" 1865
Paducah Kentucky

Some of the 44" Wis Infty coming in that were sent out to diferent places of holding election to keep the peace The union men carried the election in Paducah by a small majority. the opposition carried it in the country. F.J.B. & I went riding on the Cairo road, two miles. a very pleasant evening~

WEDNESDAY AUGUST 9" 1865
Paducah Kentucky

I received a letter from the Surg. Gen'l. requiring Invoices & Receipts relating to property borne on my Returns of June 11th 1865. I made and forwarded the triplicate. I wrote a letter to Dr. J.W. Martin late Surg. 52" Ind. in regard to a statement Dr. Mercer says Col. Pease made. McGregor & I went to Dist Hd. Qrs. to get our Commissions, but no one at the office.

THURSDAY AUGUST 10" 1865
Paducah Kentucky

One of the 44" Wis Infty. was to be drumed out of service at 10. A.M. but it rained, and it was posponed til tomorrow. H.H. Hunter was on trial to day Dr's Ball & Mercer testified in court that he was insane I put in most of the day reading except in the P.M. I slept two hours, to brighten my ideas.

FRIDAY AUGUST 11" 1865
Paducah Kentucky

The man of the 44" Wis was drumed out to day in presence of 44" Wis & 49" Ills Infty. The finding and sentence of the Court Martial was not read. Lt. A. McGregor was mustered out to day. F.J.B. J.J. Willis & I had a fine water mellon then went riding on the Cairo road, some boys on mules.

SATURDAY AUGUST 12" 1865
Paducah Kentucky

I attended sick call, and made weekly Reports Lt. A. McGregor left for home this morning. The weather a little more pleasant this morning, than for some time past. Dr. Allen, Med. Inspector came to day and will inspect our camp soon nothing unusual in camp to-day~

SUNDAY AUGUST 13" 1865
Paducah Kentucky

Dr. Mercer received a 20. days leave of absence and is going home Tuesday next. a protracted meeting going on here in town. I met with Tom Odin & C.S. Baldwin of Co. "K,, on the street drunk and making considerable noise. I had Joe Elder make a detail and send them to prison, in the absence of Major or Adj't. I made application for three days leave to go to Cairo for pay.~

MONDAY AUGUST 14" 1865
Paducah Kentucky

My leave of absence came back at noon and I started down at noon on the Str Beardstown an Ills river packet. paid $.3.00 arrived 7.P.M. the most of the gun boats down near Cairo, and mak a brilliant appearence at night. I stoped at the St. Charles found Cairo in its usual condition, Muddy~

TUESDAY AUGUST 15" 1865
Cairo Illinois

I paid $.2.00 at the St. Charles for lodging & breakfast. went to the pay masters Major W.E. Emerson and he paid me $.143.00 for the month of March / 65. I bought a gold pen for Zue ($.3.75) I expected Dr Mercer down but he didn't come. Saw Gen'l I.N. Haynie, Dr Castle, Harry Moore & Will Moore. came up on str Irene paid $.2.00.

WEDNESDAY AUGUST 16" 1865
Paducah Kentucky

I got my photographs, (half Doz, $.8.00) sent four home by Dr. Mercer also a letter containing $.20.00 and a gold pen. I settled up with Frank J. Burrows to-day. I paid him $.42.45. Dan'l Morris got into a scrape with Sam'l Elkins last night and got cut up. I got my boots fixed, and Rifle repaired to day.

THURSDAY AUGUST 17" 1865
Paducah Kentucky

I went over to Mrs Swifts and settled up with her my board account, paid her $.2.50 squared. Mr Christman is very ill. I got my horse and went up to the rolling Mill to the gov't sale of horses & Mules awhile to day. I made a certificate and sent to Mrs Dida Reed in refrence to Lt. Reeds death. I rece'd an offer of $.75.00 to discharge a man of Co "K,, signed "T.T.,, I remoddled my bunk to day.~

FRIDAY AUGUST 18" 1865
Paducah Kentucky
I attended sick call at 6.A.M. had but one attendant. Two Negroes to be hung here next Monday for committing a rape on a white lady near Columbus, Ky. I let Nick Burns have $.5.00 to day for taking care of my horse. I bought and put up a Mosquito bar this evening.

negroes

SATURDAY AUGUST 19" 1865
Paducah Kentucky
I made weekly Reports to day, and made two certificates for furloughs for men of Co. "A,, to day. I remoddled my Mosquito bar, and read Waverly. nothing of interest in camp. I rec'd letter from Lyde. Zue is improving still. Frank Bob & Lyde have the Missouri fever, Lyde says.

SUNDAY AUGUST 20" 1865
Paducah Kentucky
The 44" Wis. received orders to muster out, to day. F.J. Burrows ordered to Dist Hd Qrs for duty as A.A.A. Gen'l. Lt. Joe. Lucas detailed regimental adj't Lt. Chalfins absconding negro was brought back to day. says he went after peaches I received a letter from and wrote to Zue to day~

MONDAY AUGUST 21" 1865
Paducah Kentucky
Frank went to Dist Hd Qrs for duty to day. I received an order to attend at the Execution of those two negroes to say when life was extinct. we went out to the scaffold at 2.P.M. followed by the 49" Ills. the 44" Wis. and many citizens were in waiting. The Execution took place a few minutes after 2.P.M. The criminals hung a little over ten minutes, after declaring their innocence to the very last.~

TUESDAY AUGUST 22" 1865
Paducah Kentucky

I performed the usual duties to day. I bought a book for a journal but when I came to copy my dairy of 1862, I found it was entirely to small. Mr. Christman died to day of Typhoid Fever. I wrote to Frank to know what peaches could be put up for at Salem. Weather is pervasive wind blew most all day not in the evening.

WEDNESDAY AUGUST 23" 1865
Paducah Kentucky

After my usual duties were performed, I went down town and bought another blank Book for a Journal. paid $.3.50. I commenced transcribing my diaries to day. Mr. Christman was burried this evening. rumor says we will be mustered out soon but traceable to no reliable source.

THURSDAY AUGUST 24" 1865
Paducah Kentucky

I have been very studious to day writing in my journal. Dr. Ball wishes to recommend me as his successor as chief Medical Officer of the District West Ky., but I am not aspiring to any such annoyances. the 44" Wis. hope to get off next saturday for home All hope they may get off soon.~

FRIDAY AUGUST 25" 1865
Paducah Kentucky

This morning at breakfast F.J. Burrows received a letter from Capt. E.B. Harlan stating that the order for our Muster out was made on the 21st inst. I came to camp and told it. it was soon received, and with it another order suspending it until further orders. then the faces of all began to lengthen out. some of them soon were as long as a man's arm.

SATURDAY AUGUST 26" 1865
Paducah Kentucky

Nothing very exciting in camp to-day. every body seems rather Serious, since the Excitement and disappointment of yesterday. I have been in qrs most all day writing Joe Lucas Act. Adj't has monopolized the dispensary to-day with his writing~

SUNDAY AUGUST 27" 1865
Paducah Kentucky

I was put on duty to day as Chief Medical Officer of the District of Western Ky. I have been writing most of the day. I sent one man of Co. "G,, to Pest House with Small-pox I saw Capt Lockwood at the C. Commission rooms he emersed 12 of the boys to day, in the river

MONDAY AUGUST 28" 1865
Paducah Kentucky

I relieved Dr. Ball to day receipted for some plunder got a wagon and team and hauled it to my quarters I wrote A.J. Phelps Med Director of Dep't of the change The 44" Wis mustered out to day. We got notification that the pay master would be here to morrow. a menagerie in town to-day.

TUESDAY AUGUST 29" 1865
Paducah Kentucky

I left my measure, and order for a pr of pants to day. pay master telegraphed he would be here to day. The Mustering officers received orders to day to Muster out the 49" Ills. The officers are very busy making out Muster & pay rolls and Muster Out rolls. I wrote Dr Mercer that we had orders to muster out. all are jubilant again. almost every individual of the Reg't. is anxious to be mustered out of service.

WEDNESDAY AUGUST 30" 1865
Paducah Kentucky

The pay master came this morning to pay off the Reg't. The 44" Wis. Infty left this evening for home. All hands are busy making rolls to muster on to morrow, for pay, and muster out rolls. I received a letter from Frank & Zue and wrote to them, that we had orders to muster out.

THURSDAY AUGUST 31" 1865
Paducah Kentucky

I attended my usual duties and made personal and monthly Reports, and collected personal reports from other Surgs at this post. it rained in the A.M. Major Fenno U.S. Pay-master paid off the regiment. he paid me $.439.70 cts. for Apl, May & June. Dr. A. Thomas of Smithland came in and I forwarded some papers for him to Col. A.J. Phelps Med.

Director. have considerable drunkenness in camp.~ We are to be relieved from duty here by the 4" U.S.C. Art. Ky. from Columbus Ky and they are not ordered up yet I dont think. I will be succeeded by Dr. James Thompson of that Regiment he was Dr Ball's Senior but was not put on duty here owing to ill health. think he has sent in his resignation in consequence.~

FRIDAY SEPTEMBER 1ST 1865
Paducah Kentucky

Dr. R.M. Humble called this morning. he is in charge of the Pest House at this place. I paid the Mess $.20.20 for board for August. 200 of the 4" U.S.C. Arty. Ky. came this morning from Columbus Ky. Some of the reports came in this morning and I have some ready to forward to Col. A.J. Phelps Medical Director Dep't. of Ky. I took a little horse back ride this afternoon.~

SATURDAY SEPTEMBER 2" 1865
Paducah Kentucky

The Military Commission dissolved and Col. Moore took command of the regiment this A.M. Dr. Wm. A. Mayfield of the Post Hospital called in the A.M., and Dr. Humble in the P.M. I rec'd an order relieving me from duty as Chief. Med. Officer Dist. West Ky. got my pants $.18.00. Rec'd letter from J.F.B.

SUNDAY SEPTEMBER 3" 1865
Paducah Kentucky

I attended sick call at the Reg't. went to breakfast, then attended sick-call at the 4" Ky. Then I visited the Chaplain at the Christian Com. rooms and found him very sick.~ I rec'd letters from Frank & Zue stating that Little Charlie Williams died last Wednesday morning. I rec'd notice that my accts were settled with the Med. Dept.

MONDAY SEPTEMBER 4" 1865
Paducah Kentucky

I attended sick call at both Reg'ts to day. then visited the Chaplain and found him much better. I bought a vial case for medicines to-day $.3.00. Co's "A,, & "H,, have their muster out rolls, ready. I finished transcribing my diary of 1862. this P.M., and wrote to Zue

TUESDAY SEPTEMBER 5" 1865
Paducah Kentucky

Dr. S.F.F. Mercer returned this morning from home on time barely, and done well to even do that. I attended both sick calls this morning. The colored Reg't will use as much medicine in one day as our regiment will require in two weeks. The muster out roll are not complete yet. I went riding this evening in the uper part of town.~

WEDNESDAY SEPTEMBER 6" 1865
Paducah Kentucky

Dr. James Thompson Surg. 4" U.S.C. Art. (Ky) came this morning, and Maj. Hale brought him over and I turned over the public property to him and he moved it back to Dist Hd Qrs again I attended the sick calls at both Reg'ts I think Dr Thompson is an ornamental appendage

THURSDAY SEPTEMBER 7" 1865
Paducah Kentucky

I attended the sick calls at both regiments this morning. Dr. Thompson seems to take no interest in the welfare of the men of his Reg't. I made Invoices, and got Receipts of him, and made Monthly Returns of the property I visited Capt Lockwood this evening he is sick again

FRIDAY SEPTEMBER 8" 1865
Paducah Kentucky

I attended the sick calls, then we packed up the Medicines, and Dr. Mercer took them to the Post Q.M. to be shiped to Louisvill Ky. I called upon Dr Thompson and informed him that I had no medicine to treat his Reg't, any longer. I bought a trunk $.9.00. Lt Livesay had $.100.00 stolen and the boy[s] are donating to him.

SATURDAY SEPTEMBER 9" 1865
Paducah Kentucky

I attended the sick calls of both Reg't this morning the last time I propose to visit the 4", and made weekly reports. considerable drinking in camp to day. Tom Odin and Lloyd Buffington fought this evening.~ The Regt was Mustered Out this afternoon by Capt Shaw. I was mustered out at 7.P.M. with the field and Staff of the Regiment.

SUNDAY SEPTEMBER 10" 1865
Paducah Kentucky

I prescribed for my own Regt only this morning. My application to be relieved from the duty of prescribing for the 4" USC. came back without an endorsement. I started Charley home this morning by Wm. E. Farrow Dr. Mercer & Lockwood went along. I gave Billy $.10.00~

MONDAY SEPTEMBER 11" 1865
Paducah Kentucky

No order yet for us to depart though it was telegraphed for last thursday. F.J. Burrows was relieved from duty as A.A.A. Gen'l at Dist. Hd Qrs. Seven of Lt. Chalfins prisoners escaped last night. Col. Moore gave me permission to go home to morrow. I packed up this P.M.

TUESDAY SEPTEMBER 12" 1865
Paducah Kentucky

I attended sick call this morning, then got my things down to the Wharf. I met F.J. Burrows and F.A. Niles there. we went aboard the Str Ada Lyon, arrived at Cairo Ills. at 2.P.M. We called upon B.F. Marshall. We put up at the St. Charles Hotel & went to bed, to be called at 2.A.M. for the train

WEDNESDAY SEPTEMBER 13" 1865
Cairo Illinois

We were called at 2.A.M. and after waiting an hour or so we started. The train was crowded with officers and men of the 13" Ills Cav. We got our breakfast at Centralia, saw Col. Pease. we were behind time and I had to wait at Odin for the Noon freght I got home, found Zue had gone to New-Middleton I helped Frank mak fence. Wm C. Farrow & Dick Davis got in with the horses. Sarah Cooper & R.M. Lovell came

THURSDAY SEPTEMBER 14" 1865
Salem Illinois

I went out to New-Middleton on the 9.A.M. train after Zue. found her sick with headache, also Mrs Moody sick. I saw Mr Sealy on the train going to Flora. We returned on the 9.P.M. train. it was behind time Major Gauen telegraphed that the Regt would be up on the 5.P.M. train for Springfield Illinois.~

FRIDAY SEPTEMBER 15" 1865
Salem Illinois

After breakfast Frank got a buggy we hitched up Charley and I went with him to Sandoval, then Started to Patoka on an electioneering tour We went three miles and stoped at Mr. Douglass for dinner. my horse wouldn't eat, and we returned to Salem R.M. Lovell left to day for Monticello Ills.

SATURDAY SEPTEMBER 16" 1865
Salem Illinois

I borrowed $.20.00 of Frank, and left $.400.00 at home and started for Springfield Ills. stoped at Sandoval until 2.P.M. took dinner there. saw Frank [Burrows] at Patoka We arrived at Decatur Ills. at _P.M. no train on the G.W. R.R., a bridge broke down East of here. I stoped at the Central Hotel. Robt Kelly Tom McTigue et al there

SUNDAY SEPTEMBER 17" 1865
Decatur Illinois

A train was made up here, and went down to the break. returned and left for Springfield at 7.A.M. I went on board, and we arrived at Springfield at 10.A.M. Saw some of the officers at the American House. I stoped at the St. Nicholas Hotel. Saw Col. Stephenson of the 152nd Ills. rained from early morning until 3.P.M. saw a good many of our men they are camped near Camp Butler without Shelter

MONDAY SEPTEMBER 18" 1865
Springfield Illinois

I settled and left the St. Nicholas Hotel. Met F.J.B. and Lt. A.S. Chalfin and went back there for dinner Afternoon we went out to Oak Ridge Semitary 2. Miles north of the City registered, our names and viewed the grounds. I ordered a Suit of clothing at Woods & Henklis paid $.5.00 price $.97.00

TUESDAY SEPTEMBER 19" 1865
Springfield Illinois

I stayed in town all forenoon Frank & Col. Moore went to camp. Capt Cogan returned from St. Louis. Lt. A.K. Dement rejoined the regiment he is just from Montgomery Ala. I got my pay Acct's. went out to Camp Butler with Capts Cogan & Daniels. Dr. Mercer staid in Springfield to night

WEDNESDAY SEPTEMBER 20" 1865
Camp Butler Illinois

I prescribed for the sick this morning and went to town with a hack load of the officers R.M. Lovell & Hoskinson came in to day going to St Louis to buy cattle. Maj Gauen turned over the arms we went to the mustering officer, Capt. Hall, and got certificates. I saw Col Allen. Bob & Hoskinson left for St. Louis Mo.

THURSDAY SEPTEMBER 21" 1865
Springfield Illinois

We went to the depot, and Col. Moore hired a train, and we rode over on the engine, and brought in the Regiment, and were paid off by Maj McCaughey and got our final discharges except Co. "G,, their rolls were incomplete I rec'd $.544.70. settled my acc'ts. got my suit of cloths paid $92.00 more, and repaired to the depot. bade Col Moore and the boys good-by, and left at 6.P.M. for St Louis, and arrived there at Midnight.

FRIDAY SEPTEMBER 22" 1865
St. Louis Missouri

I met Bob & Hoskinson at the Everett House. I bought $.30.00 worth of books, $.56.00 worth of Medicins, $.44.00 worth of instruments, & a hat $.4.00 and left on the P.M. train for home.~ Gen'l. U.S. Grant was on the train We took supper at Odin. Saw Gen'l. John A. Logan there I got home at 7.P.M. R.M. Lovell stoped with me.

SATURDAY SEPTEMBER 23" 1865
Salem Illinois

Chaplain, John H. Lockwood came to town last night, and came around for his horse this morning. he stoped over one day at Decatur Ills. I sold him my Saddlebags for $.5.00 I helped him off. Albert Allmon called. We hitched up and went to the farm, for corn Potatoes tomatoes etc. in P.M.

SUNDAY SEPTEMBER 24" 1865
Salem Illinois

I went to meeting in the A.M. with Frank & the girls. Old, Mr. Covington preached. appearanced of rain in A.M. We went again in the P.M. Rev T.F. Houts preached. R.M. Lovell went out home this morning and rode [one] of our horses. They didn't find any cattle at St Louis to suit them.

MONDAY SEPTEMBER 25" 1865
Salem Illinois

I was at home and read most all day My box of Medicines came from St. Louis I opened it and found it all right the druggests had failed to put in any scales, as I directed, also one or two other articles. I sent Zue up town and got some domestic and will have some clothing made, as I thing[k] of attending the lectures this winter

TUESDAY SEPTEMBER 26" 1865
Salem Illinois

Frank, got a horse and buggy, and went on an electioneering trip to Centralia I went with him. We went by Sandoval. Saw Col. Pease, was at his house of business saw Dr. Green down there. We returned by Walnut Hill. Tom went to Omega after the horse Bob rode home.

WEDNESDAY SEPTEMBER 27" 1865
Salem Illinois

I rec'd a dun for tax on my income of 1863. Tom returned Sick. Margret had another chill to day. Frank bought a Watermelon to day for $1.00 that weighed 41 1/2 lbs. I hitched [horses] to the wagon Lyde & Zue and I went out to the farm. they cleaned up the house, and I got some tomatoes

THURSDAY SEPTEMBER 28" 1865
Salem Illinois

I read and wrote most of the day. Went up town and got some Aromatic Sulph Acid, and made some Quinine Pills. Frank went down to Raccoon precinct, and rode Charley thinks he is not a very desirable Saddlehorse. Albert Allmon Married this evening and left, for Cairo, via St. Louis

FRIDAY SEPTEMBER 29" 1865
Salem Illinois

I wrote most of the forenoon. The girls went up to Dave Meyers' to a Sewing Fraud and Col. Jas. S. Martin and Uncle Tom Black went to Centralia on an Electioneering Tour. this is the last day before the precinct meetings Afternoon Tom & I went to the farm and gathered some corn it rained on us. I went up to D.P. Meyers after the girls and, took supper up there.

SATURDAY SEPTEMBER 30" 1865
Salem Illinois

I wrote most of the forenoon transcribing my diary of 1863. Then went to the Livery Stable hired a buggy and harness and hitched Charlie up at 4.P.M. and drove him out to New Middleton on a visit Zue went with me. We found Mrs Moody Sick with the chills. Mr Moody was gone to Xenia to the Lodge (Masonic). I saw Ike Lear there

SUNDAY OCTOBER 1" 1865
New Middleton Illinois

I hitched up Charley to the buggy and Mr. Moody and I went down to Mr Costelows, found the Whole family except himself in bed sick with the Ague. We gathered some grapes and returned then we went to the Old-Dutchtown-Mill, and returned for dinner. afternoon we started home, stoped at Mr. Prudens, came home and went to church.

MONDAY OCTOBER 2" 1865
Salem Illinois

I went out to the farm, and gain the hack and Lyde, Lute, Tom, & Zue & I went to the woods and gathered some grapes we picked off and put up 4. Gallons for winter in Molasses. I went back to the farm in the evening for the boys. Frank has been cutting corn to day

TUESDAY OCTOBER 3" 1865
Salem Illinois

Frank and I went to work and finished the fence in front of the house to-day, and cleaned up the rubbish from the street. R.M. Lovell came in to-day. I wrote to and sent T.D. Clark $.20.00 to day, the tax on my income for the year 1863.

WEDNESDAY OCTOBER 4" 1865
Salem Illinois

I hitched up the hack and Lyde Tom Zue & I went out after grapes Zue had a chill and we had to hurry back we picked off 4.Gallons Frank and Bob went over to the fair now in opperation, here. Mr Hammond and Mary came in this evening to go to the fair to-morrow

THURSDAY OCTOBER 5" 1865
Salem Illinois

We hitched up to the hack and Frank, Bob, Lyde, Lute, Julia, Mary, Zue & I went over to the fair Hammond & Mary accompanied us. We stayed two or three hours and got some checks and returned for dinner. afternoon we went back then was not much of interest on exhibition. I saw Lt. A.S. Chalfin. I went up town with Zue & bought her a dress, 10. yds domestic & a basket; she is not well.

FRIDAY OCTOBER 6" 1865
Salem Illinois

Mother and Margret went up to D.P. Meyers to spend the day. Frank is painting the hack to day. Lute & Julia went out to Mr Pruden's yesterday, eve. Zue had a very hard chill to day; Lyde and I papered the hall. Frank returned $.200.00 he borrowed the other day for Lydick Bros.

SATURDAY OCTOBER 7" 1865
Salem Illinois

I cleaned up my old Pill bags, and labeled some of the vials. Frank is still painting the Hack, and I transcribing my diary. Zue's taking quinine to day. I loaned Bob, Charley and my saddle to ride home this evening. We got a Bbl of Molasses this evening. they are not good as the sample

SUNDAY OCTOBER 8" 1865
Salem Illinois

Frank and Lyde went to church. I stayed at home and gave Zue, Quinine every hour and a half until after chill time and she didn't have it. There seems to be a gread[t] deal of Intermittent Fever in the country this season, though not fatal

MONDAY OCTOBER 9" 1865
Salem Illinois

We went to the depot to meet Maj. Gen'l. John. A. Logan but learned that he was coming by private conveyance we then went out west of town with the band to meet him but he came another road. The delegates convened and nominated Jas. S. Jackson for county Clerk by majority. We went to the fair ground at 1.P.M. and heard Logan's speech. Bob & Wood. Lovell and Nan, were in There was a good turn out of people to day.

TUESDAY OCT. 10" 1865
Salem Illinois

Frank and Tom went out horse hunting to-day. Geo. & Margrett went home this P.M. I put the 2nd coat of paint on the hack. Mother went out home with Margret to stay a while as Margret has been sick for some time and is not able to be up.

WEDNESDAY OCT. 11" 1865
Salem Illinois

Frank sent up to Mr Larrimers and got his gun and we killed a hog, and then he took Old Bose out to the woods and relieved him of any further trouble in this country. Mother came in from Georges, and I cut up and salted the pork in the evening.

THURSDAY OCT. 12" 1865
Salem Illinois

Zue & I started at 9.A.M. in the buss to the R.R. stoped over at Sandoval 'til 1.P.M. arrived at Ramsey at 4.P.M. I hired a horse & buggy, for $.3.00 and started to J.S. Moody's. The road was bad and night overtook us and was very dark. We got lost and mist the road but finaly arrived. found all sick with chills.

FRIDAY OCT. 13" 1865
Fillmore Illinois

Jim & I went to Mr. Frick's and left the horse & buggy to be taken to Ramsey according to agreement. We stoped at Mr. Bliss', and found him sick. Then Jim & I rode about on the prairie hunting his old mare, and looking at the country I think some of locating here to practice medicine as soon as I can make a trip to St. Louis to get some more Medicines etc.

SATURDAY OCT. 14" 1865
Fillmore Illinois

Jim & I rode over to Mr. Whitten's to try to buy a cow and calf for Jim. then we went to John. Knowles found his mare and returned. I was called to Mr Bliss' found Mrs Bliss with congestive chill. I stayed til it was off. then went to Jim's and got Zue and returned to Bliss' to stay all night. had him send for Dr Jones.

SUNDAY OCT. 15" 1865
Fillmore Illinois

Dr. Jones came from Ramsey and we prescribed together for Mrs Bliss. I stayed until after noon then went to Jim's he had gone to Bliss' I went to hunt his mare again, didn't find her, so I went to Mr Lane's and got his hack to go to Ramsey to morrow. I concluded to locate here.

MONDAY OCT. 16" 1865
Fillmore Illinois

We were up at 4.A.M. got breakfast and started for Ramsey, but arrived after the train had gone, so we waited til 3.P.M. and went on the freight train to Sandoval. heard men hurrah for Jeff Davis at Ramsey to day. saw Mr. Richmond of Memphis on the train to night. we got home at 7.P.M.~

TUESDAY OCT. 17" 1865
Salem Illinois

I made a trade with Old Muzzy this morning, then got a horse and buggy and went to New Middleton and returned at 2.P.M. and made arrangements to go to St. Louis. I made a bill for medicines and other things I wanted to get. I bartered Grimes for his buggy to day but he wouldn't sell it so I got ready and started on the evening train.

WEDNESDAY OCT. 18" 1865
Saint Louis Missouri

I bought of Jacob. S. Merrell $.72.55cts worth of medicines then a pill Machine $.4.50 Tongue Depressor $.2.50, then of Hooker & Co. a buggy for $.250.00 paid $.5.00 for having Frank's watch repaired, and started home at 3.P.M. Med Dr. Mercer on the train returning from Missouri. I got home at 7.P.M.~

THURSDAY OCT. 19" 1865
Salem Illinois

I got a deed from Mother for the "Neal forty" and let Old. J.S. Muzzy have it at $.160.00 settled the judgement he had against me and $.72.00 on one against O'Neill & Me, and I got released from it altogether. I took the receipt to Noah Brubaker's to be applied on the judgement. My medicines came.

FRIDAY OCT. 20" 1865
Salem Illinois

I hitched to the wagon and took our trunk and three boxes to Sandoval to be Expressed to Ramsey. then went to the depot and got my Buggy. Express charges $.6.00. then went and bought a set of harness $.28.00. Frank & I took a ride. then I extracted 8. teeth for Lyde 2. for Lute and one for Tom.

SATURDAY OCT. 21" 1865
Salem Illinois

We hitched up Charley, and Zue & I started at 9.A.M. we stoped a few minutes at Margrets, then stoped an hour at noon. then drove on until we got above Bahain's Station. then tried to stop for the night, but was sent from house to house until we came to the Hericane Timber. then I got out and led the horse through and arrived at Jim's at 10.P.M. having drove 50 miles.

SUNDAY OCT. 22" 1865
Fillmore Illinois

Jim & I hitched up to the buggy and went over near Mr. Todd's and got some grapes. In the evening we went down to Mr Martin Bost's to see him. The weather is pleasant, and looks like Indian Summer. Jim has a fine crop of corn, and broom corn~

MONDAY OCT. 23" 1865
Fillmore Illinois

I hitched Charley & Old Mike to Jim's wagon and went to Ramsey and got our trunk and my boxes of Medicines. got back at 2.P.M. opened the boxes and found all right, none of the bottles broken. at night I had a call to Mr Thos. Spears'~

TUESDAY OCT. 24" 1865
Fillmore Illinois

Zue & I went to Hillsboro. I bought a lamp, and lantern, oil & can. I made application for a liscenes to practice medicine, and sent $.14.30cts to the New Havens Arms Co. for barrell, sleeve & spiral spring for my rifle. We returned at 3.P.M. found that we had went several miles out of the way.

WEDNESDAY OCT. 25" 1865
Fillmore Illinois

Zue & I went over to Hammond Cadwells to see if we could engage boarding in the evening we Succeeded. then went on to Mr Bliss' on a visit, and I was called into Mr Shutts to see a young lady with chills, and was called in to see John Owen's as we returned home. he is sick with chills. the health is improving some but quite a number of cases yet.

THURSDAY OCT. 26" 1865
Fillmore Illinois

I helped Jim shut up his poorch, and floor it, and make a room of it. Make his house considerable warmer beside the room. I was called to Henry Haake's (the dutchmans) to see a sick child. We were at home the rest of the day. I made some Pills.

FRIDAY OCT. 27 1865
Fillmore Illinois

I went with Jim to the woods. I took my trunk & boxes to Mr. Cadwells, then to the woods and got some poles for rafters for Jim's stable, and blocks to set it on. he is needing a stable very much.~ the wind blew hard and was very disagreeable~

320

SATURDAY OCT. 28" 1865
Fillmore Illinois

Zue & I moved over to Mr. Cadwells to board. I went back twice to Jim's after my medicines and saddle etc. then I put my things in order Geo. Bliss came down to spend the evening. we are tolerably well pleased with our boarding place, so far.

SUNDAY OCT. 29" 1865
Fillmore Illinois

I was called to a Mr. Hall's to see an old lady Mr Cadwell went with me. Hall, was Cadwell's first wife's father. Zue & I went to Lutheran church at Bost-Hill, but we got there while they were singing the last hymn. Mr. Frick's family got there at the same time. We returned and found Mr & Mrs Cadwell absent. they had gone down to old Mr Hall's to see the old lady.~

MONDAY OCT. 30" 1865
Fillmore Illinois

I read most of the day. Jim was down. I prescribed for Thos. Spears and got one dollar In the evening I went to the Post Office and rece'd a letter from Lt. A. McGregor he is married and in business at Sparta Ills. we wrote some. Mr & Mrs Cadwell went visiting, and left us to keep house.

TUESDAY OCT. 31" 1865
Fillmore Illinois

I read most all day. I wrote to Mc and went over to the Post Office in the A.M. In the afternoon Zue & I went riding in a S.W. direction, past Millers black smith shop and came back by old Jake Bost's and then to the mill, and out by the M.E. Church. We havent much to do and we spend a portion of the time in riding about seeing the country learning the roads, and enjoying ourselves as best we can. There is not much in the way of amusement here, and we are not acquainted with any one scarcely, and can't go visiting hence we ride about and see the country and that even is not very interesting. at least it is rather monotonous~

WEDNESDAY NOVEMBER 1" 1865
Fillmore Illinois

I hitched to the buggy and took Zue and Mrs Cadwell up to Mr. Bliss'. then I went up the prairie by John Knowles' and back to Jim's and then home and to Bliss' after Zue & Mrs C. brought them home at 3.P.M. then went to Henry Haake's after night his wife and hired hand were sick. evening pleasant and the night very light.~

THURSDAY NOVEMBER 2" 1865
Fillmore Illinois

I put in most of the day reading Mr. Cadwell went to Vanburensburg after groceries. Zue finished her cloak to day Wm Knowles called and got some medicine for his children sick with ague. not very much doing now health improving.

FRIDAY NOVEMBER 3" 1865
Fillmore Illinois

I read most all day in, "Churchill on children" Mr Lane came over this morning and got some medicine in the afternoon Zue & I went riding up on the prairie above Mr Bateman's saw some very fine country, though to far from timber we returned at dark after a drive of twelve miles~

SATURDAY NOVEMBER 4" 1865
Fillmore Illinois

I asked what our board would be. Mr Cadwell said $.3.00 apiece, and I paid him $.6.00 Zue had head ache and was in bed most all day with it. Nothing said about the price of horse feed or stable rent. I read most of the day. Windy, cloudy, and disagreeable to day

SUNDAY NOVEMBER 5" 1865
Fillmore Illinois

I read most of the day. Weather clear & cold in the evening I hitched up to go to Jim's and was called to John Owens'. Zue went with me and after calling there a few minutes we went on to Jim's and staid until 9.P.M. There was no church in the neighborhood to day that we were aware of, so we had to drag it through as best we could, at home & visiting

MONDAY NOVEMBER 6" 1865
Fillmore Illinois

I read until 2.P.M. then started to Jim's, but met old Jake Bost and turned back and extracted some teeth for him. then went to Jim's and helped him raise his stable George Bliss was there and helped. Zue had the head ache most of the day~

TUESDAY NOVEMBER 7" 1865
Fillmore Illinois

I hitched up and took Mr Cadwell to the Election I have not been here long enough to entitle me to a vote. I saw about forty men there, but there was no drinking nor fussing as I expected to see. all was even quiet. We returned by noon by Jim's but we did'nt stop.

WEDNESDAY NOVEMBER 8" 1865
Fillmore Illinois

I hitched up and Zue and I went to Hillsboro, got my gun barrell & sleeve & Magazine. got some medicines, also some articles for Mrs Cadwell I got Charley shod before. got some cards printed and returned home. we arrived at dark. Hillsboro is not a very pretty place.~

THURSDAY NOVEMBER 9" 1865
Fillmore Illinois

I went over to Miller's black smith shop and put the new barrell in my gun. then started [to] the mill and broke the dash off my buggy. and then I went to Sam'l Harris blacksmith shop and got it fixed, and returned home in the evening and, was called to Mrs. Emory's to see a sick child. Mr Cadwell commenced gathering his corn to day~

FRIDAY NOVEMBER 10" 1865
Fillmore Illinois

Zue & I took my Rifle out and we had a Shooting Match this forenoon. in the evening we went up to Jim's, and I went with him to hire a hand to work at his broomcorn to-morrow. I loaned him $.10.00 we took supper then came home at 7.P.M.

SATURDAY NOVEMBER 11" 1865
Fillmore Illinois

I paid Mr Cadwell $.6.00 for board, up to this date. I took the buggy to the creek and washed it off. after dinner I went and got some grapes. then Zue and I went riding and put up some cards on the old Shelbyville road, 4 miles east of here.~

SUNDAY NOVEMBER 12" 1865
Fillmore Illinois

We got up late, and had breakfast at 9.30.A.M. and Zue & I went to Bost Hill to church. we returned by Jim's. nobody at home in the evening when we returned. Mr & Mrs Cadwell had gone visiting to Mr Halls.~

MONDAY NOVEMBER 13" 1865
Fillmore Illinois

Zue & I went out posting up cards. We went West five miles to the East fork bridge, then South to the Vanburensburg road, then East to the burg, then North East to Mr Prathers at the junction of the Old Shelbyville, and Hillsboro roads~ then back home. we put up about 20. cards to day. I went to the Post Office and got two letters, one from Art. and one from Hellen I wrote to J.W.C., F.J.B. & Chicago Republican.

TUESDAY NOVEMBER 14" 1865
Fillmore Illinois

I was at home most of the day. Jim came along and Zue went with him to the saw-Mill. I had call to John Owens, then and went to Jim's in the evening. Nothing of interest going on. We have one continued monotony here without variations.

WEDNESDAY NOVEMBER 15" 1865
Fillmore Illinois

I read until 10.A.M. then I hitched up and Zue & I went out riding, and puting up cards We went North East to Donalson's Store. then West to East Fork School house then home by 2.P.M. the roads are good, and the weather pleasant for driving, and we put in the time

THURSDAY NOVEMBER 16" 1865
Fillmore Illinois

I had a call to Mr. Stephen Harris' to see his son. I saw a Dr. Allen there. I stoped at Lane's. P.M. Zue & Mrs Cadwell went up to Jim's. I made some Quinine Pills. put them on the stove to dry them, and scorched the Molasses in them.

FRIDAY NOVEMBER 17" 1865
Fillmore Illinois

I read most of the forenoon, then had a call to Owen's. in the evening Zue & I went out riding. we went south west to Millers and beyond then East, and back by Jake Bost's and the Mill and then home. the road is not good in the woods it is broken. the weather is pleasant enough for September~

SATURDAY NOVEMBER 18" 1865
Fillmore Illinois

I read until noon. then Zue & I went up to Jim's and staid a couple of hours. was called upon twice for Medicine. I stoped at Owens as we returned. at night Miss Valley Fauke & Charley Shutts and George Bliss & Ellen came in and spent the evening.

SUNDAY NOVEMBER 19" 1865
Fillmore Illinois

We were at home until noon, then went riding, three miles west, then north to the new road, then home. Mr & Mrs Cadwell went to Mr Hall's to day. during our absence Mr Williams [came] after medicine, said he would be back to morrow "either in A.M. or P.M." and wished me to be at home.

MONDAY NOVEMBER 20" 1865
Fillmore Illinois

I went to the office and got some letters my paper didn't come. afternoon we went riding, then to Jim's, to spend the evening. Mr & Mrs Cadwell came up and sat 'til bed time. the night was very cool. we beat them home and were in bed, when they came.

TUESDAY NOVEMBER 21" 1865
Fillmore Illinois

Mr Cadwell had four hands gathering corn to day. I wrote some letters. afternoon we went riding, east to Shutt's cane mill then north, and west by Jim's, then South to the prairie near Millers, then north to the road. I stoped at McDowells to lance a rising on Ben's wife's breast, then home after a drive of eight-miles.

WEDNESDAY NOVEMBER 22" 1865
Fillmore Illinois

Six hands here gathering corn to day I took my Rifle and went out and had some target practice at 140 yds distance made some good shots. P.M. Zue & I went to Nokomis arrived at Sundown, farther than we thought got lost in returning. got home at 11.P.M.~

THURSDAY NOVEMBER 23" 1865
Fillmore Illinois

Zue had head ache in the forenoon. in the afternoon I took my Rifle and went out and killed four squirrels. The weather is warm and pleasant, the finest fall I ever saw in my life for doing business. We have scarcely had a disagreeable day even yet.

FRIDAY NOVEMBER 24" 1865
Fillmore Illinois

I read during the forenoon in the evening Zue & I catched Charley and she rode him and we went squirrel hunting again. I killed but one. In the evening Mr. Camp came and stoped to stay over night. And Mrs Cadwell was just tickled allover about it

SATURDAY NOVEMBER 25" 1865
Fillmore Illinois

I was called up and went to Mr. Bliss' this morning before breakfast, to see Mrs Bliss. Then Zue & I went to Vanburensburg and got Some Ammunition. after we returned we went hunting. then went to Jim's to Spend the evening. Mr Camp is here again to night. I think he is imposing on good nature. on Hammon at least.~

SUNDAY NOVEMBER 26" 1865
Fillmore Illinois

Zue & I went over to Bost Hill to church this A.M. to Jim's for dinner. then to Fillmore church at 4.P.M. to hear Mr. Snell preach, (the new circuit rider) everybody seems to be pleased with his appearence. We had bad order in church Mr. Camp here again for the night.

MONDAY NOVEMBER 27" 1865
Fillmore Illinois

Mr Camp bade us a final farewell and took his final departure. Zue had a chill and was very sick most all day. I went to the office and got my paper (Chicago Republican) of the 23" inst. and some letters one from Lute & one from F.J. Burrows.

TUESDAY NOVEMBER 28" 1865
Fillmore Illinois

I read most of the day, then wrote to Lt. Chalfin, also to Arthur Moody and advised him to come to Nokomis and get a Job. Jim's says there is a good prospect.~ Weather cloudy and prospect of rain. think our fair weather is about gone.~

WEDNESDAY NOVEMBER 29" 1865
Fillmore Illinois

I cleaned up Cadwells old shot gun and went out and killed two squirrels. it took me half the day to do it, but we get so little fresh meat here, it would justify if it took all-day, to do it. Martin Bost & boys were gathering corn here to day. I read at night to make up the time lost to day while hunting~

THURSDAY NOVEMBER 30" 1865
Fillmore Illinois

I hitched up and went to Jim's, and took him in and we went to Wm. Walcotts to a sale he wanted to buy a cow and I a feather bed, as we have determined to go to Keeping house in January next. We bought nothing Then we went to Irving a small town on the St Louis, Alton, & Terra Haut R.R. We saw Tom Jones at the sale today. We returned and eat supper at Jim's, then I came home and eat again.

FRIDAY DECEMBER 1" 1865
Fillmore Illinois

Weather pleasant Mart Bost & his boys here again gathering corn to-day. Zue & I went up to Jim's and staid 'til bed time. he has sold a portion of his broom corn, to a man from Nokomis. he has seven acres that might have been worth something to him if he could have got it saved but hands were scarce and hard to get, every body is behind.

SATURDAY DECEMBER 2" 1865
Fillmore Illinois

I paid Mr. Cadwell $.6.00 for another week's board. Shutts boys are here gathering corn Mr Cadwell is getting most through with his corn. The weather is pleasant and a fine time for gathering corn or doing any kind of work on a farm.

SUNDAY DECEMBER 3" 1865
Fillmore Illinois

We got up and fixed to go to Bost Hill to church but it rained so we could'nt go. We were at home all day reading, Writing, etc. and put in the day the best we could under the circumstances, a dull day indeed with us, and no way to help it~

MONDAY DECEMBER 4" 1865
Fillmore Illinois

School commenced this morning up here. Mr & Mrs Bateman were here for dinner. weather disagreeable. I went to the office and got a letter from Col Edward Prince stating that there was pay due me for the time I was at Springfield Ills, and that he could collect it for me if I desired him to do so.

TUESDAY DECEMBER 5" 1865
Fillmore Illinois

I read most of the day. Jim came down in the afternoon. I wrote letters to day, and mailed to Col. Edward Prince, T.J.B., J.F.B., F.J.B. & R.M.L. I put in the time in reading and writing I am keeping up correspondence, with a number of my old army friends, and family friends. hence it takes considerable writing. it will eventually decline.

WEDNESDAY DECEMBER 6" 1865
Fillmore Illinois

It rained from early in the morning until night. I was at home all day and didn't put up a dose of medicine for any one. several men in for boots and repairing. the weather is getting rather disagreeable now. perhaps we will pay now for our nice fall weather.

THURSDAY DECEMBER 7" 1865
Fillmore Illinois

I read until noon, then hitched up, to go and see Al. Austin but Charley got scared and run down the hill, kicked and broke one of my buggy shafts and one side of the dash off. I then went on horse back. found Austin quite low and his recovery quite doubfull~ left him Quinine & Iron

FRIDAY DECEMBER 8" 1865
Fillmore Illinois

I took my shaft to Sam'l Harris' to get it mended but he was going to be baptised to day and couldn't do it til evening, when I went and got it done. I made some 3. gr. Quinine Pills with Simple Syrup to day. it makes the whitest, and prettyist pills I ever saw.~

SATURDAY DECEMBER 9" 1865
Fillmore Illinois

I paid Mr Cadwell $.6.00 to day for board, up to this date. Zue & I made 240 Quinine pills. afternoon I hitched up and drove Charley as far as Mr. Fricks to see if he would work to the buggy again. he didn't like it but went never-the-less. then Zue got in and we went up to Jim's, and paid them a visit that was not due yet, nor likely to be.

SUNDAY DECEMBER 10" 1865
Fillmore Illinois

We went to Fillmore church at 11.A.M. and heard Mr. Bliss preach, its rather dry music. There was several rowdies there who behave very badly. It is not uncommon for them to be drunk at meeting, and even drink whiskey in church in time of preaching here.

MONDAY DECEMBER 11" 1865
Fillmore Illinois

This is mail day but we got no letters. I went hunting but found no game. afternoon Zue & I went riding, and stoped at Jim's. In the evening we went to Mr Shutts' to pay them a visit Mr. & Mrs. Cadwell went also. Shutts libel at Bliss' use. had a lively evening.

TUESDAY DECEMBER 12" 1865
Fillmore Illinois

I wrote to Lute and went to the office. the wind blew cold, and very hard from the west. I was in doors most all day reading the papers, 'though not very much news of interest in them, yet they help to while away the time a little.

WEDNESDAY DECEMBER 13" 1865
Fillmore Illinois

I rode Charley over to Lane's, then hitched him to the buggy and went to Mr Shutts', and brought Miss Valley Fauke down to help Zue & Mr Cadwell make some Shuck caps, or turbans I went and got shucks for them, in the evening I went and took her home again. The weather is quite cold to-day, it would be very disagreeable riding very far in it.~

THURSDAY DECEMBER 14" 1865
Fillmore Illinois

I hitched up and Zue & I started down to Mulberry Grove on a visit. We got very cold and had to stop at Vanburensburg and warm then it was Eight miles farther and took us until almost night to get there. We surprised and stoped with Aunt Betsy for the night. all were well & glad to see us.

FRIDAY DECEMBER 15" 1865
Mulberry-Grove Illinois

We staid at Aunt Betsy's until near noon then she went with us to Aunt Eliza Cambell's for dinner, where we had another plasant visit. her daughter had just returned from Salem Then we went three miles west to Isaac Enloe's and surprised and staid with them. all well.

SATURDAY DECEMBER 16" 1865
Mulberry-Grove Illinois

9 ~ 5

We left Enloe's at 9.A.M., came to town and stoped with Aunt Betsy
for dinner again, then left for home stoped at the Burg and warmed
and drove home by Sundown. found that Arthur Moody had come up
during our absence, and was at Jim's now.~

SUNDAY DECEMBER 17" 1865
Fillmore Illinois

I hitched up and we went up to Jim's and spent the day. Saw Art
and heard from home. the weather is more pleasant than it has been for
a week I think we we are going to have some more fine weather now
perhaps for a while at least. The health is very good and but little doing
in my line of business.~

MONDAY DECEMBER 18" 1865
Fillmore Illinois

I paid Mr. Cadwell to day for last weeks board $.4.00. then went to
the shop and got a pr of Shoes put on Charley behind, and the dash of
my buggy repaired again~ I bought some feathers of Wm Knowles for a
bed to-day at, 60cts per lbs. I found Zue sick with head ache

TUESDAY DECEMBER 19" 1865

Ramsey

Fillmore Illinois

I went with Arthur to Ramsey to get his Valise returned at 2.P.M.
very hungry and had to wait til sundown, for a very meagre dinner. I
would'nt ask Art to stop. I thought he could go to Jim's and get it sooner
than by stoping here. This wont do much longer.

WEDNESDAY DECEMBER 20" 1865
Fillmore Illinois

It was snowing when I got up this morning and continued blustering
all day. I went to Lane's and tried to get board. I then went and killed a
squirrel, We have had but one Shoulder of a hog, in the way of fresh
meat since we have been here ourselves, family, hired hands and all to
gether

THURSDAY DECEMBER 21" 1865
Fillmore Illinois

It is cold and clear this morning. I went down to Wm Knowles this morning and took a bed tick to put feathers in. I paid Mrs Knowles $.10.00 and told her I wanted 25. lbs. I killed a squirrel.~ In the evening Zue and I went up to Jim's and staid until 9.P.M. Charley theatened to kick, and I had to lead him, and whale him before he would go along peaceably~

FRIDAY DECEMBER 22" 1865
Fillmore Illinois

Clear & cold this morning. I went to Lane's and let him have $.10.00 in gold to send to Vandalia to morrow, for sale he paid me $.10.00 on it, the ballance to be paid when sold. Cadwell got a quarter of beef this evening the first fresh meat, we have had except a shoulder of a hog since we have been here, but they cant cook it.

SATURDAY DECEMBER 23" 1865
Fillmore Illinois

I paid Mr. Cadwell $.6.00 board to this date. Mrs "C,, informed us that we would get but two meals pr day after this. I went to Wm Knowles, and old Mr. Richmonds and trid to get board but failed. so we concluded to go to Salem to morrow. we went up to Jim's a little while but he was gone to Nokomis with broom corn.

SUNDAY DECEMBER 24" 1865
Fillmore Illinois

We started at Sun up for Salem in the buggy we found the roads tolerable good until after dark, when froze and was very slipry. We arrived at 7.P.M. found all well. they were not looking for us Jim McKee was there. And we are anticipating a happy christmas, to-morrow~

MONDAY DECEMBER 25" 1865
Salem Illinois

We were at home all day, and had a good dinner Frank had some Oysters for dinner George & Margrett came in. McKee was here for dinner. Margret staid, and we all went to the M.E. Church in the evening to a distribution of christmas presents to the sunday school scholars. I hitched up, and took most of the women folks up, and brought them back. I had to whip Charley first.

TUESDAY DECEMBER 26" 1865
Salem Illinois

I hitched up Charley and had to whip him before he would work. I took Margret up to Dave Myres, and then Zue & I went out to Middleton it commenced raining when we were about half-way. We found all well. We put up the Melodion and had some Music.

WEDNESDAY DECEMBER 27" 1865
New-Middleton Illinois

More snow fell last night. Mr Moody made Zue a pair of Shoes to-day. "We all" went to Mrs Ward's and took dinner. I called on Dr. Irwin this evening. at night we went to church. Ed. Jackson professed religion. The Presbyterian are having a protracted meeting.

THURSDAY DECEMBER 28" 1865
New-Middleton Illinois

I hitched up, had a scrape with Charley, then came to Salem, and out to Georges after mother but she could not come. Margret had no girl and was not well enough to get along alone. Uncle Mark & Bob came He, Frank and the girls went to John Cunningham's to a party this evening.~

FRIDAY DECEMBER 29" 1865
Salem Illinois

Frank hitched to the wagon and Bob, Frank, Lyde, Julia, Zue & I went out to Margrets to take dinner. we staid 'til 4.P.M. then returned to town, and Bob, Frank & the girls went to Mr Haines to spend the evening. Zue & I staid at home. Uncle Mark Lovell went down to Hays prairie to collect some money. this has been a merry christmas with most of us this time.~

SATURDAY DECEMBER 30" 1865
Salem Illinois

We were in town all day. I went up town and called upon Capt. J.S. Jackson and D.P. Myres. I saw Uncle Robt Black he wants us to come out and see him, but we cant go now. Uncle Mark Lovell returned from Hays prairie Misses Sue Hall & Kate Beaver called in the evening, and others.

SUNDAY DECEMBER 31" 1865
Salem Illinois

We all went to church at 10.A.M. and heard Rev Mr Mosser preach a sermon for the Bible cause. afternoon I was unwell, and sick at dark. Madeline & Em. came down. Lizzy & Charles Black and Miss Sue Patterson came in at dark and went to night meeting. This is the first time I have spent the Holidays at home for four years.

APPENDIX A

SUPPLEMENTAL MATERIAL WRITTEN BY DR. BLACK

[History of the 49th Illinois Infantry by James A. Black, written sometime between September 15 and December 29, 1865.]

History of Forty-Ninth Infantry

The Forty-Ninth Infantry Illinois Volunteers was organized at Camp Butler Illinois, December 31st 1861, by Colonel William. R. Morrison February 3d 1862, ordered to Cairo Illinois. 8th moved to Fort. Henry, and was assigned to Third Brigade, McClernand's Division. 11th moved to Ft. Donelson. 13th engaged the enemy, losing 14. Killed and 37 wounded. among the wounded was Colonel Morrison commanding the Brigade. Remained at Ft. Donelson until March 4" when moved to Metal Landing and 6th embarked for Pitsburg Landing, Tennessee. Disembarked at Savanah. 21st moved to Pittsburg Landing.

Was engaged in the battle of Shiloh, April 6th & 7th 1862, losing 17. Killed and 99. wounded. Among the latter were Lieutenant Colonel Pease, Commanding regiment, and Major Bishop. Was engaged in the Siege of Corinth, and on the 4th of June, moved to Bethel, and was assigned to Brigadier General John A. Logan's First Division, District of Jackson. Major General John A. McClernand commanding.

March 10th 1863 moved from Bethel Tennessee by rail via Jackson and Grand Junction to Germantown, and 12th to White's Station and was assigned to the Fourth Brigade Colonel W.W. Sanford, First Division Brigadier General W.S. Smith, Sixteenth Army Corps, Major General S.A. Hurlbut commanding.

August 24th to Helena, Arkansas, to join General. F. Steel's Expedition against Little Rock Arkansas. 28th assigned to Brigade of Colonel True, and September 2nd Joined the main Army at Brownsvile Arkansas.

September 10th participated in the Capture of Little Rock ~

November 15th 1863 moved, by rail to Duval's Bluff, and from thence returned to Memphis Tennessee, arriving November 21st.

January 15th 1864, three fourths of the regiment Re-enlisted and were mustered as Veteran Volunteers

Assigned to Third Brigade Colonel S.H. Wolf. Third Division Brigadier General A.J. Smith of the 16" Army Corps. ~

January 27th moved to Vicksburg Mississippi and accompanied Major General Sherman in the Maredian campaign returning to Vickbug Mch 3d

March 10th assigned to Red River Expedition. 14th participated in the capture of Fort De Russey, Louisiana. April 9th engaged in the battle of Pleasant Hill Louisiana.

Returned to Memphis June 10th 1864. June 24th ordered to Illinois for Veteran furlough The detachment of Non-Veterans remained, commanded by Captain John A Logan participating in the battle of Tupelo, July 14" and 15" 1864 ~

After Expiration of Veteran furlough rendesvouzed at Centralia Illinois and proceeded, Via. Cairo, and Memphis to Holly-Springs, rejoining the command.

August 12th participated in the Oxford expedition and returned to Memphis August 30".

Embarking for Jefferson Barracks Missouri and arriving September the 30" Moved to Franklin Mo. and drove the enemy from the place. Moved with the army in pursuit of General. Price, and returned to St. Louis November 18" 1864. Arrived at Nashvill Tennessee December 1st. Took part in the battle of Nashville December 15" and 16th ~ December 24" ordered to Paducah Kentucky to "Muster Out" the non veterans. Since which time the regiment has been doing garrison duty

"Mustered Out" September the 9th 1865 at Paducah Kentucky, and arrived at Camp Butler Illinois September 15th 1865 for final payment and discharge. ~ Which was comemrated on Thurday September 21st, 1865. ~

[Resolution written in response to a Peace Resolution adopted in the Illinois State Legislature.]

Bethel Tennessee= February 17" 1863=

Where as our government is now engaged in a struggle for the perpetuation of every right dear to us as American citizens, and requiring the united effort of all good true and loyal men, in its behalf=

And wheras, we the officers and soldiers of the 48th and 49th regiments Illinois Volunteer Infantry, and a battalion of the 11th and 12th Illinois Vol. Cavalry have learned of the action of certain Members of the Illinois legislature, and others, who are <u>inimical</u> to the government.

Therefore Resolved= that we fully endorse the Sentiments expressed by our fellow soldiers at Corinth Miss= approving the action of the State Officers of Illinois= And hereby tender to Governor Richard Yates= and Adjutant Gen'l Fuller our warmest thanks for their untiring zeal in organizing= arming, and equiping the army which Illinois has sent to the field= and for their timely attention to the wants, of our sick and wounded Soldiers= And we assure them of our Steady and warm support in their efforts to Maintain for Illinois the proud position of permanent loyalty which she now occupies=

Resolved= that we have read with feelings of deepest regret certain treasonable and libelous resolutions, introduced into the Illinois legislature= known as the "Peace Resolutions"

Resolved= that while we know that our patriotic State Shelters a few "Malignants," who can Stoop to any infamy however disgusting= yet we cannot refrain from expressing our astonishment that a Majority of the legislature who heretofore had a respectable Social position should by a vote endorsing said resolutions proclaim to the world that they are forever associated with treason= and with Men who have attempted to dissever our glorious Union=

Resolve= that while we respect an open enemy, who risks his life on the field of battle= we have no language to express, our utter loathing and detestation of the dastardly wretches, who by said resolutions, and actions encourage rebellion and attempts to overthrow that government which has been the Star of hope= to the oppressed of every land= and are cowardly stabbing the honest Soldier in the back= who is giving his Services= and his life's blood, if need be for the upholding of the proud flag of his empereled country

Resolved= that these our opinions so expressed are not intended, nor expected to produce any effect upon the traitors of the Illinois legislature as we well know that, honor, patriotism, virtue, and every manly instinct can no more be appreciated by them= than the divine Strains of Mozart= by the Hottentots. But on the contrary we address ourselves to all, who value the blessings we enjoy under our benign government as pearls of greater value, than the sordid and selfish interests of the traitors of the Illinois legislature= who are basely doing the bidding= and lending themselves to their Masters at Richmond=

Resolved= That the preservation, and future Stability of free institutions demand that unconditional Submission to the laws, under the constition be obtained and that all preparations for an armistice can only result in the destruction of liberty and reduce our country to a State of Anarchy=

Resolved= That a copy of these resolutions be forwarded for publication to The Missouri democrat, Chicago Tribune and Springfield Journal=

Capt. L. W. Moore Chairman Com.

[Resolution concerning death of Captain Alexander described in the August 13, 1863, entry of the diary.]

Germantown Tennessee
Aug 16" 1863=

At a meeting of the officers of the 49th Illinois Infty held at Germantown Tenn, to give expression to their Sentiments in regard to the untimely death of Captain Thomas Alexander of Co 'I.' 49" Ills Infty Vols=

Col. P. Pease was called to the chair, and after stating the object of the meeting, appointed the following committee on resolutions

Capt Wm P Moore
Capt J W Cheney
Capt L. Kurghoff
Lieut S. Sondag
Lieut. H.W. Kerr

The committee submitted the following Preamble, and resolutions= which were unanimously adopted=

Whereas, It has pleased the Supreme Ruler of the Universe to call from our midst, our beloved brother officer= Captain Thomas Alexander, who met his death as a true Soldier= at the hands of Miscreants and Assassins= on the 13" inst

Therefore be it= Resolved 1st That in the death of Capt Alexander, our regiment lost one of its brightest ornaments= and our cause one of its bravest defenders= 2nd that as a true gentleman and Soldier, the character of Capt Alexander is above reproach and that he was in all things a faithful and devoted officer 3" That we deeply Sympatise with the bereaved parents, family and friends of the deceased= and that we his late companions, in arms, will ever cherish and respect his memory, for his heroic and patriotic deeds while living. 4" That a copy of the proceedings of this meeting be forwarded to the parents of the deceased= Also one to the Randolph County Democrat= and Missouri Democrat with a request that they be published=

A. McGregor Lt. Co "B,, Sec.ty=

[Medical orders and correspondence concerning Surgeon James A. Black while on duty at Smithland, Kentucky, The District of Western Kentucky]

Head Quarters Post
Smithland Ky Feby 15th 1865.

Special Order
No. 24.

Major Fred. W Ferris Surgeon 13th U.S.C.H. Art. is hereby releived from duty as Post Surgeon, at this Post, and will report to his regimental Commander for duty

Jacob. E. Gauen
Maj 49 Ills Vet Vols Infty
Com'n'd'g Post. ~

--

Head Quarters Post.
Smithland Ky Feby 15th 1865

Special Order

No. 25

Ass't. Surg. J.A. Black 49th Ills. Infty. Vols. is hereby assigned to duty as Post Surgeon, at this Post, and will be obeyed and respected accordingly

Jacob E. Gauen

Major 49th Ills. Vet Vol Infty

Comndg Post

--

Head Quarters District West Ky

Medical Director's Office

Paducah Ky Jany 4th 1865

Dr Ferris

13th U.S.C.H. Art.

Sir,

You will please have forwarded immediately to this office your Personal Report and that of Dr. Mott and Dr Black, alsow your Weekly Report for the week ending Dec 31st 1864, and Monthly Report of Sick and Wounded.

Very Respectfully yours

Henry. W. Davis

Surgeon U.S. Vols

and Medical Director

Dist West Ky.

Dr. Black will please read this and act upon it, if Dr Ferris is absent

Henry W Davis

Medical Director

Dist West. Ky.

--

Head Quarters District West Ky

Medical Director's Office

Paducah Ky. Jany 4th 1865

Dr Black
Asst Surg 49th Ills Vol Infty
I have forwarded to you two Vaccine Crusts and one Instrument.
you will please Send me a receipt for them. Please be saving of the Virus
and Vaccinate the Command as early as posible

Very Respectfully
your Obt. Servant
Henry W Davis
Medical Director

--

Dist West Ky
Medical Director's Office
Lexington Ky. Jany 11th 1865

General Order
No. 1.
Every Medical Officer, Surgeon, Assistant Surgeon, and Contract
Physician, in the Military District of Kentucky, will forward to this
office, on the last day of each month, a Personal Report, giving, name, in
full, rank and regiment, where stationed, with what troops Serving, and
date of Commission or Contract.

Every officer falling[failing] to make this Report will be Considered
absent without leave and reported accordingly

J.G. Hatchett Surg U.S.V
Med. Director Mil Dist Ky

J.A. Black
Ass't. Surg 49th Ills Infty.

--

Head Quarters Post of Smithland Ky
Feby. 10th 1865.

Special Order
No.
J.A. Black Asst Surgeon 49th Ills Infty Vols. is hereby ordered to
proceed to Paducah Ky. to procure Medicines and Hospital Supplies, for

the Detachment of the 49th Reg't. Ills. Vol. Infty. stationed at this place and return

The Quartermaster's Department will furnish transportation

Jacob E Gauen
Major 49th Ills Vol Infty
Commanding Post.

--

Head Quarters Dist West Ky
Medical Director's Office
Paducah Ky Feby 16th 1865

Ass't Surg Jas A. Black
Post Surgeon
Smithland Ky.
Sir

Owing to the frequent erors of omissions and commissions in the Reports Sent to this office, causing vexatious delays in the transmittal of business to Head Quarters, I am induced to try in this letter to give Such instructions, relative to each report, due this office, as will prevent error, delay, and confusion in future.

The Chief Surgeon at each Post, will on the last days of each month, collect the "Personal Reports" of Each Medical officer. The personal report will embody the name, in full, date of Commission or Contract, and where and with what troops Serving. Also the name of the officer with whom the Contract was made. A duplicate of the Personal Report will be sent direct to the Medical Director Mil. Dist Ky. Lexington Ky on the last day of each month.

It is the duty of the Post Surgeon to collect all Reports and examine them before forwarding them to this office, and when error exists, he will return them for correction

All "Weekly Reports," of Commands and Hospitals will be forwarded every Saturday morning

"Monthly Reports" of 'Sick and Wounded' will be forwarded, to this office before the third of the succeeding month.

Monthly Statements of 'Hospital Fund' will be made out in duplicate and have the Post Commissary's endorsement attached and forward to this office before the third of the Succeeding Month.

I have the honor to be
Very Respectfully
Your Obt Servant
Henry W Davis
Surgeon US Vols
Medical Director
Dist West Ky

--

Head Quarters Post Surgeon
Smithland Ky Feby 18th 1865

Special Order
No.1.
Ass't. Surg. W.W Piper 13th U.S.C.H. Art. is hereby ordered to
report at these Head Quarters for duty immediately

Asst Surg J A Black
Post Surgeon

Approved
Jacob. E. Gauen
Major 49th Ills Vet Vol Infty
Commanding Post of
Smithland Ky

--

Head Quarters Dist of Western Kentucky
Paducah Ky. Feby 18th 1865.
Medical Director's Office

Asst Surg J A Black
Post Surgeon
Smithland Ky
Sir,
Hereafter you will make out, every Saturday morning, a weekly
report, of all troops that have died at your Post, during the week, giving
the name rank Company, Regiment, disease and at what place he died

Very Respectfully
Yours Obt. Servant

Henry. W. Davis
Surgeon US Vols
Medical Director
Dist West Ky

--

Head Quarters Post
Smithland Ky Feby 19th 1865

Special Order

No. 26

Asst Surg Jas A. Black 49" Ills Inft is hereby ordered to Paducah Ky on business conected with the Medical department of this Post, and will return immediately

The quartermaster's department will furnish transportation

Jacob E. Gauen
Major 49th Ills Infty
Comnd'g Post

--

Head Quarter's, Post Surgeon
Smithland Ky Feby 20th 1865

Special Order

No. 2.

Surgeon Fred W Ferris 13th U.S.C.H. Art., and (recent) A A Surgeon John W. Mott U.S.A. will furnish this office a certified Statement of the number of patients and authorized Hospital attendants in each of their respective Hospitals from day to day during the month of January 1865, and the amount of rations drawn for them from the A.C.S. during the month

I Am Very Respectfully
Your Obt Servant
Jas A Black
Asst Surgeon 49" Ills Infty
Post Surgeon

Approved
Jacob. E. Gauen
Maj 49" Ills Infty
Comndg Post

--

Head Quarters Dist West Ky
Medical Director's Office
Paducah Ky March 3rd 1865

Asst Surg Jas. A. Black
Post Surgeon Smithland Ky
Sir,
In reply to your Communication of the 1st inst. asking information in regard to admitting Citizens to the Pest House I would respectfully state that such cases treated in the Pest House will be charged to the City

Henry W Davis
Surg US Vols
Medical Director
Dist West Ky

--

Head Quarters Department of Kentucky
Medical Director's Office
Louisville Ky. March 6th 1865

Circular
No. 2
Surgeons in charge of U.S.A. general and Post Hospitals in the Department of Kentucky will make out, and forward promptly every Saturday morning Weekly reports of the Hospitals under their charge. In addition to the copies for the Surgeon General, and Asst Surg. Genl U.S.A., a triplicate copy will be forwarded for file in this office By order of

Major General Palmer
Alonzo J Phelps
Surgeon US Vols
Med. Director Dept of Ky

To W.W. Piper
The above report will be sent through this office
Henry. W. Davis
Surg. U.S. Vols
Med. Director Dist West Ky

--

Head Quarters Department of Kentucky
Medical Directors Office
Louisville Ky. March 8th 1865

Circular

No 3

The attention of Medical officers in this Department is called to the necessity of the thorough Vaccination of all men under their charge.

Vaccination must be practiced on all Soldiers joining their Posts, or entering the Hospitals, except in cases whose pathological condition might forbid it, or where recent Vaccination has been successful.

All recruits, whether Volunteers or drafted men, must be vaccinated as soon as they pass inspection by Examining Surgeons whether they have good Vaccine Scars or not.

Medical Officers will report Monthly to this office, the number of Vaccinations and re-vaccinations instituted under their charge

Good vaccine virus may be obtained from the Medical Purveyor at Louisville on requisition approved at this office.

By order of
Major General Palmer
Alonzo. J. Phelps
Surgeon U.S. Vols
Med. Dir. Dept of Ky

Henry W. Davis
Medical Director
Dist West Ky
To
Ass't Surg J.A. Black
Post Surgeon
Smithland Ky
I.M.D.O.D.W. Ky. Mch 10th 1865

--

Surgeon General's Office
Washington D.C. March 15th 1865

Circular
No 2.

Medical Directors will in future require of all medical officers under their direction a strict compliance with the following instructions

In all cases, either in Hospital or in the field, in which death is supposed to result from the employment of anaesthetical agents, a detailed report of the attendant circumstances will be transmitted by the medical officer in immediate charge of the patient, through the ordinary channels to the Surgeon General

Medical officers in charge of Hospitals and Surgeons in chief of Division will endorse on the report of their subordinates their opinions of the facts.

Together with the report a Sample of the Anaesthetic agent employed will be forwarded for analysis

Joseph K. Barnes
Surgeon General

--

Head Quarters District Western Kentucky
Paducah Ky March 19th 1865

Asst Surgeon Black
Surgeon in Chief

Smithland
Ky
Sir
You will appoint a Board of Medical Officers, consisting of three members yourself acting as chairman to examine all candidates for Leave of Absence, Furlough or discharge who will place their approval on all papers relating to the above cases, prior to forwarding to this office for endorsement

Henry. W. Davis
Surg US Vols
Medical Director Dist W. Ky

--

Head Quarters District Western Ky
Paducah Ky March 19th 1865

Asst Surg Jas A Black
Surg in Chief
Smithland Ky
Sir,
You will please report to this Office in writing by what authority Surgeon F W Ferris 13th U.S. Ky. Art Col'd and acting Post Surgeon Smithland Ky is absent, from his Post and Command

Henry W Davis
Surgeon U.S. Vols
Medical Director
Dist West Ky

--

Head Quarters District Western Kentucky
Medical Directors Office
Paducah Ky March 29th 1865

Surgeon Jas A Black
Smithland Ky

Sir

I send three <u>Crusts</u>. Please carry out the order relative to Re-vaccinating your Command, and all others at the Post.

Resptly
Henry W. Davis
Medical Director
Dist West Ky

--

Head Quarters District Western Ky
Medical Director's Office
Paducah Ky March 30th 1865

Special Order
No. 63 Extract****

ll S Baird Wolff Surgeon Post Paducah James Thompson Surgeon Post of Columbus and Ass't Surg Jas A. Black Surgeon Post of Smithland will report to this office as soon as possible the completion of Vaccination of the troops under their charge, the number of primary cases, number Vaccinated, success, and other facts of interest to the Medical Department

*** By Command of **
Brig Gen'l Sol Meredith
Henry W. Davis
Surgeon US Vols
Med. Director Dist. W. Ky.

--

Head Quarters Department of Kentucky
Medical Director's Office
Louisville Ky April 12th 1865

Sir

You are hereby directed to forward to this office, on the last day of every month, through the Head Quarters of the District in which you may be serving a Personal report in accordance with the following form

Station

Date

Sir

I have the honor to transmit the following personal report

Name

Rank and Regiment

Date of Contract or Commission

With What Troops Serving

Station

Changes of duty during the month giving numbers, date and source of orders

Official Signature

All communications to this office must be properly folded and indorsed, giving station date, name, and rank of writer, and Synopsis of the contents of the letter or report

Very Respectfuly
your Obedient Servant
A.J. Phelps
Col. U.S. Vols
Medical Director
Dept of Kentucky

J.A. Black
Ass't Surg. 49 Ills Infty
Smithland Ky

--

Head Quarters Post of Smithland
Smithland Ky. Apl 25th 1865

Special Order
No 24

Extract

ll ll Asst Surgeon James A Black 49" Ills Vet. Vol Infty is hereby relieved from duty as Post Surgeon. He will immediately turn over to his successor all books and records in his possession, pertaining to the

Medical Department of the Post Service and report to the Commanding officer of the 49" Ills Vet Vol Infty for duty ~

By order of Lt. Col. J.T. Foster
Commanding Post
H.E. Smith
Lt and Post Adjutant

To
Asst Surg Jas A. Black
49" Ills Vol Infty

--

Head Quarters District Western Kentucky
Paducah Ky April 30th 1865

Special Order
No 67

Extract

ll Asst Surgeon James. A. Black will proceed to Smithland Ky, and investigate the condition of the Hospital Fund due the 13th US Hy Artilery Col'd And the amount due the Pest Hospital at Smithland Ky

Asst. Surg. James. A. Black is authorized to draw upon the present Post Surgeon for all papers connected with the settlement of the above Fund for the months of January February and March 1865.

By Command of
Brig Gen'l Sol Meredith
Henry W Davis
Surgeon US Vols
Medical Director
Dist Western Ky

To
Asst Surg. J.A. Black

--

Head Quarters District West Ky
Medical Director's Office
May 4th 1865

Special Order
No 69
Asst Surg. James. A. Black 49th Ills Infty Vols will report at District Head Quarters at 8.A.M. this inst. as Surgeon to the Expedition, projected by Genl S Meredith

> By Command of
> Brig Gen'l Sol Meredith
> Henry W. Davis
> Surgeon US Vols
> Medical Director
> Dist West Ky

To
Asst Surgeon
James A Black
49" Ills Infty Vol.

--

> Head Quarters Post Surgeon
> Paducah Ky June 10th 1865

James A Black
Asst Surg 49th Ills Infty
Sir
You will please visit daily and treat the sick of the US Military in this city, in addition to your other duties

> Respectfully etc
> James M. Ball
> Surgeon 44 Wis Vol. Infty
> Post Surgeon Paducah

--

> Head Quarters District Western Kentucky
> Paducah Ky. June 26th 1865

Special Order
No. 79

Extract

Ass't Surgeon Jas. A. Black 49th Re'g Ills Infty Vols is hereby ordered to proceed to Smithland Ky. on business connected with the Medical Department.

By Command of
Col S G Hicks
Commanding Dist West Ky
Henry. W. Davis
Surg US Vols
Medical Director D.W. Ky.

To
Asst Surgeon
Jas A Black
49 Ills Infty Vols

--

Head Quarters Post of Paducah
Paducah Ky. August 21st 1865

Asst Surgeon Jas A. Black
49" Ills Infty Vols
Sir
The Colonel Commanding directs that you attend the Execution of those two Negroes at 2.P.M. this 21st day of August 1865, as it is customary for a Surgeon to be present on such occasions

By order of Col Geo. G. Symes
Commanding Post.

J.H. Bigferd
Lieut. & Post Adj't

--

Head Quarters Dist Western Ky
Paducah Ky. Aug 27th 1865

General Order
No. 31

Extract

ll Surgeon James. M. Ball 44" Wisconsin Infantry Vols. is hereby relieved from duty as Chief Medical Officer of the District of Western Ky. and will report to the Commanding officer of his Regiment

He will transfer all papers public property etc. pertaining to this Department to Ass't Surgeon James A. Black of the 49" Reg't Ills Vol Infty

ll ll Asst Surgeon James A. Black 49th Ills Infty Vet Vols is hereby temporarily announced as Chief Medical Officer of the District of Western Ky and will be obeyed and respected accordingly

By order of
Col James M McArthur
F.J. Burrows
1st Lieut and a.a.a.g.

Asst Surg J.A. Black
49 Ills Inft. Vet Vols

--

Head Quarters Dist West Kentucky
Paducah Ky. Sept 2nd 1865

General Order
No. 34

Extract

ll Asst Surgeon James A Black 49th Ills Vet Infty, is hereby relieved as Chief Medical Officer of the Dist of Western Kentucky

He will transfer all paper, public property etc. to Surgeon James Thompson 4th USC. Art. Ky.

ll ll Surgeon James Thompson 4th U.S.C. Art. Ky is hereby announced as Chief Medical Officer of the District of Western Kentucky

He will be obeyed and respected accordingly

By Command of
Col James M McArthur
F.J. Burrows
1st Lieut and a.a.a.g.

To
James. A. Black
C.M. Officer Dist. W. Ky

--

Head Quarters Post of Paducah
Paducah Ky. Sept 2nd 1865

Special Order
No. 185

Extract

ll ll ll Asst Surgeon James A Black 49th Ills Vet Vol Infty. is hereby directed to visit and prescribe for the convalescents of the Detachment of 4th USCA Ky at this Post.

By order of
Col. J.M. McArthur
Albert. O. Damon
1st Lieut and Post Adjt.

To
Asst. Surg. J.A. Black
49th Ills. V.V. Infty.

Address of Soldier Friends

Col. P. Pease - Columbus Ohio
Chaplain John. H. Lockwood - Beloit, Mitchell Co Kan
Lieut Fred. A. Niles - Fontana - Pension Dept Washington
Lieut H W Kerr - Carlinville Ills
Capt Wm Pagan - Carlinville Ills
Capt Joseph Laur, Knob Prairie, Jefferson Co Ills
Capt Louis Kurghoff - Nashville Ills
Adjt. Frank. J. Burrows, Williamsport Penn
Capt Jacob Fischer = New Hanover, Monroe Co Illinois
Capt J.W. Cheney Detroit Mich
Mrs Mary C Harlan No. 1124 South Sixth St Springfield Ill
Thos O. Hoss - 133 North Main St Wichita Kan
Lieut W.W. Bliss Co. "G,, Washington DC Int Dept.
Chas. Bliss Co. "G,, Washington DC War Dept.
Pady Burns Alton Ills
Col W.P. Moore Kansas
Capt L.W. Moore Belleville Ills

RECORD OF PAY

Date	Post or Station	By whom paid	Months	Days	Amount
1862					
Janry 16	Camp Butler Ills	Major	2	32	31.63
August 17	Bethel Tenn	"	6	-	102.00
1863					
Jany 31	Bethel Tenn	"	2	.	34.00
Aug 24	Memphis Tenn	Ferney	10	-	621.80
Oct 15	Little Rock Ark	Burn	2	.	234.80
Nov 25	Memphis Tenn	Maybarn	2	-	283.30
1864					
Jany 26	Memphis Tenn	Reynolds	2	.	224.30
June 24	Memphis Tenn	Jamison	4	-	445.11
July 4	St Louis Mo	Ballard	2	-	233.95
Sept 8	On Steamer	Turney	2	.	222.21
Nov 24	St Louis Mo	Emmerson	2	-	220.00
1865					
March 4	Cairo Ills	Reaynes	2	-	220.80
June 5	Paducah Ky	Adams	2	-	217.85
Aug 15	Cairo Ills	Emmerson	1	-	143.00
" 31	Paducah Ky	Turner	3	-	433.70
Sept 21	Springfield Ills	McCaughey	2	14	541.70
					4156.67

APPENDIX B

Facts to Complement James Black's History of Forty-Ninth Infantry

Organization: 10 companies plus field and staff officers

Initial Recruitment: September - December, 1861

Mustered: December 31, 1861

Mustered Out: September 9, 1865

Ceremonial Discharge: September 21, 1865

Active Service: 1,362 days

Total number of men who served in Regiment: 1,376

Deployment: Western Theater of the Civil War, including service in Arkansas, Illinois, Kentucky, Louisiana, Mississippi, Missouri, and Tennessee

The 49th Regiment records a proud history of service during the Civil War. The men of the Regiment were drawn primarily from twelve Southern Illinois counties, although every county in the southern third of the state was represented. By war's end the Regiment had participated in four major campaigns and numerous battles including Fort Donelson, Shiloh, Corinth, Tupelo, and Nashville. Regimental service also included protection of railroad lines, occupation and pacification duties in conquered territory, pursuit and engagement of Rebel guerrillas and routine garrison duties. When the Regiment was called upon they did their duty. The Regimental records list 7 officers and 72 enlisted men killed in action, 5 officers and 170 enlisted men died of disease for a total of 254. This number does not include the accidental deaths or murders, nor does the total include men taken prisoner, men missing, or deserters. Likewise, the total of 254 does not take into account men discharged because of disability (many because of wounds received).

APPENDIX C

THE ADVOCATE

J W. & E. L. MERRITT, ... Editors.

SALEM, MARION COUNTY, ILLINOIS

THURSDAY, JANUARY 28, 1864.

Horrible Murder.

This community was shocked on Friday of last week at the news of the murder of one of its oldest and most respected citizens. About five o'clock in the evening of that day, a rumor came to town that Mr. Willis H. Black had been shot and murdered in the neighborhood. At first the report could scarcely be credited. It seemed impossible that so amiable and respected a citizen could have come to his death by violence at the hand of a fellow creature. But it was too true. The news was confirmed and about six o'clock in the evening the mortal remains of our respected neighbor were brought to his late residence. The ball had entered his pistol shots taking effect in his brain and death immediately ensued. The inhuman wretch who had inflicted so severe an injury upon this community had escaped.

The facts attending this terrible and harrowing murder of one of our most exemplary and peaceable citizens, as developed at the Coroner's Inquest are as follows:

It appears that the Deputy Provost Marshal, in his search for deserters on Friday, had requested Mr. Black to accompany him. This he did. Two deserters were known to be in this neighborhood, and the Deputy Provost Marshal understanding that they were engaged in going for a load of corn about five miles south of town started in pursuit. The company with the Deputy Marshal, consisted of himself, Mr. Cress,

O'Neil, who has acted as a detective, Mr. Willis H. Black, and a man named Yates, who served as a guide. These occupied a carriage and after riding nearly five miles south of Salem, they espied the two deserters, of whom they were in search, approaching seated on a load of corn, they had gathered. When the two vehicles met coming from opposite directions they came close together and stopped. Mr. O'Neil got out of the carriage on one side and the Provost Marshal on the other, and the former at once announced to the deserters his intention to arrest them. Upon this, the latter, one or both drew their revolvers and began firing. At this moment Mr. Black alighted from the carriage and as he did so received a ball from the revolver of one of the deserters on the left cheek, a little below the eye. Also, another wound was made, the ball entering his right side, the ball ranging up and passing through the upper part of the heart, and lodging under the skin directly over the heart. The ball in the check ranging upward penetrated the brain and was instantly fatal. Our poor friend fell to the ground without uttering a word. He was left in a moment. Several shots were exchanged by the several parties, but without other effect. The deserters fled to a piece of woodland and Mr. O'Neil, following, was recalled by the Provost Marshal crying out that Mr. Black was killed.

As soon as it was known in town, and in the surrounding country in what direction the murderers had fled, a number of citizens started in pursuit; but up to the present writing, no traces have been discovered of their refuge. On Friday night an inquest was held upon the remains of the murdered deceased, by the Coroner of the County, James H. Lackey,

Esq. The verdict of the jury rendered was that the deceased came to his death from pistol shots, fired by the hands of one Thomas and John Jennison."

Thus has been taken away in the midst of his usefulness an old friend, a respected citizen and an honest man, a christian. It certainly could not have been the desperado, from whom a worse death could have been inflicted. We forget to mention that the names of the two deserters are John Connolly alias Thomas and John Jennison. We hope every good citizen will aid in giving such information as may lead to their apprehension and punishment.

Article from Salem, Illinois newspaper, The Advocate, describing the death of James Black's father, Willis, on January 22, 1864. In February 2, 1864, diary entry James received word of Willis' death.

APPENDIX D

Correspondents

Personal correspondence was most important to James A. Black. During his three years, eight months, twenty-three days of service in the Union Army he wrote 207 personal letters, and received 184. In his diary James kept a record, usually by personal initials, of letters written, letters received. The following identification of correspondents is listed alphabetically arranged by last initial. Example: F.J.B. is listed under B. Most identifications are certain but some are surmised.

1. A.F.A. Unidentified. Probably from Wayne County, Ill., as noted on Jan. 19, 1863.
2. A.K.A. Unidentified. Probably from Wayne County, Ill., as noted on Jan. 19, 1863.
3. Art Arthur Moody, Zue's brother.
4. F.M.A. Unidentified.
5. M.A. Unidentified. May be James' cousin, Martin V. Allmon.
6. S.B.A. May be Samuel B. Arnold.
7. B.N.B. Unidentified.
8. E.A.B. Unidentified.
9. F.J.B. Frank J. Burrows, friend from Salem, Ill., also in Co. D of 49th.
10. J.F.B. James' brother, Joseph Frank Black, often called Frank. He served in the 111th as Lt. Colonel. Born in 1837.
11. J.W.B., Doctor Unidentified.
12. L.H.B. James' sister, Lucy Hensley Black, born in 1846. Also called Lute.
13. S.J.B. Unidentified.
14. T.C.B. James' brother, Thomas C. Black, born in 1848.
15. T.J.B. James' uncle, Thomas Jefferson Black, brother of Willis.
16. Wm. B. James' uncle, William Renick Black, brother of Willis.
17. W.H.B. James' father, Willis H. Black.
18. W.W.B. William W. Bishop, Lt. Colonel of 49th, from Centralia, Ill.

19. E.W.C. Dr. E.W. Charles, from Columbia, Ill., discharged from Co. A, 49th on Dec. 10, 1862.

20. J.W.C. Captain James W. Cheney, Co. D, 49th, from Vandalia, Ill.

21. Cephline Unidentified.

22. Lt. Chalfin Lt. A.S. Chalfin, Co. A, 49th, from Waterloo, Ill.

23. Rev. Cliff Unidentified.

24. Ella Ella Moody, daughter of John and Jane Moody. Ella's sister Missouri Jane, will marry James in 1865.

25. Frank Depending on time or place could be brother, J.F.B., or Frank J. Burrows.

26. E.G. Ephraim Glathent is described on Nov. 8, 1863.

27. E.B,H. Lt. Emery B. Harlan, Co. D, 49th, from Salem, Ill.

28. M.M.H. James' aunt, Martha M. Higgason, probably sister of his mother, Emilla.

29. R.H. Unidentified. May be Robert Hensley.

30. W.W.H. May be Dr. William Hill of Salem, Ill., with whom James had studied medicine. James is writing him at the time he is studying for medical examination.

31. Hellen Hellen Moody, younger sister of Ella and Missouri Jane Moody.

32. J.R. Higgason John R. Higgason, husband of Martha, identified under M.M.H.

33. Martha M. Higgason Wife of J.R. Higgason, same as #28.

34. Wm. Holmes Soldier of Co. D, 49th, from Omega, Ill. Discharged with disability Nov. 28, 1862.

35. Ella Holton Former Ella Moody married George Holton.

36. John Keen, Jr. Son of John Keen in whose Wayne County, Ill., home James boarded before enlistment.

37. R.M.L. Robert M. Lovell, cousin of James. His mother, Polly, sister of James' mother, Emilla. Robert was in the 111th with Joseph Frank Black. He was from Omega, Ill.

38. Lyde Lawrence Unidentified.

39. Lucy, Aunt Lucinda Woodward, sister of James' father, Willis.

40. Lute Lucy H. Black, sister of James. Same as #12.

41. Lyde Ann Eliza Black, sister of James, born in 1844 or 1845.

42. A. McGregor   Andrew J. McGregor, Co. B, 49th, from Sparta, Ill.
43. E.M.   Ella Moody, same as #24 and #35.
44. Em M.   May be Emit Merritt.
45. Zue M.   Missouri Jane Moody, daughter of John and Jane Moody, called Zue. Will marry James in 1865. Same as #47 and #58.
46. S.F.F.M.   Dr. Stephen F. Mercer, Surgeon of 49th, from Salem, Ill.
47. Z.M.   Zue Moody, same as #45.
48. Arthur Moody   Same as #3.
49. Helen Moody   Zue's younger sister. Same as #31.
50. James S. Moody   Zue's older brother, a resident of Fillmore, Ill.
51. C.R.O'N.   Charles R. O'Neill, Co. D, 49th, from Omega, Ill. Discharged with disability June 1, 1862, after being wounded at Ft. Donelson. Married to James' mother's sister, Harriett.
52. K.R.   Unidentified.
53. Min___ Seymore   Unidentified.
54. Lt. J.L. Stanley   Co. B, 49th, from Columbia, Ill.
55. & 56. M.W. and M.D.W.   Undoubtedly both sets of initials refer to James' older sister, Margaret D. Black, who married George Williams.
57. John C. Wilson   Co. D, 49th, recruit from Decatur, Ill., who was in Baltimore, Md., in Jan., 1865.
58. Zue   Missouri Jane Moody who marries James in 1865. Same as #45 and #47.

APPENDIX E

Glossary

The reader surely will be impressed with the precise word choice found in the Civil War diary of James A. Black. James understood the power of words and chose them wisely, sparingly. Not surprisingly, a few words reflect the language of the past, and the modern reader may have difficulty with their meaning. For ease of reading the archaic words are defined. The purist is encouraged to reference the defined words, read them in context, and search for other possible meanings.

Likewise, a few nonmilitary abbreviations may need definition. They are included.

The words are listed alphabetically, followed by definition and diary date location for the initial usage of the word.

ague a fever with shivering and chills(January 31, 1862)

bbl. abbreviation for barrel(August 4, 1862)

black leg a swindler; especially a dishonest gambler(June 13, 1865)

catchpenny using sensationalism or cheapness for appeal(January 25, 1862)

deponent one who gives evidence, especially in writing(December 11, 1863)

Exquisite one who is overly fastidious in dress or ornament(June 8, 1865)

"French" French leave: an informal, hasty, or secret departure (August 23, 1862)

gate given the gate - dismissed(October 2, 1863)

hhd. abbreviation for hogshead, a large cask or barrel(March 25, 1864)

in season at the right time(August 9, 1863)

inst. from the word instant: occurring in the present or current month(June 3, 1863)

lawn a fine sheer linen or cotton fabric(March 7, 1862)

lay be covert in action(April 25, 1865)

parole in military a watchword given only to officers of the guard and of the day(July 26, 1862)

parole in pacification the promise of a prisoner of war to fulfill stated conditions in consideration of his release(May 5, 1865)

pest hospital a hospital for an epidemic disease associated with high mortality(December 15, 1863)

promiscuously intermingled(October 25, 1863)

repaired returned(September 30, 1864)

sanitaries items related to health(May 14, 1862)

sinecure a position that requires little or no work(March 21, 1862)

sutler a civilian provisioner to an army post(January 24, 1862)

swimingly very well(January 1, 1862)

tattoo a call sounded shortly before taps as notice to go to quarters(January 3, 1862)

to wit   namely(December 16, 1863)

ult.   from the word ultimo: occurring in the month preceding the present(January 18, 1863)

U.S.C.   James Black's abbreviation for United States Colored Troops

varioloid   mild form of smallpox, in persons who have been vaccinated or had smallpox(December 29, 1863)

vice   in the place of(October 19, 1862)

viz.   that is to say: namely(March 15, 1862)

ACKNOWLEDGEMENTS

Thanks to my aunt, Lucille Black, for giving me the diary of Dr. James A. Black. She is the widow of Harry R. Black to whom the diary was given around 1960, when he was researching and compiling the Black family genealogy.

Richard Qualls

Thanks also to Jack Moore, Howard Purcell, Richard Qualls and many other individuals who made this endeavor possible.

ABOUT THE AUTHOR

Benita K. Moore earned her B.S. degree from Southern Illinois University and her M.A. degree from the University of Illinois. She taught History at the high school in Galesburg, Illinois, for 30 years. She is a native of Southern Illinois from which the 49th Infantry came. Benita worked over three years to transcribe and edit this diary.

Printed in the United States
127231LV00004B/1/P

9 781434 393678